52.

500

California Heartland

Writing from the Great Central Valley
Gerald W. Haslam & James D. Houston, Editors

Capra Press   Santa Barbara

Grateful acknowledgment to the National Endowment for the Arts
for assistance on this publication.

Library of Congress Cataloging in Publication Data:

Main Entry Under Title:
California Heartland.
    1. American Literature California Central Valley.
2. Central Valley, California Literary Collections.
I. Haslam, Gerald W. II. Houston, James D.
PS571.C2C22   810'.809794'5   78-18337
ISBN 0-88496-083-3
ISBN 0-88496-084-6 pbk.

CAPRA PRESS
631 State Street
Santa Barbara, California 93101

ACKNOWLEDGMENTS
(sources for all selections, listed in order of appearance)

"*Earth Diver,*" "*He-Who-Is-Above,*" and "*Coyote Death,*" *from Wintu Myths* by Constance G. DuBois and D. Demetrocopoulous, UNIVERSITY OF CALIFORNIA PUBLICATIONS IN AMERICAN ARCHAEOLOGY AND ETHNOLOGY, Vol. 28, No. 5. Berkeley, 1931.

"Origin of the Mountains," from TRIBES OF CALIFORNIA by Stephen Powers, Washington, 1877.

"Birth of the Sacramento," and "Dancing Song for a Wedding," from THE CALIFORNIANS: WRITINGS OF THEIR PAST AND PRESENT, Vol. I, edited by Robert Pearsall and Ursula Spier Erickson. Hesperian House, San Francisco, 1961.

"The Repeopling of the World," and "Creation of Man," from *Miwok Myths,* by Edward W. Gifford, UNIV. OF CALIF. PUBLICATIONS IN ARCH. AND ETH., Vol. 12. Berkeley, 1916.

"Thunder and Lightning," from *System and Sequence in Maidu Mythology,* by Roland B. Dixon, JOURNAL OF AMERICAN FOLKLORE, Vol. XVII, 1903.

"The Race Between Antelope and Deer," from *Myths of South Central California,* by Alfred Kroeber, UNIV. OF CALIF. PUBLICATIONS IN ARCH. AND ETH., Vol. 4. Berkeley, 1907.

"Song of the Spirits," from CREATION MYTHS OF PRIMITIVE AMERICA, Jeremiah Curtin. Boston, 1898.

"Rattlesnake Ceremony Song," and "Prayer," from HANDBOOK OF THE INDIANS OF CALIFORNIA, Alfred Kroeber. Washington D.C., 1925.

"Monday, March 30, 1772," from FRAY JUAN CRESPI, MISSIONARY EXPLORER OF THE PACIFIC COAST, 1769-1774. Translated and edited by Herbert Bolton. Univ. of Calif. Press, 1927.

"Valley Indians," from A HISTORICAL, POLITICAL AND NATURAL DESCRIPTION OF CALIFORNIA, by Pedro Fages, Soldier of Spain, 1775. Translated by Herbert Ingram Priestley. Univ. of Calif. 1937.

"The Eternal Summer of Sacramento," from ROUGHING IT, by Mark Twain. Harper and Bros., 1872.

"Firebaugh to Fort Tejon," from UP AND DOWN CALIFORNIA 1860-1864, by William Henry Brewer. Ed. by Francis Peloubet Farquhar. Yale Univ. Press, 1930.

"The Bee Pastures," from MOUNTAINS OF CALIFORNIA, by John Muir, The Century Co. New York, 1894.

"The Plains of the San Joaquin," anonymous ballad, from GARDEN OF THE SUN, Wallace Smith, (1939). California History Books, Fresno, 1960.

"The Spirit of Joaquin," from TALES OF CALIFORNIA by Hector Lee. Letter Shop Press, Santa Rosa, Calif., 1974. Reprinted by permission of the author.

"Cabeza de Vaca was a Piker," by W.H. Hutchinson, from *Hunters and Healers,* ANNUAL OF THE TEXAS FOLKLORE SOCIETY, Austin, Texas, 1971. Reprinted by permission of the author.

"The Expansive Power of Beans," by John A. Barker, from THE BAKERSFIELD DAILY CALIFOR-NIAN, June 28, 1904.

"El Viejito" and "Curanderas" from LORE OF THE CALIFORNIA VAQUERO by Arnold A. Rojas. Academic Library Guild, 1958. Reprinted by permission of the publisher.

"The Scavengers," from THE LAND OF LITTLE RAIN by Mary Austin. Houghton Mifflin, Boston, 1903.

The publisher and editors wish to express their gratitude to the National Endowment for the Arts for their assistance.

Foreword

LAWRENCE CLARK POWELL

Now that I have left California to live in Arizona, I can look back across the river to good long years that came to a natural end. Mine was a life that took me throughout the Golden State, over the mountains and down the rivers. I dwelled in town and country and on the seacoast, working, reading and writing, identifying with people present and past, seeing life through the lenses of literature and demanding that literature be true to life.

In *California Classics* (1971) I paid homage and bade farewell to the literature and landscape of my nearly natal state. Now in *California Heartland* we learn that classics keep coming into being. All that is needed for them to take form is some genius or much talent. Then come readers, and finally critics to illuminate their creation.

I first knew the San Joaquin valley as boy and youth, then in later years I paid many visits to the valley of the Sacramento. Those sandy lands which end at the Tehachapis, and that I once irrigated under the burning sun of summer, are now unrecognizably verdant. The watery northern lands are less changed. From Sutter's Buttes to Mount Shasta they await their laureate. They are rich in history and legendary, and peoples with ghosts whose voices are lost in time. If I were to live again, I would want to come to manhood in the lee of Lassen and Shasta. There it seems to me is the *cor cordium* of California. There is a deep untapped source of creativity.

Jeffers first nourished me at home and abroad, then Steinbeck and Everson. I needed no critics to discover them. Those early choices were my own. This book holds some of them and others new to me. It tells me that life never stops seeking form in literature.

This is a volume of many riches that I shall keep on the short shelf of California books that I want with me wherever I live. It is a thoughtful book of loving discernment that will lead readers to landscape and literature. This is one of the things that only books can do.

—Verde Valley

Contents

Part Three: AWAKENING

Part Four: EXPLORING

Yes, we must stress the regional again. The "nation" is a fiction as Kropotkin and others have pointed out. The region is real.
—Gary Snyder, "The Writer's Sense of Place."

Editors' Preface

THE REGION is real. It can be any region. Somewhere between the freeways and the fast-food chains, somewhere out behind the interchangeable supermarkets of America, the regions are still there. The Rockies. The Great Plains. The southwestern desert. The Mississippi Delta. New York City. New England. The subject of this book is one of those regions, the Great Central Valley of California, considered by some a subdivision of the West, but in fact a realm unto itself.

It has a shape, roughly that of an elongated football field, with mountain ranges where the bleachers would be — the Coast Range to the west, the Tehachapis to the south, the Cascades to the north, and to the east the vaulting Sierra Nevadas.

It has a character, which some dismiss from afar as "rednick," but which is much more diverse than that, comprised not only of transplanted Texans and southerners, but of transplanted Swedes, Blacks, Germans, Italians, Yugoslavs, Armenians, Portuguese, Mexicans, Japanese, Chinese and Basques, and their children, and their children's children (often mixtures) — people who share for better or for worse an interst in its two great natural resources, fertile land, and oil.

It has a history, but a short one, as America's regions go. In the expansion of the United States, California was settled late, and its central valley had to wait until the coast began to develop, then wait a while longer, for the railroad.

The valley also has a literature, a unique body of poems and songs and essays and stories, emerging from the landscape and from the lives lived there. It begins with the Indians who built creation myths from the mountain ranges that framed their world. It includes writers who were passing through on their way to somewhere else, or who based a book or story there, as well as several widely published contemporary writers whose reputations extend far beyond the borders of the valley where they were born.

We have gathered some of these works together, proceeding in the belief that there can be a meaningful relationship between a region and the writing it evokes. The place can give shape to the writing. And the writing in turn helps us see and grasp the place. And the voices remind us that a region can still have its own sounds, quite apart from whatever the national sound might be. The voices remind us that there are still tales and verses about distinct groups of people inhabiting specific parts of the country, who we are not likely to see on network television, where other tale-tellers conspire with the fast-food chains to absorb all our differences into one homogenous, coast-to-coast mythology.

PART ONE

Visioning

My words are tied in one
With the great mountains,
With the great rocks,
With the great trees...
    —from a Yokut prayer

THEY VISIONED this land, their valley, living it in their dreams and words as certainly as they dwelt upon it. Whether visions were inspired by Jimson weed extract consumed during tolache cult ceremonies among Tulamni Yokuts, or by the personal meditation of a lone Pushuni Maidu, they constituted a reality that could not be dismissed. In chants and tales, valley Indians affirmed the sacredness and depth not only of their own lives, but of all life and the forces shaping it.

They had much to affirm, for the Natives of the Great Central Valley were a chosen people, and the Heartland boasted one of the densest populations in the Americas prior to the white invasion, nearly 160,000 according to most recent estimates. "Here were to be found most of her (California's) Indians," Theodora Kroeber points out, "the predominant physical type, and the carriers of the most idiosyncratic culture. Three hundred tribelets of California's five hundred or more belong to this area."

While there was great diversity of specific tribelets within the valley, four major tribes, all members of the Penutian language family, dominated the region: Wintun and Maidu inhabited the north; Yokuts controlled the entire south, while Miwoks separated the northern and southern tribes with a relatively small east-central incursion. Alfred Kroeber describes topographical relations in his classic *Handbook of Indians of California* (1925):

> *The Penutian family occupied nearly half of California. It also held the core of the state—not only in a spatial sense but physiographically. This heart and kernel is what the geographer knows as the Great Central Valley of California and the residents as the Sacramento and San Joaquin Valleys, together with the flanking and inclosing mountains—an unbroken plain 400 miles long, and a stretch from crest to crest of nearly 500. . . . . There are few regions of the same size that nature has endowed with greater diversity of surface, altitude,*

3

humidity, soil, and vegetation than this one. But there are also few that have been so distinctly stamped by her as a compact and indissoluble unit. This unit was the Penutian empire.

Living in an area that had, according to their own oral histories, never suffered a famine, valley Natives were considered wealthy as well as peaceful. Despite its general lack of rainfall, the region was rich in rivers, lakes and marshes, with drainage from the nation's largest snowpack in the Sierra Nevadas to the east. As a consequence it was also rich in fish and waterfowl, being a migration path for salmon, steelhead, ducks and geese. On the land, elk, antelope and deer roamed in large numbers, sharing the region's abundant vegetation with people, only to be harvested in turn by them. So rich was their environment and so balanced their reaping, that tribal hunting and gathering obviated the need to develop husbandry or farming.

The Yokuts, a large, varied tribe that dominated the entire San Joaquin Valley, were typical central California Indians. Of medium height and weight, their skin was light copper brown, their hair black. Despite bodies that appeared soft, they were, according to scientific tests, stronger than their white counterparts. Theodora Kroeber calls them "the ultimate realization of the heartland people in feature and form, in the extreme rounding of face and body and in a temperament that fitted the ample curves like a second skin." A stable people, their demeanor tended to be reserved, yet courteous toward outsiders.

If restraint characterized their public lives, their spiritual lives knew no such bounds. Living in a vitalistic cosmos, they ritually sought to transcend their human limitations. The Great Valley was their home; they were part of it, products of the same life force that created and sustained even the trees and rocks. So they visioned, seeking to be "seized by the sacred," as Mircea Eliade phrases it.

It was through poetry that the inner rhythms of life might most commonly manifest themselves, so it tended to be reserved for religious uses. Indians sang their poems, danced them, allowing rhythmic repetition to expand their sensitivities. Moreover, they sang to effect virtually every important phenomenon. As Mary Austin points out, "it is not (merely) the words which are potent, but the states of mind evoked by the singing."

Rhythm and repetition were the major devices used by singers of poetry. An apparently simple verse such as the following Yokut Death Song—

All my life
  I have been seeking
  Seeking.

—repeated to the rhythms of a rattle, might invade one's being with the most profound spiritual consequences. "Poetry," A. Grove Day explains, "was not a pastime. Poetry was power."

When, for example, all humanity was destroyed by a massive flood in the Miwok tale called "The Repeopling of the World," Coyote first dreamed, then followed instruction given him during his dream and sang. His song repopulated the world.

It was not uncommon for songs to be included in tales, especially when powerful totem animals such as Coyote or Condor, or other strong spiritual symbols such as lightning, were involved in the story, as is illustrated in the Wintun "Songs of Spirits." The Yokut "Rattlesnake Ceremony Song," part of an elaborate shamanistic ritual, guarantees vipers will give a rattle-warning throughout the next year to those who participate.

Just as poems were often sung to influence events on a spiritual level, tales were most often employed to explain the world as valley Natives found it. Many people today understand their contemporary situations to be the products of history; similarly Indians of the valley understood that certain mythical events explained the origin and continuing basis of their lives. These myths are in no sense false for they relate how a reality came into existence, providing a sacred, metaphoric history. Thus the existence of the earth proves the success of Earth Diver's quest, just as Earth Diver's success explains the existence of the earth. The race between Antelope and Deer explains why they range differently just as the fact they range differently validates the race. It is a world view lost to most of the whites who have settled the Great Central Valley, making it nearly impossible for them to understand the Natives they displaced.

The tales included here are concerned with sacred origins, with supernatural forces that created everything. The primordial power of such beginnings could be recaptured, *ab origine,* when they were explained in tales or reenacted in rituals. The stories told by valley Natives were not mere tales, their songs not mere poems. Rather they linked Heartland people with the power underlying all existence.

Earth Diver

(WINTU)

At first all was water. A water-fowl thought that there must be earth below. So all the water-fowls dived for it. Finally Turtle said he would try. He made himself a waterproof suit to travel in under water. Then he got much rope. He said, "If I jerk on the rope pull me out. If there is no earth I shall come to the surface all alone." Finally they pulled him up. He was helpless when he came to the surface. His mouth and ears were all plugged up with mud. They saw mud under his nails. His eyes were wedged with mud. There was mud in his mouth. They got a little mud this way. They dried it and made an island. It grew and became the world.

Origin of the Mountains
(YOKUT)

Once there was a time when there was nothing in the world but water. About the place where Tulare Lake is now, there was a pole standing far up out of the water, and on this pole perched a hawk and a crow. First one of them would sit on the pole a while, then the other would knock him off and sit on it himself. Thus they sat on top of the pole above the waters for many ages. At length they wearied of the lonesomeness, and they created the birds which prey on fish such as the kingfisher, eagle, pelican, and others. Among them was a very small duck, which dived down to the bottom of the water, picked its beak full of mud, came up, died, and lay floating on the water. The hawk and the crow then fell to work and gathered from the duck's beak the earth which it had brought up, and commenced making the mountains. They began at the place now known as Ta-hi-cha-pa Pass, and the hawk made the east range, while the crow made the west one. Little by little, as they dropped in the earth, these great mountains grew athwart the face of the waters, pushing north. It was a work of many years, but finally they met together at Mount Shasta, and their labors were ended. But, behold, when they compared their mountains, it was found that the crow's was a great deal the larger. Then the hawk said to the crow, "How did this happen, you rascal? I warrant you have been stealing some of the earth from my bill, and that is why your mountains are the biggest." It was a fact, and the crow laughed in his claws. Then the hawk went and got some Indian tobacco and chewed it, and it made him exceedingly wise. So he took hold of the mountains and turned them around in a circle, putting his range in place of the crow's; and that is why the Sierra Nevada is larger than the Coast Range.

He-Who-Is-Above
(WINTU)

This world came to an end three times. The first people were all short men; the next never walked, they just rolled; the last were all tall as pines.

He-who-is-above was not satisfied, so he set to work and made Wintu. The first place where they were made was on the flat near Campbell Creek. He made a man and a woman and put them on the island (informant explained he meant the United States by the island). |He made different pairs and each pair he put in a different place on the island. The man and woman of each pair talked the same language.

He made them early in the morning. The woman went to get water, the man went to get a spear pole. It was the same all over the island.

Then the younger generation came.

He-who-is-above put deer on the island. The deer would not sleep, they traveled about night and day. He-who-is-above said, "What shall I do about it?" Then he took a fishline and fishhook and baited it with an acorn. Deer found the acorn and ate it. Thus He-who-is-above caught deer. However, the deer broke away, so He-who-is-above had to give up. The hook can still be found in the deer's head.

He-who-is-above planted different acorn trees, different berries, different clovers; he put fish in the rivers, he made all kinds of animals for the Wintu.

All Indian tribes increased all over this island. There were no whites.

Coyote and Death

(WINTU)

A long time ago, when the first people lived, all of them came together and decided to build a staircase to heaven. They set to work. Buzzard was their leader. He said, "When people are old and blind they will go to heaven and become young and healthy again. There will be a camping place there with plenty of wood and a spring."

Coyote came along. They were working. Coyote said, "Nephews, what are you doing?" They paid no attention to him. Then he said, "Get in the shade and rest. It is too hot to work." So finally they did. They told Coyote what they were doing. Coyote said, "It would be a good idea to have people die. People can go to burials and cry. It would be nice."

"Your idea is not good," they said.

Coyote argued in favor of death. Then Buzzard and the others said, "When acorns ripen they will have no shells. Snow will be salmon flour."

Coyote was against this too. He said, "Acorns should have shells so that the boys and girls can shell them and throw them at each other in the evening and have a good time. Snow should be cold, and when people go out to hunt in it they will die. That is the way it will be good."

Finally all the people became very angry and destroyed their work.

Birth of the Sacramento

(MAIDU)

The Maidu who used to live around here were happy and rich. But then a whole lot of water came down here and the whole Sacramento Valley was turned into an ocean. Most of the people were drowned. Some tried to swim away but the frogs and salmon caught them and ate them. Only two people got safe away into the Sierras.

Great Man blessed these Maidu with many children, and all the tribes arose. One wise old chief ruled all of them. This chief went to the Coast Range but was disconsolate because the Sacramento Valley was still under water. He stayed there for nine days without any food, thinking about the water that covered the plains of the world.

This thinking and fasting changed him. He was not like a man. No arrow could hurt him. He could never be killed after that. He called out to Great Man and told him to get rid of the flood waters. Great Man tore open the Coast Range and made the waters flow down to the ocean. This flow of water was how the Sacramento River began.

The Repeopling of the World

(MIWOK)

Chief Eagle said, "Where is Coyote? Where is Coyote? He must try to resurrect the people. What shall we do about our dead people? Who is going to help us? Tell Coyote to think." Thus spoke the chief. "Tell Coyote to think intently. All human beings are dead." So said Eagle to Coyote.

Coyote said, "I do not know how I shall bring them back to life." Thus spoke Coyote, when he answered Eagle. "But," he continued, "I will try to bring them back. I will try to bring them back."

He went to the top of a rock and slept. He dreamed that he saw a skeleton. Then he went to the chief and told him that he had seen a skeleton in his dream. The chief sent him back, saying, "That may help us. Go back and sleep again. If you dream again do not arise. The skeleton may talk to you."

Coyote said, "No one helps the chief. He feels lonely. He mourns each day for the dead Indians." Then Coyote dreamed of the skeleton again. The skeleton awakened him and told him to sing. The skeleton said, "If you sing, the people will return."

Coyote sang in a great cave. The skeleton told Lesisko [translated as "devil" by the interpreter] that Coyote was singing in the cave. Coyote sang, "Come back, all of you girls. Come back. Come back. Come back. Come back, all of you old people. Come back. Come back. Come back. Come back, all of you women. Come back. Come back. Come back." Thus sang Coyote, when he called the people back after Eagle asked him to resurrect them.

Prairie Falcon told Coyote to try hard to bring about the return of mankind. Coyote sang and cried for days and nights. Eagle cried. He said to Prairie Falcon, "I do not think Coyote will bring your people back." Coyote said, "The skeleton told me that, if I sang loudly each morning, some of the people would return, but not all." Then Coyote went to the chief and said, "The skeleton told me that by singing loudly every morning some of the people would return, but not all." The chief felt a bit better after he had this word from Coyote.

Coyote said, "I think that I shall bring my people back. I think that I shall." Thus he spoke, when he talked with the chief. He felt very happy, when he said this to the chief. Then he continued, "I will go back to the cave and sing."

Then he sang. He sang in the morning. First he brought one old man back to life. He tried to talk to the old man, but the latter would not answer him. The old man did not even shake his head. Coyote said, "I will try some more singing."

Coyote then visited the chief and told him, "I shall bring the people back but they will not be the same people. They will be very nearly the same people, but they will be a little different." The chief laughed.

Then Coyote ran around the rock shouting, ran around the rock shouting. He felt glad that he had resurrected the people. He said, "I brought back my grandson. Now there are many people. Now there are many people. Now there are many people. I brought them back. Now they are nearly the same as they were before."

Then he climbed a hill. He ran around the hills and shouted. He went around the hills and shouted. Eagle said, "He has made the same people. Coyote has done well." Thus spoke Chief Eagle, for he was glad to see the people alive again. Coyote still shouted and danced in his joy.

The chief said to Hummingbird, "Go back and look at that mountain." Then Hummingbird went. All of the people returned. The chief was glad to see his people. He said that the various kinds of baskets must return. The chief was glad. He said, "Coyote did it all." The chief told Chief Prairie

Falcon, "Coyote secured the return of the people through the help of the skeleton." Then Coyote shouted, because he was glad that he had brought back his people. Thus spoke Coyote. Thus spoke Coyote.

Chief Eagle said, "He brought back the people." Coyote said to Prairie Falcon, "We have saved our people. They have returned to their places. I have brought my people back." He told no one. He just thought about it, when he brought the people back. No one told him what to do. When he saw the people, he was glad. Coyote said, "I do not know what happened to us. I do not know what it was, that killed our old folks. I do not know whence the water came." Thus spoke Coyote, while he was running.

Prairie Falcon said, when he answered his brother, "Yes, that is all right." Coyote shouted and shouted, when he secured the baskets, various sorts of baskets, the various sorts in which the people cook. He shouted and shouted, after he had brought back everything together with the people. He was glad to have his people again. Then he stopped shouting. He stopped shouting. He said, "It is all right. It is all right." But when he spoke he shouted again. Then he became accustomed to shouting and he still continued to do so. Because he was glad to see the people, he shouted.

Thunder & Lightning

(MAIDU)

Great-man created the world and all the people. At first the earth was very hot, so hot it was melted, and that is why even to-day there is fire in the trunk and branches of trees, and in the stones.

Lightning is Great-Man himself coming down swiftly from his world above, and tearing apart the trees with his flaming arm.

Thunder and Lightning are two great spirits who try to destroy mankind. But Rainbow is a good spirit who speaks gently to them, and persuades them to let the Indians live a little longer.

Creation of Man

(MIWOK)

After Coyote had completed making the world, he began to think about creating man. He called a council of all the animals. The animals sat in a circle, just as the Indians do, with Lion at the head, in an open space in the forest. On Lion's right was Grizzly Bear; next Cinnamon Bear; and so on to Mouse, who sat at Lion's left.

Lion spoke first. Lion said he wished man to have a terrible voice, like himself, so that he could frighten all animals. He wanted man also to be well covered with hair, with fangs in his claws, and very strong teeth.

Grizzly Bear laughed. He said it was ridiculous for any one to have such a voice as Lion, because when he roared he frightened away the very prey for which he was searching. But he said man should have very great strength; that he should move silently, but very swiftly; and he should be able to seize his prey without noise.

Buck said man would look foolish without antlers. And a terrible voice was absurd, but man should have ears like a spider's web, and eyes like fire.

Mountain Sheep said the branching antlers would bother man if he got caught in a thicket. If man had horns rolled up, so that they were like a stone on each side of his head, it would give his head weight enough to butt very hard.

When it came Coyote's turn, he said the other animals were foolish because they each wanted man to be just like themselves. Coyote was sure he could make a man who would look better than Coyote himself, or any other animal. Of course he would have to have four legs, with five fingers. Man should have a strong voice, but he need not roar all the time with it. And he should have feet nearly like Grizzly Bear's, because he could then stand erect when he needed to. Grizzly Bear had no tail, and man should not have any. The eyes and ears of Buck were good, and perhaps man should have those. Then there was Fish, which had no hair, and hair was a burden much of the year. So Coyote thought man should not wear fur. And his claws should be as long as the Eagle's, so that he could hold things in them. But no animal was as cunning and crafty as Coyote, so man should have the wit of Coyote.

Then Beaver talked. Beaver said man would have to have a tail, but it should be broad and flat, so he could haul mud and sand on it. Not a furry tail, because they were troublesome on account of fleas.

Owl said man would be useless without wings.

But Mole said wings would be folly. Man would be sure to bump against the sky. Besides, if he had wings and eyes both, he would get his eyes burned out by flying too near the sun. But without eyes, he could burrow in the soft, cool earth where he could be happy.

Mouse said man needed eyes so he could see what he was eating. And nobody wanted to burrow in the damp earth. So the council broke up in a quarrel.

Then every animal set to work to make a man according to his own ideas. Each one took a lump of earth and modelled it just like himself. All buy Coyote, for Coyote began to make the kind of man he had talked of in the council.

It was late when the animals stopped work and fell asleep. All but Coyote, for Coyote was the cunningest of all the animals, and he stayed awake until he had finished his model. He worked hard all night. When the other animals were fast asleep he threw water on the lumps of earth, and so spoiled the models of the other animals. But in the morning he finished his own, and gave it life long before the others could finish theirs. Thus man was made by Coyote.

The Race Between Antelope and Deer

(YOKUT)

The antelope and the deer were together. The antelope said: "I can beat you running." The deer said: "I think not." The antelope said: "Well, let us try." The deer said: "We shall run for six days," and the antelope agreed. The deer said: "Let us go south and run northward." Then they went far to the south "across the ocean" (or Tulare Lake), in order to run northward to the end of the world. The antelope said: "This will be my path on the west here. You take the path on the east." The deer agreed. They they started. Their path was the milky way. On the other side where the antelope ran there is a wide path; on the other side there are patches. That is where the deer jumped. The antelope had said: "If I win, all this will be my country and you will have to hide in the brush." The deer said: "Very well, and if I win it will be the same for me." Then they ran and the antelope won. So now he has the plains to live in, but the deer hides in the brush.

Songs of Spirits

(WINTU)

I
LIGHTNING
I bear the sucker-torch to the western tree-ridge.
Behold me! first born and greatest.

II
OLELBIS (THE CREATOR)
I am great above.
I tan the black cloud.

III

HAU (RED FOX)

On the stone ridge east I go.
On the white road I, Hau, crouching go.
I, Hau, whistle on the road of stars.

IV

POLAR STAR

The circuit of earth which you see,
The scattering of stars in the sky which you see,
All that is the place for my hair.

Dancing Song for a Wedding

(YOKUT)

Who put the trees on the hills?
     Coyote did it. Coyote did it.
     Coyote did it. Coyote did it.

Who put the acorns up there?
     Coyote did it. Coyote did it.
     Coyote did it. Coyote did it.

Who made the marriage song?
     Coyote did it. Coyote did it.
     Coyote did it. Coyote did it.

Who now shall marry this woman?
     Him says Coyote. Him says Coyote.
     Him, him says Coyote, him, him!
     Him him him him him him him!

Rattlesnake Ceremony Song

(YOKUT)

The king snake said to the rattlesnake:
Don't touch me!
You can't whip me,
Lying with your belly full,

Rattler of rock pile,
Don't touch me!
There's nothing you can do,
Lying with your belly full
Where the ground squirrel holes are thick.
Don't touch me!
What can you do to me
Rattlesnake in the tree clump,
Stretched in the shade?
You can't do anything.
Don't touch me!
Big valley rattler,
You whose white eye
The sun shines on,
Don't you touch me!

A Prayer

(YOKUT)

Do you see me!
See me, Tüüshiut!
See me, Pamashiut!
See me, Yuhahait!
See me, Eshepat!
See me, Pitsuriut!
See me, Tsuksit!
See me, Ukat!

Do you all help me!
My words are tied in one
With the great mountains,
With the great rocks,
With the great trees,
In one with my body
And my heart.
Do you all help me
With supernatural power
And you, day,
And you, night!
All of you see me
One with this world.

PART TWO

Discovering

*The great central valley and mountain
region of California is a country full
of telltale landscapes that show at a
glance to the traveler the general
topographical structure of the whole
land. In the gently mountainous regions
of even the more rugged of our Eastern
states one may wander for many days, and
see many picturesque or imposing landscapes, without getting any clear notion
of the complex water system of the country
through which he journeys. . . . But in
the typical central Californian landscape,
as viewed from any commanding summit, the
noble frankness of nature shows one at a
glance the vast plan of the country.*

From California *(1886)*
by Josiah Royce

THE VALLEY TRIBES had no written language. Their tales and songs and prayers passed from one generation to the next by word of mouth. Written accounts begin with the Spaniards, with the missionaries and military men who came looking for foundation sites, and later, looking for deserters from the coastal enclaves.

Fray Juan Crespi was a Franciscan priest, born on the Spanish isle of Mallorca. He had already travelled on foot from San Diego to San Francisco with Portolá on the first overland exploration of the Western coastline. Three years later, in March 1772, travelling with Captain Pedro Fages, he was in the first party of Europeans to view the Great Central Valley.

Fages had orders to establish a mission near Point Reyes, north of the Golden Gate. Searching for a way to get there by land from Monterey, he led his party up the eastern shoreline of San Francisco Bay until they reached Carquinez Straits, which forced them further inland. After resting near what is now Concord, they climbed a spur of Mount Diablo and came upon "a great plain as level as the palm of the hand," and a river so wide that Crespi calculated it to be "the largest that has been discovered in New Spain."

They camped near what is now Antioch. Crespi named the river San Francisco (later changed to San Joaquin), and the next day, knowing they could get no further north without boats, they started back toward Monterey to report what they had found.

Crespi's diary contains the full record of this expedition, and thus might be rightly called the earliest piece of valley writing. Another version of this same expedition is found in Fages' account, compiled for the Mexican Viceroy in 1775, which gives us one of the earliest descriptions of the region's original inhabitants.

During the next century our images of valley life come from soldiers, trappers, pioneers, and the various adventurers who followed the

Spaniards into California. The 19th century traveller best known to modern readers is probably Mark Twain, who passed through the Sacramento Valley in 1864-65, leaving us one of his choice asides on the climate and the view. In that same period, two other travellers recorded their impressions, in two books that have since become classic west coast travel narratives. William Brewer gathered the material for UP AND DOWN CALIFORNIA 1860-1864 while working as field leader of the first California Geological Survey team. John Muir, the legendary Scotsman, naturalist, and founder of the Sierra Club, included "The Bee Pastures" in his MOUNTAINS OF CALIFORNIA. Brewer, moving through the sparsely settled and as yet unirrigated lower San Joaquin, finds himself surrounded by the bleak emptiness of an undernourished landscape, while Muir, encamped between the Merced and Tuolome rivers, seems to have come up the land of promise so many travellers were looking for.

Like every region of the west, 19th Century valley life produced its share of legends, legendary figures, and tall tales. Hector Lee, one of America's most prominent folklorists, recounts the tale of the bandit/hero Joaquin Murieta, whose adventures, in this version of the legend, took him from the banks of the Stanislaus, to Marysville and Stockton, and finally south to Tejon Pass, where he met his death.

In a lighter vein, W. H. Hutchinson, a leading western historian, has resurrected a short-lived myth from the 1870s, wherein three Spanish deserters from the De Soto expedition supposedly crossed the continent, from Florida to the region near Oroville, some three hundred years before the Gold Rush. And John A. Barker, an early Bakersfield resident, revived another kind of yarn. "The Expansive Power of Beans," first published in the *Bakersfield Daily Californian* in 1904, comes from the world of mining country tall tales that gave Mark Twain such lasting gems as "The Celebrated Jumping Frog" and Baker's "Bluejay Yarn."

The period of settlement, from the 1860s onward, is represented here by Arnold A. Rojas, Mary Austin, and Frank Norris.

Rojas was born in the San Joaquin near the turn of the century. Of Spanish and Indian descent, he spent his life as a working cowboy, starting out on the vast Kern County cattle ranches. His four books, published between 1953 and 1964, reach back into the ranching days of the 19th century and the all-but-forgotten lore and skills of the vaqueros who taught him to rope and ride.

Mary Austin was another kind of settler. Raised and educated in Illinois, she moved to Kern County with her family in 1888. On the northern slope of the Tehachapis she began to pursue her chosen career as a writer, focussing first on California lives and landscapes. "The Scavengers" comes from THE LAND OF LITTLE RAIN, the first (1903) of her thirty-five published books, and in many ways still her best. Looking at the same country William Brewer found so stark and unforgiving, she sees touches of loveliness mingling with the relentlessness of the heat and the buzzards. She discovers the awesome balancings of death and life.

Frank Norris was the first nationally known writer whose major work was directly associated with the valley. His novel THE OCTOPUS was published in 1901, and it announces themes that will recur in valley writing throughout the 20th century: the lives lived by people drawn to its rich soil, and their battles for shares of the produce and profits.

Set in and around Tulare in the 1880s, this novel has its origins in a land swindle engineered by the Southern Pacific Railroad ("The Octopus"). The protagonists are local wheat ranchers, fighting to protect their hard-won holdings. One irony is that most of Norris's detail is based upon impressions gathered while visiting the much smaller San Benito Valley, a mountain range to the west, around Hollister and San Juan Bautista. Thus, readers who know the region feel slightly betrayed. The presence of a Spanish mission near Tulare, for example, is plainly ridiculous. Yet the struggle he set there was based upon a very real and brutal one, which became the focus of national attention after the notorious Mussel Slough Affair on May 10, 1880, outside the town of Hanford, when a U.S. Marshal and railroad-backed landholders shot it out with members of a local settler's league. A dramatic moment in California history, it became a crucial scene in the novel, symbolic of the conflict that Norris enlarged to epic literary proportions, making THE OCTOPUS an enduring piece of American naturalistic fiction.

Monday, March 30, 1772

FRAY JUAN CRESPI

We set out from this valley and entered some medium-sized hills of pure earth and pasture. We ascended a pass to its highest point in order to make observations, and we saw that the land opened into a great plain as level as the palm of the hand, the valley opening about half the quadrant, sixteen quarters from northwest to southeast, all level land as far as the eye could reach. Below the pass we beheld the estuary that we were following and saw that it was formed by two large rivers. Where these united to form the estuary we saw a good-sized island; each one of the rivers seemed to us to have a width of about a quarter of a league. We saw also that one of these rivers, the one to the south, was formed by two other rivers as wide as the principal one, a quarter of a league, and that the place where they united must be about eight leagues distant from the pass.

We made out that these three arms or three large rivers were formed by a very large river, a league in width at least, which descended from some high mountains to the southeast, very far distant, all that part of it which the eye reached descending from the east, and then dividing into three rivers. These three flowed to the north, making several windings, and afterwards they formed only two, one of which divided into two others, and the three then united to form once more the great river which entered the bay or round lake of which I have already spoken.

Besides the above we saw from the summit of the pass large groves of trees, very distant. It seemed to us that none of them were in the beds of those large rivers mentioned, though we judged they were on arroyos which empty into these rivers.

This examination concluded, we descended from the pass in order to go on and finish the day's march, which covered on this day ten leagues, all of level land, and we halted on the bank of a small arroyo of half salty water, about a quarter of a league distant from one of the large rivers, which we went to examine, finding the water fresh and still, and apparently with no current, on account of being very deep and having steep banks.

One league before halting, as it was nearly midday, I stopped to observe the latitude, and it was thirty-nine degrees and thirteen minutes. I gave to this great river the name of my Father San Francisco, so that he may intercede with His Divine Majesty for the conversion of all the immense body of heathen that no doubt must be on the banks of the great stream, which it seems must be the largest that has been discovered in New Spain.

Valley Indians

CAPTAIN PEDRO FAGES

The plain of San Francisco extends from the mouth of the river to a village named Buenavista near the Portezuelo de Cortés, where there are many grapevines; it is about one hundred and sixty leagues long and from twenty to thirty leagues wide. In it there are numerous reed patches and ponds, and it is very fertile. The natives, who live in spherical houses, are accustomed, in order to avoid the inconvenience attendant upon the rains when they are heavy, to move to drier land during the wet season; when this has passed they return to their dwellings. The slope of the sierra which lies toward Monterey is rather bare of trees, but abounds in seeds, and there are numerous villages near its streams. The range where it extends inland from the other side of the river is very high, and its peaks are always covered with snow. On its slopes there are many trees of great variety growing in good soil, and there are numerous wild buffaloes living in the dense parts of this forest.

THE COSTUME OF THE INDIANS

The captains wear their cloaks adorned with feathers, and a great coiffure of false hair folded back upon their own. The common Indians wear a small cloak which reaches to the waist; in their hair they interweave cords or bands with beads, among the folds of which they bestow the trifles which they need to carry with them. The most common of these small articles is a small horn of the antelope containing tobacco for smoking, wrapped in leaves. They gather great harvests of this plant, and grind large quantities of it mixed with lime, from this paste forming cones or small loaves which they wrap in *tule* leaves and hang up in the house until quite dry. They assert that as a food it is very strengthening, and that they can sustain themselves on it for three days without other nourishment; they usually partake of it at supper.

The arrangement of their villages is like a chain, not continuous, however, but broken, and in front of their dwellings they erect storehouses or barns in which to keep their seeds, implements, and so forth.

They have stone mortars very like the *metates* of this kingdom, jars of the same material, and trays of all sizes made of wood or reeds artistically decorated with fibrous roots of grass which always keep their natural color, which is variable according to the species.

They sleep upon skins of animals, and cover themselves with other skins.

The figure and form of these Indians is graceful; both men and women are taller than ordinary. The men have the custom of smearing their heads in the form of a cross (the efficacy and mysteries of which are yet unknown to them) with white mud. The women observe in their dress the styles of San Luis Obispo, but with greater neatness and decency; they have also the fashion of wearing the hair in a toupé with a braid.

Firebaugh to Fort Tejon

(from *Up and Down California,* 1860-64)

WILLIAM HENRY BREWER

Visalia.
Sunday, April 12, 1861

Monday, April 6, we started on and rode thirty-one miles without any incident. We stopped that night at Hill's Ferry, a dirty place, where a drunken "Secesh" made an uproar the whole night. A few *vaqueros* were managing a lot of wild Spanish cattle, to get them on board the ferryboat, and gave us some specimens of horsemanship and lassoing that were decidedly fine.

Tuesday we came on to Firebaugh's Ferry — a long fifty miles, a weary ride, and we had nothing to eat the entire day. Nor was this all. In crossing a slough early in the morning, a mixture of very muddy water and very sticky mud, Kate and Gabb got mired. They got out safely, but both cut a sorry figure, wet and covered with sticky mud, the former from head to tail, the latter from head to foot. We pushed on, the sun came out and dried them, and the mud was brushed off.

Firebaugh's was even a harder place than Hill's. I ought to have mentioned that near our Sunday's stopping place a murderer had just been arrested, and that at Hill's four horses had just been stolen. When we got to Firebaugh's we found more excitement. A band of desperadoes were just below — we had passed them in the morning, but luckily did not see them. Only a few days before they had attempted to rob some men, and in the scrimmage one man was shot dead and one of the desperadoes was so badly cut that he died on Monday. Another had just been caught. Some men took him into the bushes, some pistol shots were heard, they came back and said he had escaped. A newly made grave on the bank suggested another disposal of him, but all were content not to inquire further. This semi-desert plain and the inhospitable mountains on its west side are the grand retreats of the desperadoes of the state. It is needless to say that knife (newly ground) and six-shooter are carried "so as to be handy," but I trust that I will ever be spared any actual use for them.

Wednesday we came on to Fresno City — only eighteen miles, but there was no other stopping place for forty miles, so we had to stop. The country had been growing more and more desolate. We had left the trees behind at

Hill's, except occasional willows along the sloughs, and this day, for sixteen miles we rode over a plain of absolute desolation. The vegetation that had grown up last year, the wet year, was dead, and this year none has started. Sometimes no living thing cheered the eye, nothing in sight alive for miles. We crossed the slough ten miles above Firebaugh's, where there is a ferry, and a solitary shanty stands, the only house for the eighteen miles. We then struck across the plain in the direction of Fresno City, without track or guide, and at last that place loomed up.

Fresno "City" consists of one large house, very dilapidated, one small ditto, one barn, one small dilapidated and empty warehouse, and a corral. It is surrounded by swamps, now covered with rushes, the green of which was cheering to the eye after the desolation through which we had passed. These swamps extend southeast to Tulare Lake. We got into the place after much difficulty, but our animals had to content themselves with eating the coarse rushes that grew on the edges of the swamp. The cattle and horses that live on this look well.

Thursday we came on to Kings River, forty miles. Two men came with us, and in taking us across the swamp by a "better way," the horses came through safely, but Kate got mired again and Gabb had to get off and wade it and lead her. A mule mires much easier than a horse, having so much smaller feet. This day's ride was even more tedious and monotonous in its features. The land was wetter, so was green, but we were nearer the center of the plain, which is here not less than sixty miles wide! We rode upward of thirty miles without any tree or bush—except once a single small willow was visible for two hours, but we passed nearly two miles from it; it was a mere speck.

Hour after hour we plodded on. The road was good but a dead level—no hill or ridge ten feet high relieved the even surface—no house, no tree—one hour was but like the next—it was like the ocean, but it depressed the spirits more. The coast ranges were dim in the haze on the west; the snows of the Sierra Nevada eighty to a hundred miles distant on the east were hardly more distinct; while north and south the plain stretched to the horizon.

About six miles from Kings River we struck a belt of scattered oaks— fine trees—and what a relief! For, except a few cragged willows, shrubs rather than trees, in places along the soughs, we had seen no trees for the last 130 miles of the trip! We crossed Kings River, a swift deep stream, by ferry, and stopped at a house on the bank, the most like a *home* of anything we had seen for two hundred miles. The owner was a Massachusetts Yankee, and his wife a very intelligent woman—I noticed an atlas of the heavens hanging up in the sitting room—but she was a Kentuckian and smoked *cigarritos* as industriously as we did pipes.

Friday, April 10, we came on here, twenty-five miles, crossing an open plain of nearly twenty miles. The morning was clear, and the view of the snowy Sierra most magnificent. Tomorrow we push on, and anticipate a rough time for the next four or six weeks.

Visalia is a little, growing place, most beautifully situated on the plain in an extensive grove of majestic oaks. These trees are the charm of the place. Ample streams from the mountains, led in ditches wherever wanted, furnish water for irrigating. We have stopped here two days to allow our animals to rest and get inspiration for our trip ahead. The Indian troubles east seem quelled, so we apprehend no trouble on that score. The ringleader was killed near here yesterday morning, and another detachment of soldiers has just left to further punish those in the mountains.

One sees many Indians here in various stages of civilization, but generally rather low. On Kings River we visited a camp of the Kings River tribe. They were hard looking customers. They lived in a long building, made of rushes carefully plaited together so as to shed the rain, making a long shed perhaps sixty or eighty feet long. The children were entirely naked; the adults all with more or less civilized clothing. All have very dark complexions, nearly as black as negroes.

Fort Tejon.
May 5.

Monday, April 13, we left Visalia and came on to Tule River, about thirty miles, still along the plain, here very barren, but the Sierra rose quite near us. We stopped at a little tavern and store, with miserable accommodations, but poor as it was, it was to be our last for near a hundred miles. I spent the evening in reading *Les Miserables* — a returned miner was reading *Shakespeare*. I question if the next generation here will care for Shakespeare, or any other author, growing up in ignorance, far from school, church, or other institution of civilization. The Tule River is a small river, easily forded, with wide stretches of barren sand on either side.

Tuesday we came on thirty miles and stopped at Coyote Springs, about six or seven miles from White River. The road this day was through a desolate waste — I should call it a *desert* — a house at Deer Creek and another at White River were the only habitations. The soil was barren and, this dry year, almost destitute of vegetation. A part of the way was through low barren hills, all rising to about the same height — in fact, a tableland washed down into hills. We stopped at a miserable hut, where there is a spring and a man keeps a few cattle. He was not at home, but his wife was, and she gave us something to eat, and we slept out upon the ground near our mules. The woman was a fat, ignorant thing, with four little girls who looked like half-savages; in fact, they were scarcely better than Indians.

Wednesday we came on thirty-five miles to Kern River, the most barren and desolate day's ride since leaving Fresno, and for thirty miles we saw no house. We continued among the low barren hills until we came near Kern River—here we had to leave the road and go down the river nine or ten miles to find a ford. We followed a few wagon tracks, left the hills, and struck down the plain. The soil became worse—a sandy plain, without grass, in places very alkaline—a few desert or saline shrubs growing in spots, elsewhere the soil bare—no water, no feed. We saw some coyotes (wolves) and antelope. Night came on, and still we found neither grass nor river ford. Long after dark, when we began to get discouraged and to fear we would have to stop without water or feed for ourselves or animals, we heard some dogs bark. Soon we saw a light and soon afterward struck a cabin. Here we found some grass, went into the house, made some tea, and then slept on the river bank. Here in a cabin lived a man, wife, and several children, all ragged, dirty, ignorant—not one could read or write—and Secessionists, of course.

Kern River is a wide swift stream, here about twenty or twenty-five rods wide, with a treacherous sandy bottom. I dared not risk our animals in it without seeing what it was, so I hired the man to cross it first with his horse. We crossed safely, but it was up to the horses' sides most of the way. That day, Thursday, we came on thirty miles to the mouth of this canyon. From Kern River we saw the mountains on all sides of us—the Sierra on the east, the Coast Range on the west, the two joining on the south—the high peaks, some of them capped with snow, rising like a vast amphitheater. The morning was cloudy and clouds hung over the highest peaks. In about six miles we crossed the last slough of Kern River, then struck south for the mountains, across a complete desert. In places there were patches of alkali grass or salient desert shrubs, in others it was entirely bare, the ground crusted with salt and alkali, like snow—the only living thing larger than insects for many miles was a rattlesnake that we stopped and killed.

The storm came up black behind us; it stretched like a wall across the valley from mountain to mountain; the clouds grew lower on the peaks. We hurried up our tired and jaded animals, who seemed almost worn out. The storm struck us; but instead of rain it was wind—fierce—and the air was filled with dust and alkali. It was fearful, like a sandstorm on the desert. Sometimes we could not see a hundred yards in any direction—all was shut out in clouds of dust. In the midst of this storm my tired horse fell flat with me and got away; luckily he was too tired to run, and I easily caught him again.

At last the rain set in and wet us thoroughly. It was night when we struck the mouth of the Cañada de las Uvas, and found a house. They would not keep us at first, no accommodations, but at last we prevailed and stopped. We got some supper, shivered in the cold, then went to bed. Our host, a young man, with Indian servants, generously gave us his room. There were but two rooms in the house. He, a Spaniard, and two squaws occupied the other room — with a pack of cards and a bottle of whiskey to heighten the pleasure of a social evening.

The last few miles the plain had risen rapidly, until the mouth of the canyon where we were had an elevation of over a thousand feet. The country had improved on this slope, with some grass, while on striking the mountains all was green. All changed, and what a relief! We had ridden on this plain *about three hundred miles!*

The Eternal Summer of Sacramento

(from *Roughing It*)

MARK TWAIN

I have elsewhere spoken of the endless Winter of Mono, California, and but this moment of the eternal Spring of San Francisco. Now if we travel a hundred miles in a straight line, we come to the eternal Summer of Sacramento. One never sees Summer-clothing or mosquitoes in San Francisco — but they can be found in Sacramento. Not always and unvaryingly, but about one hundred and forty-three months out of twelve years, perhaps. Flowers bloom there, always, the reader can easily believe — people suffer and sweat, and swear, morning, noon and night, and wear out their stanchest energies fanning themselves. It gets hot there, but if you go down to Fort Yuma you will find it hotter. Fort Yuma is probably the hottest place on earth. The thermometer stays at one hundred and twenty in the shade there all the time — except when it varies and goes higher. It is a U. S. military post, and its occupants get so used to the terrific heat that they suffer without it. There is a tradition (attributed to John Phenix) that a very, very wicked soldier died there, once, and of course, went straight to the hottest corner of perdition, — and the next day he *telegraphed back for his blankets*. There is no doubt about the truth of this statement — there can be no doubt about it. I have seen the place where that soldier used to board. In Sacramento it is fiery Summer always, and you can gather roses, and eat strawberries and ice-cream, and wear white linen clothes, and pant and perspire, at eight or nine o-clock in the morning, and then take the cars, and at noon put on your furs and your skates, and go skimming over frozen Donner Lake, seven thousand feet above the valley, among snow banks fifteen feet deep, and in the shadow of grand mountain peaks that lift their frosty crags ten thousand feet above the level of the sea. There is a transition for you! Where will you find another like it in the Western hemisphere? And some of us have swept around snow-walled curves of the Pacific Railroad in that vicinity, six thousand feet above the sea, and looked down as the birds do, upon the deathless Summer of the Sacramento Valley, with its fruitful fields, its feathery foliage, its silver streams, all slumbering in the mellow haze of its enchanted atmosphere, and all infinitely softened and spiritualized by distance—a dreamy, exquisite glimpse of *fairyland,* made all the more charming and striking that it was caught through a forbidden gateway of ice and snow, and savage crags and precipices.

The Bee Pastures
(from *The Mountains of California*)

JOHN MUIR

The Great Central Plain of California, during the months of March, April, and May, was one smooth, continuous bed of honey-bloom, so marvelously rich that, in walking from one end of it to the other, a distance of more than 400 miles, your foot would press about a hundred flowers at every step. Mints, gilias, nemophilas, castilleias, and innumerable compositae were so crowded together that, had ninety-nine per cent of them been taken away, the plain would still have seemed to any but Californians extravagantly flowery. The radiant, honeyful corollas, touching and overlapping, and rising above one another, glowed in the living light like a sunset sky—one sheet of purple and gold, with the bright Sacramento pouring through the midst of it from the north, the San Joaquin from the south, and their many tributaries sweeping in at right angles from the mountains, dividing the plain into sections fringed with trees.

Along the rivers there is a strip of bottom-land, countersunk beneath the general level, and wider toward the foot-hills, where magnificent oaks, from three to eight feet in diameter, cast grateful masses of shade over the open, prairie-like levels. And close along the water's edge there was a fine jungle of tropical luxuriance, composed of wild-rose and bramble bushes and a great variety of climbing vines, wreathing and interlacing the branches and trunks of willows and alders, and swinging across from summit to summit in heavy festoons. Here the wild bees reveled in fresh bloom long after the flowers of the drier plain had withered and gone to seed. And in midsummer, when the "blackberries" were ripe, the Indians came from the mountains to feast—men, women, and babies in long, noisy trains, often joined by the farmers of the neighborhood, who gathered this wild fruit with commendable appreciation of its superior flavor, while their home orchards were full of ripe peaches, apricots, nectarines, and figs, and their vineyards were laden with grapes. But, though these luxuriant, shaggy riverbeds were thus distinct from the smooth, treeless plain, they made no heavy dividing lines in general views. The whole appeared as one continuous sheet of bloom bounded only by the mountains.

When I first saw this central garden, the most extensive and regular of all the bee-pastures of the State, it seemed all one sheet of plant gold, hazy and vanishing in the distance, distinct as a new map along the foot-hills at my feet.

Descending the eastern slopes of the Coast Range through beds of gilias and lupines, and around many a breezy hillock and bush-crowned headland, I at length waded out into the midst of it. All the ground was covered, not with grass and green leaves, but with radiant corollas, about ankle-deep next the foot-hills, knee-deep or more five or six miles out. Here were bahia, madia, madaria, burrielia, chrysopsis, corethrogyne, grindelia, etc., growing in close social congregations of various shades of yellow, blending finely with the purples of clarkia, orthocarpus, and oenothera, whose delicate petals were drinking the vital sunbeams without giving back any sparkling glow.

Because so long a period of extreme drought succeeds the rainy season, most of the vegetation is composed of annuals, which spring up simultaneously, and bloom together at about the same height above the ground, the general surface being but slightly ruffled by the taller phacelias, pentstemons, and groups of *Salvia carduacea,* the king of the mints.

Sauntering in any direction, hundreds of these happy sun-plants brushed against my feet at every step, and closed over them as if I were wading in liquid gold. The air was sweet with fragrance, the larks sang their blessed songs, rising on the wing as I advanced, then sinking out of sight in the polleny sod, while myriads of wild bees stirred the lower air with their monotonous hum — monotonous, yet forever fresh and sweet as everyday sunshine. Hares and spermophiles showed themselves in considerable numbers in shallow places, and small bands of antelopes were almost constantly in sight, gazing curiously from some slight elevation, and then bounding swiftly away with unrivaled grace of motion. Yet I could discover no crushed flowers to mark their track, nor, indeed, any destructive action of any wild foot or tooth whatever.

The great yellow days circled by uncounted, while I drifted toward the north, observing the countless forms of life thronging about me, lying down almost anywhere on the approach of night. And what glorious botanical beds I had! Oftentimes on awaking I would find several new species leaning over me and looking me full inthe face, so that my studies would begin before rising.

About the first of May I turned eastward, crossing the San Joaquin River between the mouths of the Tuolumne and Merced, and by the time I had reached the Sierra foot-hills most of the vegetation had gone to seed and become as dry as hay.

All the seasons of the great plain are warm or temperate, and bee-flowers are never wholly wanting; but the grand springtime — the annual resurrection — is governed by the rains, which usually set in about the middle of November or the beginning of December. Then the seeds, that for six months have lain on the ground dry and fresh as if they had been gathered into barns, at once unfold their treasured life. The general brown and purple of the ground, and the dead vegetation of the preceding year, give place to the green of mosses and liverworts and myriads of young leaves. Then one species after another comes into flower, gradually overspreading the green with yellow and purple, which lasts until May.

The "rainy season" is by no means a gloomy, soggy period of constant cloudiness and rain. Perhaps nowhere else in North America, perhaps in the world, are the months of December, January, February, and March so full of bland, plant-building sunshine. Referring to my notes of the winter and spring of 1868–69, every day of which I spent out of doors, on that section of the plain lying between the Tuolumne and Merced rivers, I find that the first rain of the season fell on December 18th. January had only six rainy days — that is, days on which rain fell; February three, March five, April three, and May three, completing the so-called rainy season, which was about an average one. The ordinary rain-storm of this region is seldom very cold or violent. The winds, which in settled weather come from the northwest, veer round into the opposite direction, the sky fills gradually and evenly with one general cloud, from which the rain falls steadily, often for days in succession, at a temperature of about 45° or 50°.

More than seventy-five per cent of all the rain of this season came from the northwest, down the coast over southeastern Alaska, British Columbia, Washington, and Oregon, though the local winds of these circular storms blow from the southeast. One magnificent local storm from the northwest fell on March 21. A massive, round-browed cloud came swelling and thundering over the flowery plain in most imposing majesty, its bossy front burning white and purple in the full blaze of the sun, while warm rain poured from its ample fountains like a cataract, beating down flowers and bees, and flooding the dry watercourses as suddenly as those of Nevada are flooded by the so-called "cloud-bursts." But in less than half an hour not

a trace of the heavy, mountain-like cloud-structure was left in the sky, and
the bees were on the wing, as if nothing more gratefully refreshing could
have been sent them.

The Plains of the San Joaquin
(Anonymous 19th-century ballad)

Don't go, I say, if you've got any brains,
You'll stay far away from the San Joaquin plains.
At four in the morning they're hustling up tools.
Feed, curry, and harness ten long-eared old mules.
Plow twenty-four miles through sunshine and rain,
Or your blankets you'll roll on the San Joaquin Plain.

They'll work you eight hours and eight hours more,
You'll sleep in a bunkhouse without any door;
They'll feed you on mutton, sow-belly, and sheep,
And dock you for half of the time that you sleep,
Twenty-four hours through sunshine and rain
or your blankets you'll roll on the San Joaquin Plain.

The Spirit of Joaquin
HECTOR LEE

In a little cabin on the Stanislaus River in central California lived a young
Mexican. He was a very handsome young man, apparently of a good
family, who had come up from Sonora, Mexico, to farm and perhaps pan a
little gold in this new land of El Dorado. With him was his lovely young
bride, Rosita. Or perhaps her name was Carmelita; the stories differ, and
no one is quite sure. And with them also was his brother.

Together, in that little cabin by the river, they lived through a quiet,
happy summer. They took a little gold from the stream, and they talked
about how they would plant some corn when spring came. They knew
nothing of the Californian's laws, and when it was explained to them that it
was illegal for Mexicans to own mining claims or take gold from the
California rivers, they merely shrugged and went on with their work. God
had put the gold there. It belonged to everybody. And they took only the

little that fortune put into their hands to pay for their work.

The Californians were angry about this, and one night a small group of men, drunk on liquor and mad with hatred, burst into the cabin on the river. Angry words, threats, and a fight! Joaquin's brother was shot down immediately. And Joaquin's beautiful wife — innocent, frightened, helpless — was brutally attacked and then murdered. They tied him to a post out in the yard, stripped him to the waist, and with a horsewhip lashed him until the blood came. As he stood their straining at the ropes, each time the leather whip cut across his bear chest and shoulders, he swore an awful vengeance. He memorized the ugly faces of his attackers and swore that he would kill them every one, and all the other Americans that he could. Then he slumped into unconsciousness, and his assailants left him for dead.

We are told that the next day he disappeared, that he drifted north after that, but no one knows for sure where he went. The marks of the whiplash gradually healed, but the memory of his pain and the hatred for his enemies seemed to grow stronger. The next time he appeared it was as a bandit. As an outlaw he gathered around him a band of other Mexicans who had grievances. And he took in some who wanted quick profit and were not afraid to kill for it. The handsome young Mexican soon became the respected and feared leader of bold and ruthless outlaws. Always splendidly dressed, he rode at the head of his band on a magnificant horse, and his very name struck fear to any who might stand in his way. The men who had killed his wife and brother one by one disappeared, and everyone knew what had happened to them.

He was a cruel and deadly enemy of his foes, but he was never known to turn down a friend who needed help. Many poor Mexicans received his generous help, and they thanked him and asked the saints to bless him. Whenever he needed a place to hide, they sheltered him and kept his secrets. He had become their Robin Hood.

In 1851 he and his gang settled about three miles north of Marysville. They stole horses, robbed immigrant wagons, held up stage coaches, and killed whoever got in their way or were so foolish as to try to capture them. The vigilantes organized a large force to hunt him down, so Joaquin quietly slipped away and went further north and wintered near Mount Shasta. After that, he was always on the move. At San Jose a posse almost cornered him, but he got away. Some say he went to Carmel Mission, and it is said that a priest at the mission painted his picture.

There was such a picture. Perhaps it was painted by a priest. It shows a man supposed to be named Joaquin, with wild eyes, a fierce moustache, and a cruel face. Other artists later copies this picture — or some other — and in each successive portrait the outlaw became more dashing, more handsome, more gallant, and his costume became more colorful and splendid. These pictures only reflect the growing legend.

There is a telling of how a cattle buyer was camped by a little stream one night as he was driving his cattle to market in one of the San Joaquin Valley towns. Five young Mexicans rode into his camp just at dusk and asked for some supper. He obligingly gave them food, and they spread out their bedrolls and slept by his camp that night. The next morning, when they awoke, he was cooking breakfast for them.

"Well, how is Senor Joaquin this morning?" he asked.

The young leader looked startled and suddenly became tense. One of his companions drew his gun, looked a long time at the cattle man, and then grinned. "So you theenk you know heem?"

"Yes, I knew him the minute he rode in last night," said the cattle man. The Mexican then asked why the drover hadn't killed him last night when he was asleep to collect the reward.

"Why, that's easy, friend. I don't like to kill men. And I don't want the reward. Besides, you fellers never did me any harm. If every man that deserved to hang went supperless, there'd be empty chairs at more tables than mine," said the cattle man. Joaquin smiled and promised the man that he would never be sorry. And the people say that from that day on, this man never lost a head of cattle to any Mexican bandits.

The reward for the outlaw grew. It attracted many adventurers, some of whom gave their lives to the vengeance of Joaquin. With increasing interest and satisfaction he read the reward notices. One beautiful Sunday morning in Stockton, while the bells were ringing for church and the fine ladies and gentlemen were walking to worship, a handsome young Mexican came riding along the street on a beautiful black horse. He was wearing a fashionable sombrero, flashing buckles, and spurs of silver. He stopped here and there to look in the shop windows. The young ladies cast admiring glances his way and thought, "What a rich young man he must be."

He rode over to the side of the building where some posters had been nailed to the wall. One of the posters read: "Reward: $5,000 for the bandit Joaquin." The stranger got off his horse, took a pencil out of his pocket and wrote something over the poster. Then he remounted his horse and rode away. The ladies and gentlemen rushed up to look at the poster to see what he had written. On the reward notice he had crossed out the $5,000 and had written under it, "I will give $10,000," and it was signed, "Joaquin."

This romantic bandit was said to be the kind of man who couldn't live long without love, and there were many beautiful ladies willing to share his company. One in particular was a fiery beauty called Antonia la Molinera. She ran away with him, dressed like a man, and rode with him in the hills. She fought beside him on the raids. It was said that they were happy for a time. But after awhile she fell in love with another member of Joaquin's gang, and one night she slipped away with him and they disappeared.

Once again Joaquin swore vengeance, and everybody knew he would keep his word. For months he followed their trail from village to village and from ranch to ranch. At last he found the man and killed him. The girl knew her turn would surely come, that she would never be safe until Joaquin was caught; so secretly she sent word to the man who was most likely to capture the bandit, and she told him where Joaquin's hideouts were.

That man was Captain Harry Love, a hunter of men and an adventurer who had come up from Texas. He yearned for the excitement of the hunt and hungered for the reward money that stood on Murieta's head. The state legislature authorized Captain Love to organize a posse of rangers to track down the outlaws and paid them $150 a month, with the rangers furnishing their own horses and outfits.

The orders were to get Joaquin and as many of his gang as possible, and particularly a wanton killer known as Three-Fingered Jack, who was riding with him at the time. Love had learned from the treacherous Antonia where Joaquin's hide-out camps were located, and the long hunt began. The rangers chased the bandits from one camp to another, night and day, through the hills, across the rivers, and over the mountains, gradually closing the circle. Finally, early one morning in July, 1853, the rangers came upon the last camp. They were in the mountains near Tejon Pass in the Tehachapis.* They rode quietly up over a ridge and suddenly, there below them, was a little camp hidden in a pocket in the rugged canyon. Six Mexicans were seated around the fire. Breakfast was being prepared, and some were already eating. A seventh man—slender, graceful, with dark eyes and long black hair—was standing a little way from the campfire rubbing down a beautiful bay horse. This was Joaquin Murieta.

The rangers rode in quickly with their guns drawn and ordered the bandits to surrender. For a brief moment there was silence. No one moved. No one spoke. Joaquin's guns were hanging on his saddle several feet away from where he was standing, just out of reach. Three-Fingered Jack stood back against a rock, watching every move. He was tense and ready. Suddenly Joaquin made a dive for his guns. This was the move that sprung the action. Three-Fingered Jack whipped out his guns and began to fire. A burst of gunfire came from the other Mexicans, but their shots went wild. Love and his rangers dug spurs and lunged into the camp, firing at Jack. Their lead hit him again and again. He slumped and fell, and was dead.

Joaquin couldn't quite reach his guns without moving directly into their fire. In a flash he changed his mind and leaped on his horse. Without saddle

*Some researchers locate this showdown at Panoche Pass, west from Fresno, on the eastern face of the Coast Range.

or bridle, the horse bounded away over the hill and up among the rocks. Through the brush and over the hills he flew, with the rangers after him. Joaquin had no gun, only a dagger which he brandished in the air as he pushed the horse on. The rangers were following, shooting as fast as they could. At one precipice, where the rocks hung low overhead, Murieta was scraped off his horse, but he leaped on again and away they went.

Finally, one bullet found flesh, and the horse fell. Joaquin was now on foot. He scrambled through the rocks and behind the bushes. The shots were still coming. Three bullets entered his body, and he began to fall. He sank first to his knees, then to his elbows, and finally he lay in the sand. Then he raised one hand as if to stop the shooting and said, "It is enough. The work is done." And Joaquin Murieta fell dead. The long trail had ended.

This place in the mountains was too far away to carry the dead bodies in from, so Love and his party cut off the head of Murieta and the hand of Three-Fingered Jack to deliver as proof that they had killed the bandits and thus collect the reward. Preserved in alcohol, these frightful objects were accepted as evidence that the outlaws were dead, and on August 18, 1853, the head was placed on exhibition in San Francisco. The curious were thus enabled to see what was left of the man who but a little while before had been a living legend, Joaquin Murieta, the Robin Hood of El Dorado. For this great privilege it was necessary only to pay the small admission price of one dollar.

It was the work of only three short years to start the legend. It still lives. The name of Joaquin is seen everywhere in the great valleys of California, and the people say that the spirit of Joaquin still rides the California hills. Even a grizzled old poet of the Sierra, Joaquin Miller, took his name and wrote a poem about him.

The legend will not die. And wherever unjust laws or greedy men oppress the poor, some Joaquin Murieta or another Robin Hood will ride again.

Cabeza de Vaca Was a Piker

W. H. HUTCHINSON

Stories that stimulate idle speculation are few and far between in these parlous times. After twenty years of pondering what follows, that is all that is claimed for it.

Oroville, California, is that state's latest "best town by a dam site," because of the world's largest, at this writing, earth-filled structure, which is storing the waters of Feather River to slake the thirst of Los Angeles. The necessity of this function still is moot in the minds of many northern Californiacs, this writer among them. In 1879, Oroville was "between hay and grass," so to speak. The placer riches of the Gold Rush had been depleted; the heyday of gold-dredging was twenty years in its future; and the rise of commercial lumbering was in its infancy. The town was a torpid distributing center for the foothill and mountain country to its north and east, and summer's heat increased its somnolence by about 109° F.

On Friday, July 25, 1879, the town's *Weekly Mercury* printed the following item under the heading "A Relic of the Past," which has been paragraphed for easier assimilation:

"While chopping up an oak tree, which they had felled for the purpose of obtaining lumber to construct a cabin, James Reynolds and Joe McCarty, two miners working on Middle Fork of Feather River, last Thursday, found in a cavity in the interior of the tree a piece of parchment, 8x14 inches, both sides of which were covered with hieroglyphics, as they thought, excepting four figures, viz: 1542.

"Naturally presuming it to be something of a curiosity, the gentlemen very properly decided to preserve the parchment, which they did until Monday of this week, when a San Francisco man, who was hunting in that section, stopped at their camp and upon being shown the document offered $50 for it. The offer was accepted.

"Tuesday night the purchaser, who proved to F. M. Castronjo, of Madrid, Spain, reached this city, en route to the [San Francisco] Bay. We ran across him while in quest of items with this assault.

"He said the characters on the parchment were Spanish letters: that he, being a well-educated Spaniard, had experienced no difficulty in deciphering the writing, and informed us that it was a condensed history of the wanderings, trials and tribulations of three men named Emanuel Sagosta, Jose Gareljos and Sebastian Murilo [sic], deserters from the command of Hernando de Soto: that they were, at the time of writing, the sole survivors of a party of thirteen who ran away from the expedition on the 24th of November, 1539, and that this letter was written and placed in a knothole in the oak on the 29th day of August, 1542: that the party were discouraged at the prospect of dying in the wilderness and had no idea as to whither their steps were leading them.

"He kindly permitted us to look at the parchment, which was of a dark cream color, the writing thereon being easily perceived by the naked eye, its color being that of a faded blue. Prior to leaving this city, Mr. Castronjo had the precious article securely sealed up in a tin can to keep the air from it, and intends disposing of it to the National Historical Society of Spain.

"In response to our inquiry as to how much the tree had grown in that time, he said the miners told him that the outer edge of the cavity was about five inches within the tree, which had grown over and completely closed the hole."

Apparently Señor Castonjo had his purchase so securely encased that no scholarly *djinn* has yet unsoldered it. Neither have the state's numerous Chambers of Commerce seized upon its newsletter mention to prove that emigration from Florida to California antedated Spain's beachhead at San Diego by some two centuries.

This lack of attention is not offset by the once-prevalent legend that one of the Maidu tribelets along the lower Feather River had a distinctive ruling family long before the coming of any immigrant recorded in Hubert Howe Bancroft's *Pioneer Register*. This family was blessed with far greater height and much greater strength than run-of-the-Maidu males; it possessed far greater intelligence and far lighter skins than those it dominated. Perhaps Pocahontas had California counterparts even before Sir Francis Drake's claim gave western limits to the Virginia (*London*) Company's charter. Perhaps, too, the Maidu legend of a giant evil spirit who dwelled in the Middle Fork of Feather River near the polished granite mass they called *U - 1 - No* derived from the journey of José, Manuel, and Sebastián. *Quién sabe?*

At the time of their presumed desertion, the expedition of Hernan de Soto was in the neighborhood of Apalachee Bay in Florida. This is a long country mile or more from the Middle Fork's cutlass-slash canyon in the western flank of the Sierra Nevada. Yet the *entrada* of Cabeza de Vaca proves that mileage, terrain, and the unknown were not barriers to survival travel. So does the lesser-known journey of David Ingram, one of John Hawkins' *"saylers,"* who allegedly tramped from near Tampico, across Texas to New Brunswick, where he hailed a French vessel and was carried home to England. By these lights, the journey of Señor Castronjo's trio can be viewed as a possibility. It also can be viewed in other lights.

For instance, why were two miners felling oaks to build a cabin instead of the pine and fir and cedar that grew to the river's edge? Wasn't it providential that a "well-educated" Spaniard with surplus cash should visit their camp? Wasn't it fortunate that an inquiring reporter "ran across" Señor Castronjo and was granted an interview? Wasn't that a durable piece of parchment to survive three hundred years and thirty-seven immured in the knothole of a tree whose punkwater is a notable remedy for warts?

Assuming the parchment did survive inside a self-healing knothole, what did happen to it thereafter? Did it wind up in Madrid's *Museo Naval*, as once was rumored but never proven? Or did Señor Castronjo throw the "securely sealed up" can into the nearest Madrid gutter, aware at last that he had been sold a bill of goods by two simple miners in far-away California and convinced that a little learning is a dangerous thing?

Irrespective of the parchment's fate, the final question must be asked. How did Jim Reynolds and Joe McCarty spend those fifty golden dollars, if they got them?

The Expansive Power of Beans as Related by General Freeman

JOHN A. BARKER

One very rainy winter day in 1855 in the town of Visalia, Tulare county, a party of young men were congregated in the law office of General Freeman and Wm. G. Norris, and as usual on such occasions, some one started to tell a story. This time one was told by an amateur miner; the subject was his experience in his attempt to cook a pot of beans.

It seems that he and his partners, as was usual amongst miners in those days, took turns, week about, in keeping camp and doing the cooking. About the second day of his turn the outfit was rather grumpy because the bread was of such a consistency that, as one of them declared, if after eating a meal, he should, by accident, fall into the river, it would be an utter impossibility that he should ever rise to the surface, and abjured his partners to waste no time in searching for his corpse, but to consider him as safely buried as though he had been enclosed in a leaden sarcophagus, and to let it go at that.

It was finally suggested that, for a change, they have pork and beans; that the cook, if he allowed the beans to cook a sufficient length of time, could not help but have them soft enough to eat.

The next morning, bright and early, he had his beans out and soaking in water, and when he came to put them in the pot he was in doubt as to how much he ought to put in, or rather how full he ought to fill the pot. The other men were at work too far off for him to make any inquiry, so he thought that if he filled the pot within two inches of the top the beans would naturally settle down as they were cooked and leave plenty of room to put the bacon in. He carried out his ideas in this respect and set the pot on the fire, and went about his other work.

In about an hour he came to look at the pot. When behold! the beans were rolling over the top of the pot and had nearly covered up the fire. He at once seized a dipper and commenced dipping out the beans until he had every spare vessel about the place full of half cooked beans; and when his partners arrived for dinner he was voted a failure and banished from the kitchen. They swore he could not boil water without burning it.

General Freeman heard this story out and chipped in. "Why," said he, "you do not know the first principles of the expansive power of beans.

"When I was mining up on Greenhorn, at my mill, I had for partners in the mine Sam May, Long Moore, Leon Mathews — four including myself. We always laid off and took a holiday on Sunday. We went on Saturday evening to Whiskey Flat, now known as Kernville, and did not return until Sunday night or Monday morning. Of course we were at church all this time.

"One Saturday evening when it was my turn to cook, I told the boys not to wait for me; that I had some chores to attend to, and that I would be at the prayer meeting almost as soon as they would. We had a large open fire place that occupied very nearly the whole width of the cabin on the hearth, and we could roll an oak log in that would answer as a back log for several days. We also had a large copper kettle that would hold about forty gallons. I concluded that as the weather was cool, I would cook enough beans to last a week and not be troubled cooking them every day. So I filled the kettle nearly full of water and took the sack of beans. After I had hung the kettle on the hook that hung in the chimney, and started to empty the beans into the kettle, I slipped forward as I was in the act, and emptied the whole sack into the kettle. I thought I would let it go any way, and finished up my work and started for the church at Whiskey Flat.

"We had a protracted meeting then and we did not return home until after dark on Sunday evening.

"Our cabin was a substantial one built of pine logs, and the doors all opened toward the inside. One of us attempted to open the door. It would not budge. I tried it, and I said, 'I think some one is inside and has fastened the door.' We tried a rear door with the same results. One of us then climbed up with the intention of crawling down the chimney, but the chimney seemed choked by something. I then climbed up myself, got into the chimney, reached down to feel what I stood on, when, behold, it was beans! I then remembered what I had done, and I said, 'Boys, get an ax and split that door to pieces. The devil has been here while we were worshipping at Whiskey Flat.'

"No sooner said than done. The door was split out, and out rolled the beans. We got shovels and shoveled them out and then shoveled them into a pile away from the cabin. We found it full to the roof, and everything steaming like a Turkish bath. We had to send away for the whole tribe of Indians on the South Fork to help us get away with those beans before they got sour and created an epidemic.

"A short time after that episode, we ran out of blasting powder at the mine. In those days we knew nothing of the high and powerful explosives used in the mines of today, and as there was no powder to be got before the arrival of the next train of ox teams from Stockton, it set us to thinking of the highly expansive power of beans. I called the attention of my partners to the fact, historically established, that Pizarro, when he invaded the domain of the Incas of Peru, found great works that had been constructed by this remarkable and wonderful people, in the construction of canals for the purpose of irrigation, which exist to this day, in which their courses had been excavated for long distances by way of open work as well as tunnels through the hardest kind of rock formation and this without the aid of steel or the agency of explosives. I argued that as they had nothing but the simplest tools at their command that they must have used some of the forces provided by nature for the purpose of disintegrating the rock. Ergo, what would have suggested itself more naturally to them than the expansive power of one of the staple articles of their food, viz, beans?

"I suggested that we go to work and try an experiment by drilling four holes into the face of the drift in our mine, one at the top, one at the bottom and one on each side about half way up. We did so accordingly, and then filled the holes about two-thirds full of dry beans, rammed them in tight and forced warm water in — sufficient to saturate them well. We then tamped them hard and tight in the usual way of tamping a blast with sand. When we had that all done we leisurely sat down and awaited developments. In about a half hour we began to hear an occasional snap or crack, and soon we began to see the rock in the face of the drift begin to bulge out. Then gradually the whole face of the drift began to disintegrate and to bulge more and more, until with a crash such as would be made by a mass of falling mortar, the vein matter that formed the face of the drift fell out all broken up to the full depth of the holes we had drilled, which was about two feet. We were of course delighted. We had wrested the secret of the Incas from the oblivion in which in had been shrouded, and demonstrated the power of one of the hidden forces of nature, simplified the art of mining and provided and cheap and effectual means of unlocking the great treasure house of the Sierra Nevada. No longer were men to be killed and maimed by premature explosions of dangerous compounds; and we, the discoverers of this simple, safe and powerful agent, would go down to posterity as amongst the foremost of the great army of discoverers like Fulton, Columbus, Sir Isaac Newton and a host of others."

El Viejito
ARNOLD A. ROJAS

In the old days, *muchachos malcriados,* ill bred youngsters, were not often met with, if at all. One of the reasons why people respected their elders might have been the result of the many stories where this particular virtue was the main theme. There were few books in California and fewer people who could read them. In those days the *cuento* was relied upon to teach manners and this story is one that has been told many times through the years.

The ranch was known far and wide for its mean horses. When the ragged old man with his wizened little wife went there and asked for work, the *mayordomo* pitied them. Out of respect for the *viejito's* white hair, he assigned him a *jacalito,* little hut, and gave him a spavined, ring-boned old mare to ride when herding the goats. The old one accepted this work and the decrepit mount humbly and thankfully and took such good care of her that it was not long before her ribs filled out and her coat gleamed in the sunlight. In the morning the men would all grin when the *viejito* rode out on the old mare. She would mince out of the corral with a hump in her back; but only for a few yards, when old age and infirmities would bring her back to a more sober behavior.

The time for working the bands of horses comes in winter, long after the rodeos are over and the cattle have drifted out of the sierra into the warm lowlands. The saddle stock is culled; the older horses turned out to rest through the winter, while the four year olds are brought in and issued to the men who are to break them.

One cold morning the corral was jammed with wild-eyed broncos and the men were gathered in a group near the gate to wait for the colts to be roped and allotted to them. As each animal was caught the *caporal* called a vaquero who led it away and tied it up. The *viejito* had joined the vaqueros when the work began and stood patiently by until each man had been issued four broncos each and there was but one horse left in the corral, a *bayo lobo,* or buckskin with a coating of light hair over his black mane and tail. He had been ridden and spoiled the year before and had been turned out; sometimes horses forget about bucking after running out a year or two. The *mayordomo* was leaving when the *viejito,* seeing he was to be left out of the picture, approached him and said, "Señor, I have not been issued a *potro,* (colt)." The mayordomo was of the old school who show respect to their elders so he spoke gently.

"*Tio,* uncle," he said, "the nature of your work does not permit the riding of *caballos broncos* and for that reason I did not call on you to take one."

The *viejito* with *mucha tristesa*, very sadly, said, "I would like to earn the extra money riding the *potro* will bring."

The *mayordomo* pondered. It did not look well to give the *viejito* the spoiled horse he had kept from younger men; on the other hand to refuse him a colt would be as much as to say the old man was worthless, so much against his will the *mayordomo* told the *viejito* to take the buckskin.

The *viejito* immediately removed the saddle from the old mare and carried it into the corral where he untied the *tapa ojos* (blinds) and *jaquima* he had brought. The *caporal* threw a loop around the bronco's neck and led him into the empty corral, where, after he had choked down and fallen, the old man fastened the *tapa ojos* and *jaquima* on his head. When the loop was removed the colt stood up and the *viejito* put the saddle on, cinching it up tightly.

By that time, the men, sensing excitement, had all returned to the corral and were talking among themselves. One of them, seeing what the *viejito* was up to went up to him as he was reaching for the stirrup and said, "*Mira,* Don Luisito, here are four reales. Each of us will give you this amount so you need not ride the horse."

The old man made no answer until he had mounted the trembling buckskin and got a firm grip on the reins, then he said, "I will show you what to do with your money. Put a coin on each stirrup."

The vaquero put his coin on one stirrup while another man put a coin on the other. Then the old man put a foot on each coin and raised the blinds. The horse bucked long and hard and when he quit and stood panting the old man raised his feet and there were the coins where they had been placed. Thus did the little old man gain the respect of the hard bitten vaqueros on that ranch.

Curanderos

Back in the old days before the gringo had brought doctors, drugstores and hospitals to the San Joaquin, the *curandero,* or healer was depended upon to cure the sick. Though they were often *matasanos,* (literally, killers of the healthy) some of them were quite skillful. A curandero was anyone who professed a knowledge of healing, even if the extent of his practice was limited to *flotadas.* A *flotada,* or massage, was given for every pain or ache from pneumonia to simple earache.

Every kind of grease from beef tallow to rattlesnake oil was used as an ointment. The latter was secured in the following manner: first, a snake was found asleep stretched at full length and before it could coil, get angry and bite, it was struck on the head and killed. Next, six inches of the body was cut from both ends because the poison is in the head and tail. The snake was then cleaned, the grease removed and put in a pan or dish and set on the roof of the house for the sun to render, as the oil would be useless if rendered by artificial heat. The remainder, which consisted of the vertebrae, was hung up to dry. This was good for people who had sores; a small portion of the jerked snake would be pounded to a powder and sprinkled over the sick person's food.

The snake oil was best for deafness. The warmed oil was poured in the ears and the ears plugged. The oil would penetrate the inner parts of the ear and cure this distressing condition.

Salt was considered a cureall and oak ashes were taken internally as an anti-acid.

Cobwebs were applied to a wound to stop the flow of blood, and sugar mixed with pounded charcoal and put in the cut would heal it.

Cactus, besides being used for food was toasted and used as a poultice.

The old reliable among the herbs was *yerba del pasmo,* which, when boiled was used to wash wounds and could be found in the store house of all ranches. Chili also had medicinal value. Whenever a paisano had an *empache* (indigestion) the curandero removed the seeds from dried red chilis until he had a spoonful. These were washed in nine waters and then given to the patient to swallow. The seeds would attach themselves to the *empache* and remove it from the spot to which it was glued. Vaqueros believed that an *empache* was an undigested morsel of food which stuck to the walls of the stomach and caused the pains many were bothered with. *Yerba del pasmo* is known botanically as Waltheria Americana.

A sure cure for acute indigestion, though somewhat drastic, was the rawhide riata. There was a young vaquero who owed his life to such a rope and the stern measures of a *mayordomo.* Though this youngster never cared to have his experience mentioned in after years, this is how it came about:

The vaquero crew had left early one morning with a herd of cattle to make a *jornado,* or drive, across a long stretch of desert to a canyon where there was a ranch and some irrigated fields. It was the evening of a long summer day when they arrived at the ranch to find the *jacal* (hut) deserted. The door was open but nothing to eat could be found. The hut had not been empty long, however, because the *milpa* (cornfield) was green and had been recently irrigated.

After the cattle had been watered and had drifted up the canyon to feed, the vaqueros gathered ears of corn. They built several fires and ate the *elotes,* corn, until their hunger had been dulled. One of their number, despite warnings from the older men, ate his fill of the corn, to his sorrow.

Vaqueros go to sleep early but they had not slept long before they were awakened by the boy who was crying in pain. The mayordomo studied the situation briefly and decided on a course of action. He ordered one of the men to bring a riata. He took the rope and threw it over a low hanging limb of a giant fig tree. He then pulled both ends together, and ordered the men to bring the boy. When they were under the branch he told them to stand the boy on his head and hold his feet upright. The mayordomo then tied both ends of the riata to the boy's ankles. He took a stout stick, put it between the ropes and turned the boy around and around until the riata was twisted enough to raise him off the ground.

Then the mayordomo suddenly released the stick and the twisted rope spun so rapidly it made the boy dizzy. This proved to be an effective emetic, and the boy, having gotten rid of the offending corn, was relieved of his pain.

The Scavengers

(from *The Land of Little Rain*)

MARY AUSTIN

Fifty-seven buzzards, one on each of fifty-seven fence posts at the rancho El Tejon, on a mirage-breeding September morning, sat solemnly while the white tilted travelers' vans lumbered down the Canada de los Uvas. After three hours they had only clapped their wings, or exchanged posts. The season's end in the vast dim valley of the San Josquin is palipitatingly hot, and the air breathes like cotton wool. Through it all the buzzards sit on the fences and low hummocks, with wings spread fanwise for air. There is no end to them, and they smell to heaven. Their heads droop, and all their communication is a rare, horrid croak.

The increase of wild creatures is in proportion to the things they feed upon: the more carrion the more buzzards. The end of the third successive dry year bred them beyond belief. The first year quail mated sparingly; the second year the wild oats matured no seed; the third, cattle died in the tracks with their heads towards the stopped watercourses. And that year the scavengers were as black as the plague all across the mesa and up the treeless, tumbled hills. On clear days they betook themselves to the upper air, where they hung motionless for hours. That year there were vultures among them, distinguished by the white patches under the wings. All their offensiveness notwithstanding, they have a stately flight. They must also have what pass for good qualities among themselves, for they are social, not to say clannish.

It is a very squalid tragedy, — that of the dying brutes and the scavenger birds. Death by starvation is slow. The heavy-headed, rack-boned cattle totter in the fruitless trails; they stand for long, patient intervals; they lie down and do not rise. There is fear in their eyes when they are first stricken, but afterward only intolerable weariness. I suppose the dumb creatures know nearly as much of death as do their betters, who have only the more imagination. Their even-breathing submission after the first agony is their tribute to its inevitableness. It needs a nice discrimination to say which of the basket-ribbed cattle is likest to afford the next meal, but the scavengers make few mistakes. One stoops to the quarry and the flock follows.

Cattle once down may be days in dying. They stretch out their necks along the ground, and roll up their slow eyes at longer intervals. The buzzards have all the time, and no beak is dropped or talon struck until the breath is wholly passed. It is doubtless the economy of nature to have the scavengers by to clean up the carrion, but a wolf at the throat would be a shorter agony than the long stalking and sometime perchings of these loathsome watchers. Suppose now it were a man in this long-drawn, hungrily spied upon distress! When Timmie O'Shea was lost on Armogosa Flats for three days without water, Long Tom Basset found him, not by any trail, but by making straight away for the points where he saw buzzards stooping. He could hear the beat of their wings, Tom said, and trod on their shadows, but O'Shea was past recalling what he thought about things after the second day. My friend Ewan told me, among other things, when he came back from San Juan Hill, that not all the carnage of battle turned his bowels as the sight of slant black wings rising flockwise before the burrial squad.

There are three kinds of noises buzzards make, — it is impossible to call them notes, — raucous and elemental. There is a short croak of alarm, and the same syllable in a modified tone to serve all the purposes of ordinary conversation. The old birds make a kind of throaty chuckling to their young, but if they have any love song I have not heard it. The young yawp in the nest a little, with more breath than noise. It is seldom one finds a buzzard's nest, seldom that grown-ups find a nest of any sort; it is only children to whom these things happen by right. But by making a business of it one may come upon them in wide, quiet cañons, or on the lookouts of lonely, table-topped mountains, three or four together, in the tops of stubby trees or on rotten cliffs well open to the sky.

It is probable that the buzzard is gregarious, but it seems unlikely from the small number of young noted at any time that every female incubates each year. The young birds are easily distinguished by their size when feeding, and high up in the air by the worn primaries of the older birds. It is when the young go out of the nest of their first foraging that the parents, full of a crass and simple pride, make their indescribable chucklings of gobbling, gluttonous delight. The little ones would be amusing as they tug and tussle, if one could forget what it is they feed upon.

One never comes any nearer to the vulture's nest or nestlings than hearsay. They keep to the southerly Sierras, and are bold enough, it seems, to do killing on their own account when no carrion is at hand. They dog the shepherd from camp to camp, the hunter home from the hill, and will even carry away offal from under his hand.

The vulture merits respect for his bigness and for his bandit airs, but he is a sombre bird, with none of the buzzard's frank satisfaction in his offensiveness.

The least objectionable of the inland scavengers is the raven, frequenter of the desert ranges, the same called locally "carrion crow." He is handsomer and has such an air. He is nice in his habits and is said to have likable traits. A tame one in a Shoshone camp was the butt of much sport and enjoyed it. He could all but talk and was another with the children, but an arrant thief. The raven will eat most things that come his way, — eggs and young of ground-nesting birds, seeds even, lizards and grasshoppers, which he catches cleverly; and whatever he is about, let a coyote trot never so softly by, the raven flaps up and after; for whatever the coyote can pull down or nose out is meat also for the carrion crow.

And never a coyote comes out of his lair for killing, in the country of the carrion crows, but looks up first to see where they may be gathering. It is a sufficient occupation for a windy morning, on the lineless, level mesa, to watch the pair of them eyeing each other furtively, with a tolerable assumption of unconcern, but no doubt with a certain amount of good understanding about it. Once at Red Rock, in a year of green pasture, which is a bad time for the scavengers, we saw two buzzards, five ravens, and a coyote feeding on the same carrion, and only the coyote seemed ashamed of the company.

Probably we never fully credit the interdependence of wild creatures, and their cognizance of the affairs of their own kind. When the five coyotes that range the Tejon from Pasteria to Tunawai planned a relay race to bring down an antelope strayed from the band, beside myself to watch, an eagle swung down from Mt. Pinos, buzzards materialized out of invisible ether, and hawks came trooping like small boys to a street fight. Rabbits sat up in the chaparral and cocked their ears, feeling themselves quite safe for the once as the hunt swung near them. Nothing happens in the deep wood that the blue jays are not all agog to tell. The hawk follows the badger, the coyote the carrion crow, and from their aerial stations the buzzards watch each other. What would be worth knowing is how much of their neighbor's affairs the new generations learn for themselves, and how much they are taught of their elders.

So wide is the range of the scavengers that it is never safe to say, eyewitness to the contrary, that there are few or many in such a place. Where the carrion is, there will the buzzards be gathered together, and in three days' journey you will not sight another one. The way up from Mojave to Red Butte is all desertness, affording no pasture and scarcely a rill of water. In a year of little rain in the south, flocks and herds were driven to the number of thousands along this road to the perennial pastures of the high ranges. It is a long, slow trail, ankle deep in bitter dust that gets up in the slow wind and moves along the backs of the crawling cattle. In the worst of times one in three will pine and fall out by the way. In the defiles of Red Rock, the sheep piled up a stinking lane; it was the sun smiting by day. To these shambles came buzzards, vultures, and coyotes from all the country round, so that on the Tejon, the Ceriso, and the Little Antelope there were not scavengers enough to keep the country clean. All that summer the dead mummified in the open or dropped slowly back to earth in the quagmires of the bitter springs. Meanwhile from Red Rock to Coyote Holes, and from Coyote Holes to Haiwai the scavengers gorged and gorged.

The coyote is not a scavenger by choice, preferring his own kill, but being on the whole a lazy dog, is apt to fall into carrion eating because it is easier. The red fox and bobcat, a little pressed by hunger, will eat of any other animal's kill, but will not ordinarily touch what dies of itself, and are exceedingly shy of food that has been man-handled.

Very clean and handsome, quite belying his relationship in appearance, is Clark's crow, that scavenger and plunderer of mountain camps. It is permissible to call him by his common name, "Camp Robber:" he has earned it. Not content with refuse, he pecks open meal sacks, filches whole potatoes, is a gormand for bacon, drills holes in packing cases, and is daunted by nothing short of tin. All the while he does not neglect to vituperate the chipmunks and sparrows that whisk off crumbs of comfort from under the camper's feet. The Camp Robber's gray coat, black and white barred wings, and slender bill, with certain tricks of perching, accuse him of attempts to pass himself off among woodpeckers; but his behavior is all crow. He frequents the higher pine belts, and has a noisy strident call like a jay's, and how clean he and the frisk-tailed chipmunks keep the camp! No crumb or paring or bit of eggshell goes amiss.

High as the camp may be, so it is not above timberline, it is not too high for the coyote, the bobcat, or the wolf. It is the complaint of the ordinary camper that the woods are too still, depleted of wild life. But what dead body of wild thing, or neglected game untouched by its kind, do you find? And put out offal away from camp over night, and look next day at the foot tracks where it lay.

Man is a great blunderer going about in the woods, and there is no other except the bear makes so much noise. Being so well warned beforehand, it is a very stupid animal, or a very bold one, that cannot keep safely hid. The cunningest hunter is hunted in turn, and what he leaves of his kill is meat for some other. That is the economy of nature, but with it all there is not sufficient account taken of the works of man. There is no scavenger that eats tin cans, and no wild thing leaves a like disfigurement on the forest floor.

Shootout

(from *The Octopus*)

FRANK NORRIS

Around the bend of the road in front of them came a cloud of dust. From it emerged a horse's head.

"Hello, hello, there's something."

"Remember, we are not to fire first."

"Perhaps that's Hooven; I can't see. Is it? There only seems to be one horse."

"Too much dust for one horse."

Annixter, who had taken his field glasses from Harran, adjusted them to his eyes.

"That's not them," he announced presently, "nor Hooven, either. That's a cart." Then, after another moment, he added, "The butcher's cart from Guadalajara."

The tension was relaxed. The men drew long breaths, settling back in their places.

"Do we let him go on, Governor?"

"The bridge is down. He can't go by and we must not let him go back. We shall have to detain him and question him. I wonder the marshal let him pass."

The cart approached at a lively trot.

"Anybody else in that cart, Mr. Annixter?" asked Magnus. "Look carefully. It may be a ruse. It is strange the marshal should have let him pass."

The leaguers roused themselves again. Osterman laid his hand on the revolver.

"No," called Annixter in another instant, "no, there's only one man in it."

The cart came up, and Cutter and Phelps, clambering from the ditch, stopped it as it arrived in front of the party.

"Hey — what — what?" exclaimed the young butcher, pulling up. "Is that bridge broke?"

But at the idea of being held, the boy protested at top voice, badly frightened, bewildered, not knowing what was to happen next.

"No, no, I got my meat to deliver. Say, you let me go. Say, I ain't got nothing to do with you."

He tugged at the reins, trying to turn the cart about. Cutter, with his jackknife, parted the reins just back of the bit.

"You'll stay where you are, m'son, for awhile. We're not going to hurt you. But you are not going back to town till we say so. Did you pass anybody on the road out of town?"

In reply to the leaguers' questions, the young butcher at last told them he had passed a two-horse buggy and a lot of men on horseback just beyond the railroad tracks. They were headed for Los Muertos.

"That's them, all right," muttered Annixter. "They're coming by this road, sure."

The butcher's horse and cart were led to one side of the road, and the horse tied to the fence with one of the severed lines. The butcher himself was passed over to Presley, who locked him in Hooven's barn.

"Well, what the devil," demanded Osterman, "has become of Bismarck?"

In fact, the butcher had seen nothing of Hooven. The minutes were passing, and still he failed to appear.

"What's he up to, anyways?"

"Bet you what you like, they caught him. Just like that crazy Dutchman to get excited and go too near. You can always depend on Hooven to lose his head."

Five minutes passed, then ten. The road toward Guadalajara lay empty, baking and white under the sun.

"Well, the marshal and S. Behrman don't seem to be in any hurry, either."

"Shall I go forward and reconnoiter, Governor?" asked Harran.

But Dabney, who stood next to Annixter, touched him on the shoulder, and without speaking pointed down the road. Annixter looked, then suddenly cried out:

"Here comes Hooven."

The German galloped into sight around the turn of the road, his rifle laid across his saddle. He came on rapidly, pulled up, and dismounted at the ditch.

"Dey're commen," he cried, trembling with excitement. "I watch um long dime bei der side oaf der roadt in der busches. Dey shtop bei der gate oder side der relroadt trecks and talk long dime mit one n'udder. Den dey gome on. Dey're gowun sure do zum monkey-doodle pizeness. Me, I see Gritschun put der kertridges in his guhn. I tink dey gowun to gome *my* blace first. Dey gowun to try to put me off, tek my home, bei Gott."

"All right, get down in here and keep quiet, Hooven. Don't fire unless———"

"Here they are."

A half-dozen voices uttered the cry at once.

There could be no mistake this time. A buggy, drawn by two horses, came into view around the curve of the road. Three riders accompanied it, and behind these, seen at intervals in a cloud of dust, were two—three—five—six others.

This, then, was S. Behrman with the United States marshal and his posse. The event that had been so long in preparation, the event which it had been said would never come to pass, the last trial of strength, the last fight between the trust and the people, the direct, brutal grapple of armed men, and law defied, the government ignored—behold, here it was close at hand.

Osterman cocked his revolver, and in the profound silence that had fallen upon the scene, the click was plainly audible from end to end of the line.

"Remember our agreement, gentlemen," cried Magnus in a warning voice. "Mr. Osterman, I must ask you to let down the hammer of your weapon."

No one answered. In absolute quiet, standing motionless in their places, the leaguers watched the approach of the marshal.

Five minutes passed. The riders came on steadily. They drew nearer. The grind of the buggy wheels in the grit and dust of the road and the prolonged clatter of the horses' feet began to make themselves heard. The leaguers could distinguish the faces of their enemies.

In the buggy were S. Behrman and Cyrus Ruggles, the latter driving. A tall man in a frock coat and slouched hat—the marshal, beyond question—rode at the left of the buggy; Delaney, carrying a Winchester, at the right. Christian, the real estate broker, S. Behrman's cousin, also with a rifle, could be made out just behind the marshal. Back of these, riding well up, was a group of horsemen, indistinguishable in the dust raised by the buggy's wheels.

Steadily the distance between the leaguers and the posse diminished.

"Don't let them get too close, Governor," whispered Harran.

When S. Behrman's buggy was about one hundred yards from the irrigating ditch, Magnus sprang out upon the road, leaving his revolvers behind him. He beckoned Garnett and Gethings to follow, and the three ranchers, who with the exception of Broderson were the oldest men present, advanced, without arms, to meet the marshal.

Magnus cried aloud:

"Halt where you are."

From their places in the ditch, Annixter, Osterman, Dabney, Harran, Hooven, Broderson, Cutter, and Phelps, their hands laid upon their revolvers, watched silently, alert, keen, ready for anything.

At the Governor's words, they saw Ruggles pull sharply on the reins. The buggy came to a standstill, the riders doing likewise. Magnus approached the marshal, still followed by Garnett and Gethings, and began to speak. His voice was audible to the men in the ditch, but his words could not be made out. They heard the marshal reply quietly enough, and the two shook hands. Delaney came around from the side of the buggy, his horse standing before the team across the road. He leaned from the saddle, listening to what was being said, but made no remark. From time to time, S. Behrman and Ruggles, from their seats in the buggy, interposed a sentence or two into the conversation, but at first, so far as the leaguers could discern, neither Magnus nor the marshal paid them any attention. They saw, however, that the latter repeatedly shook his head, and once they heard him exclaim in a loud voice:

"I only know my duty, Mr. Derrick."

Then Gethings turned about, and seeing Delaney close at hand, addressed an unheard remark to him. The cowpuncher replied curtly, and the words seemed to anger Gethings. He made a gesture, pointing back to the ditch, showing the entrenched leaguers to the posse. Delaney appeared to communicate the news that the leaguers were on hand and prepared to resist to the other members of the party. They all looked toward the ditch and plainly saw the ranchers there, standing to their arms.

But, meanwhile, Ruggles had addressed himself more directly to Magnus, and between the two an angry discussion was going forward. Once, even, Harran heard his father exclaim:

"The statement is a lie, and no one knows it better than yourself."

"Here," growled Annixter to Dabney, who stood next him in the ditch, "those fellows are getting too close. Look at them edging up. Don't Magnus see that?"

The other members of the marshal's force had come forward from their places behind the buggy and were spread out across the road. Some of them were gathered about Magnus, Garnett, and Gethings; and some were talking together, looking and pointing toward the ditch. Whether acting upon signal or not, the leaguers in the ditch could not tell, but it was certain that one or two of the posse had moved considerably forward. Besides this, Delaney had now placed his horse between Magnus and the ditch, and two others riding up from the rear had followed his example. The posse surrounded the three ranchers, and by now everybody was talking at once.

"Look here," Harran called to Annixter, "this won't do. I don't like the looks of this thing. They all seem to be edging up, and before we know it they may take the Governor and the other men prisoners."

"They ought to come back," declared Annixter.

"Somebody ought to tell them that those fellows are creeping up."

By now the angry argument between the Governor and Ruggles had become more heated than ever. Their voices were raised; now and then they made furious gestures.

"They ought to come back," cried Osterman. "We couldn't shoot now if anything should happen, for fear of hitting them."

"Well, it sounds as though something were going to happen pretty soon."

They could hear Gethings and Delaney wrangling furiously; another deputy joined in.

"I'm going to call the Governor back," exclaimed Annixter, suddenly clambering out of the ditch.

"No, no," cried Osterman, "keep in the ditch. They can't drive us out if we keep here."

Hooven and Harran, who had instinctively followed Annixter, hesitated at Osterman's words, and the three halted irresolutely on the road before the ditch, their weapons in their hands.

"Governor," shouted Harran, "come on back. You can't do anything."

Still the wrangle continued, and one of the deputies, advancing a little from out the group, cried out:

"Keep back there! Keep back there, you!"

"Go to hell, will you?" shouted Harran on the instant. "You're on my land."

"Oh, come back here, Harran," called Osterman. "That ain't going to do any good."

"There — listen," suddenly exclaimed Harran. "The Governor is calling us. Come on; I'm going."

Osterman got out of the ditch and came forward, catching Harran by the arm and pulling him back.

"He didn't call. Don't get excited. You'll ruin everything. Get back into the ditch again."

But Cutter, Phelps, and the old man Dabney, misunderstanding what was happening, and seeing Osterman leave the ditch, had followed his example. All the leaguers were now out of the ditch and a little way down the road, Hooven, Osterman, Annixter, and Harran in front, Dabney, Phelps, and Cutter coming up from behind.

"Keep back, you," cried the deputy again.

In the group around S. Behrman's buggy, Gethings and Delaney were yet quarreling, and the angry debate between Magnus, Garnett, and the marshal still continued.

Till this moment the real estate broker, Christian, had taken no part in the argument, but had kept himself in the rear of the buggy. Now, however, he pushed forward. There was but little room for him to pass, and as he rode by the buggy, his horse scraped his flank against the hub of the wheel. The animal recoiled sharply, and striking against Garnett, threw him to the ground. Delaney's horse stood between the buggy and the leaguers gathered on the road in front of the ditch; the incident, indistinctly seen by them, was misinterpreted.

Garnett had not yet risen when Hooven raised a great shout:

"*Hoch, der Kaiser! Hoch, der vaterland!*"

With the words, he dropped to one knee, and sighting his rifle carefully, fired into the group of men around the buggy.

Instantly the revolvers and rifles seemed to go off of themselves. Both sides, deputies and leaguers, opened fire simultaneously. At first, it was nothing but a confused roar of explosions; then the roar lapsed to an irregular, quick succession of reports, shot leaping after shot; then a moment's silence, and last of all, regular as clock ticks, three shots at exact intervals. Then stillness.

Delaney, shot through the stomach, slid down from his horse, and on his hands and knees crawled from the road into the standing wheat. Christian fell backward from the saddle toward the buggy, and hung suspended in that position, his head and shoulders on the wheel, one stiff leg still across his saddle. Hooven, in attempting to rise from his kneeling position, received a rifle ball squarely in the throat, and rolled forward upon his face. Old Broderson, crying out, "Oh, they've shot me, boys," staggered sideways, his head bent, his hands rigid at his sides, and fell into the ditch. Osterman, blood running back from his mouth and nose, turned about and walked back. Presley helped him across the irrigating ditch and Osterman laid himself down, his head on his folded arms. Harran Derrick dropped where he stood, turning over on his face, and lay motionless, groaning terribly, a pool of blood forming under his stomach. The old man Dabney, silent as ever, received his death, speechless. He fell to his knees, got up again, fell once more, and died without a word. Annixter, instantly killed, fell his length to the ground, and lay without movement, just as he had fallen, one arm across his face.

PART THREE

Awakening

It was still dark when he awakened. A small clashing noise brought him up from sleep. Tom listened and heard again the squeak of iron on iron. He moved stiffly and shivered in the morning air. The camp still slept. Tom stood up and looked over the side of the truck. The eastern mountains were blue-black, and as he watched, the light stood up faintly behind them, colored at the mountain rims with a washed red, then growing colder, grayer, darker, as it went up overhead, until at a place near the western horizon it merged with pure night. Down in the valley the earth was the lavender-gray of dawn.

from *The Grapes of Wrath* (1939)
by JOHN STEINBECK

IN THE MID-1930s two young writers — William Saroyan and William Everson — began almost simultaneously to publish their early works. Not only were these two men born and raised in the San Joaquin, they found their inspiration through indigenous materials, and thus became the first to produce a body of work unmistakably *of* the region. Together with Carey McWilliams and John Steinbeck, who began in this same period to voice the plight of California's long-abused migrant labor force, these writers mark a clear moment in the valley's conscious life — an opening, via stories, poems, and newly voiced ideas, toward larger awareness.

William Saroyan was born in Fresno in 1908. His family, his hometown, his roots in the Armenian community there, have provided recurring images throughout his long and flamboyant career.

Saroyan's first book, THE DARING YOUNG MAN ON THE FLYING TRAPEZE, published in 1934, won him instant fame. His second, MY NAME IS ARAM, came out in 1939 and was also a hit. It is based on his own boyhood experiences around Fresno between 1915 and 1925. In stories like "The Pomegranate Trees" Aram emerges as a kind of Armenian Huckleberry Finn, and through his adventures we are offered the view of life that has shaped Saroyan's best work: a generosity of spirit, a sense of whimsy and pathos, a compassion for human error. Years later he came back to this material in the rambling autobiographical narrative, THE BICYCLE RIDER IN BEVERLY HILLS (1952):

I decided very early to love my family, and to see in each of its members something rare and good as well as the miserable and painful things that were obvious. I do not think that in writing of them I ever lied, I merely chose to notice in them the things I cherished and preferred, and to refer to the things I didn't cherish with humor and charity. The writer in the end creates his family, his nation, his culture and worth, and I believe that I have more effectively than any other

55

member of the Saroyan family created that family, which appears all through my writing but especially in the small book called *My Name is Aram.*

William Everson was born in Sacramento in 1912. Until the outbreak of World War II he farmed near Selma, south of Fresno. In 1949 he converted to Catholicism, and in 1951 entered monastic life, in the Dominican Order. As Brother Antoninus he was prominent in the San Francisco Bay Area poetry scene through the 50s and 60s, often associated with the Beat Generation writers. In 1969, after 18 years as a monk, he left the order and now lives and writes near Santa Cruz.

One of the country's most distinguished contemporary poets, Everson has also written major interpretative works on Robinson Jeffers, as well as a landmark study of west coast literature, ARCHETYPE WEST (Oyez Press, 1976). The poems included here are taken from his second book, SAN JOAQUIN, published by the Ward Ritchie Press in 1939. Composed between 1935 and 1938, these pieces arise directly from his farming experience during that era, and clearly establish the intense involvement with western landscape that has given his later poetry and scholarship such authenticity and spiritual power.

Carey McWilliams was born in Colorado in 1905. Educated at USC, he entered law practice in Los Angeles, and in 1938 became Chief of the Division of Immigration and Housing for the State of California, a post he held until 1942. Well known as editor of THE NATION, with which he was associated from 1945 until his retirement in 1975, McWilliams has also written several influential books arising from his interest in California labor practices, minority experience, and general lifestyle. Among these is FACTORIES IN THE FIELD, from which "The Wheatland Riot" is taken. Published in 1939, this collection of articles and essays could be called the documentary companion to John Steinbeck's novel, THE GRAPES OF WRATH, which appeared in the same year. Both books focus on the migratory labor struggles which had been an explosive presence in the valley for decades, and they reveal the fervor and compassion of two powerful writers striving to draw public attention to a monstrous social disaster.

Steinbeck was born in Salinas, California, in 1902, and grew up among the fields and truck farms of the fertile Salinas Valley. His best books all have agricultural settings, and throughout the 30s he wrote novels and stories and articles that championed the working man, the day laborer, the ranch hand. In THE GRAPES OF WRATH the Joads, forced off their farm by the drought and hard times of "Dust-Bowl" Oklahoma, load up their flatbed truck to make the long journey west, looking for a new and better life — one family among the thousands upon thousands of uprooted families who poured into the valley seeking work. McWilliams, remembering this era in *The American West* in *1970*, wrote, "The migration was, of course, a modern day reenactment of a familiar theme, the forced exodus of an oppressed people from their farms and homes and their flight to a distant Promised Land. The structure of the novel has its roots in the Old Testament, which perhaps accounts for its messianic tone and quality." In the scene included here, we see them at Tehachapi Pass, just before the dream that has carried them across the Southwest is shattered by the reality of crowded migrant camps, Depression wages, and greed.

The Pomegranate Trees

(from *My Name is Aram*)

WILLIAM SAROYAN

My uncle Melik was just about the worst farmer that ever lived. He was too imaginative for his own good. What he wanted was beauty. He wanted to plant it and see it grow. I myself planted more than a hundred pomegranate trees. I drove a John Deere tractor, too, and so did my uncle. It was all art, not agriculture. My uncle just liked the idea of planting trees and watching them grow.

Only they wouldn't grow. It was on account of the soil. The soil was desert soil. It was dry. My uncle waved at the six hundred and eighty acres of desert he had bought and he said in the most poetic Armenian anybody ever heard, Here in this awful desolation a garden shall flower, fountains of cold water shall bubble out of the earth, and all things of beauty shall come into being.

Yes, sir, I said.

I was the first and only relative to see the land he had bought. He knew I was a poet at heart, and he believed I would understand the magnificent impulse that was driving him to glorious ruin. I did. I knew as well as he that what he had purchased was worthless desert land. It was away over to hell and gone, at the foot of the Sierra Nevada Mountains. It was full of every kind of desert plant that ever sprang out of dry hot earth. It was overrun with prairie dogs, squirrels, horned toads, snakes, and a variety of smaller forms of life. The space over this land knew only the presence of hawks, eagles, and buzzards. It was a region of loneliness, emptiness, truth, and dignity. It was nature at its proudest, dryest, loneliest, and loveliest.

My uncle and I got out of the Ford roadster in the middle of his land and began to walk over the dry earth.

This land, he said, is my land.

He walked slowly, kicking into the dry soil. A horned toad scrambled over the earth at my uncle's feet. My uncle clutched my shoulder and came to a pious halt.

What is that animal? he said.

That little tiny lizard? I said.

That mouse with horns, my uncle said. What is it?

I don't know for sure, I said. We call them horny toads.

The horned toad came to a halt about three feet away and turned its head.

My uncle looked down at the small animal.

Is it poison? he said.

To eat? I said. Or if it bites you?

Either way, my uncle said.

I don't think it's good to eat, I said. I think it's harmless. I've caught many of them. They grow sad in captivity, but never bite. Shall I catch this one?

Please do, my uncle said.

I sneaked up on the horned toad, then sprang on it while my uncle looked on.

Careful, he said. Are you sure it isn't poison?

I've caught many of them, I said.

I took the horned toad to my uncle. He tried not to seem afraid.

A lovely little thing, isn't it? he said. His voice was unsteady.

Would you like to hold it? I said.

No, my uncle said. You hold it. I have never before been so close to such a thing as this. I see it has eyes. I suppose it can see us.

I suppose it can, I said. It's looking up at you now.

My uncle looked the horned toad straight in the eye. The horned toad looked my uncle straight in the eye. For fully half a minute they looked one another straight in the eye and then the horned toad turned its head aside and looked down at the ground. My uncle sighed with relief.

A thousand of them, he said, could kill a man, I suppose.

They never travel in great numbers. You hardly ever see more than one at a time.

A big one could probably bite a man to death.

They don't grow big. This is as big as they get.

They seem to have an awful eye for such small creatures. Are you sure they don't mind being picked up?

They forget all about it the minute you put them down.

Do you really think so?

I don't think they have very good memories.

My uncle straightened up, breathing deeply.

Put the little creature down, he said. Let us be kind to the innocent inventions of Almighty God. If it is not poison and grows no larger than a mouse and does not travel in great numbers and has no memory to speak of, let the timid little thing return to the earth. Let us love these small things which live on the earth with us.

Yes sir.

I placed the horned toad on the ground.

Gently now. Let no harm come to this strange dweller on my land.

The horned toad scrambled away.

These little things have been living on soil of this kind for centuries, I said.

Centuries? my uncle said. Are you sure?

No, I'm not, but I imagine they have. They're still here, at any rate.

My uncle looked around at his land, at the cactus and brush growing out of it, at the sky overhead.

What have they been *eating* all this time? he said.

Insects, I guess.

What kind of insects?

Little bugs.

We continued to walk over the dry land. When we came to some holes in the earth my uncle stood over them and said, Who lives down there?

Prairie dogs.

What are *they*?

Well, they're something like rats. They belong to the rodent family.

What are all these things *doing* on my land?

They don't know it's your land. They're living here the same as ever.

I don't suppose that horny toad ever looked a man in the eye before.

I don't *think* so.

Do you think I scared it or anything?

I don't know for sure.

If I did, I didn't mean to. I'm going to build a house here some day.

I didn't know that.

I'm going to build a magnificent house.

It's pretty far away.

It's only an hour from town.

If you go fifty miles an hour.

It's not fifty miles to town. It's thirty-seven.

Well, you've got to take a little time out for rough roads.

I'll build me the finest house in the world. What else lives on this land?

Well, there are three or four kinds of snakes.

Poison or non-poison?

Mostly non. The rattlesnake is poison, though.

Do you mean to tell me there are *rattlesnakes* on this land?

This is the kind of land rattlesnakes *usually* live on.

How many?

Per acre? Or on the whole six hundred and forty acres?

Per acre.

Well, I'd say there are about three per acre, conservatively.

Three per acre? *Conservatively?*

Maybe only two.

How many is that to the whole place?

Well, let's see. Two per acre. Six hundred and forty acres. About fifteen hundred of them.

Fifteen hundred rattlesnakes?

An acre is pretty big. Two rattlesnakes per acre isn't many. You don't often see them.

What else have we got around here that's poison?

I don't know of anything else. All the other things are harmless. The rattlesnakes are harmless too, unless you step on them.

All right, my uncle said. You walk ahead and watch where you're going. If you see a rattlesnake, don't step on it. I don't want you to die at the age of eleven.

Yes sir. I'll watch carefully.

We turned around and walked back to the Ford. I didn't see any rattlesnakes on the way. We got into the car and my uncle lighted a cigarette.

I'm going to make a garden in this awful desolation.

Yes sir.

I know what my problems are, and I know how to solve them.

How?

Do you mean the horny toads or the rattlesnakes.

I mean the problems.

Well, the first thing I'm going to do is hire some Mexicans and put them to work.

Doing what?

Clearing the land. Then I'm going to have them dig for water.

Dig where?

Straight down. After we get water, I'm going to have them plow the land, and then I'm going to plant.

Wheat?

Wheat? my uncle shouted. What do I want with wheat? Bread is five cents a loaf. I'm going to plant pomegranate trees.

How much are pomegranates?

Who knows? They're practically unknown in this country. Ten, fifteen, maybe twenty cents each.

Is that all you're going to plant?

I have in mind planting several other kinds of trees.

Peach?

About ten acres.

How about apricots?

By all means. The apricot is a lovely fruit. Lovely in shape, with a glorious flavor and a most delightful pit. I shall plant about twenty acres of apricot trees.

I hope the Mexicans don't have any trouble finding water. *Is* there water under this land?

Of course, my uncle said. The important thing is to get started. I shall instruct the men to watch out for rattlesnakes. Pomegranates. Peaches. Apricots. What else?

Figs?

Thirty acres of figs.

How about mullberries?

The mulberry is a very nice-looking tree, my uncle said. A tree I knew well inthe old country. How many acres would you suggest?

About ten?

All right. What else?

Olive trees are nice.

Yes, they are. About ten acres of olive trees. Anything else?

Well, I don't suppose apple trees would grow on this kind of land.

No, but I don't like apples anyway.

He started the car and we drove off the dry land on to the dry road. The car bounced about slowly until we reached the road and then we began to travel at a higher rate of speed.

One thing, my uncle said. When we get home I would rather you didn't mention this *farm* to the folks.

Yes sir. (*Farm?* I thought. *What farm?*)

I want to surprise them. You know how your grandmother is. I'll go ahead with my plans and when everything is in order I'll take the whole family out to the farm and surprise them.

Yes sir.

Not a word to a living soul.

Yes sir.

Well, the Mexicans went to work and cleared the land. They cleared about ten acres of it in about two months. There were seven of them. They worked with shovels and hoes. They didn't understand anything about anything. It all seemed very strange, but they never complained. They were being paid and that was the thing that counted. They were two brothers and their sons. One day the older brother, Diego, very politely asked my uncle what it was they were supposed to be doing.

Señor, he said, please forgive me. Why are we cutting down the cactus?

I'm going to farm this land, my uncle said.

The other Mexicans asked Diego in Mexican what my uncle had said and Diego told them.

They didn't believe it was worth the trouble to tell my uncle he couldn't do it. They just went on cutting down the cactus.

The cactus, however, stayed down only for a short while. The land which had been first cleared was soon rich again with fresh cactus and brush. My uncle made this observation with considerable amazement.

Maybe it takes deep plowing to get rid of cactus, I said. Maybe you've got to *plow* it out.

My uncle talked the matter over with Ryan, who had a farm-implement business. Ryan told him not to fool with horses. The modern thing to do was to turn a good tractor loose on the land and do a year's work in a day.

So my uncle bought a John Deere tractor. It was beautiful. A mechanic from Ryan's taught Diego how to operate the tractor, and the next day when my uncle and I reached the land we could see the tractor away out in the desolation and we could hear it booming in the grand silence of the desert. It sounded crazy. It *was* crazy. My uncle thought it was wonderful.

Progress, he said. There's the modern age for you. Ten thousand years ago it would have taken a hundred men a week to do what the tractor has already done today.

Ten thousand years ago? You mean yesterday.

Anyway, there's nothing like these modern conveniences.

The tractor isn't a convenience.

What is it, then? my uncle said. Doesn't the driver sit?

He couldn't very well stand.

Any time they let you sit, it's a convenience. Can you whistle?

Yes sir. What kind of a song would you like to hear?

I don't want to hear any song. Whistle at the Mexican on the tractor.

What for?

Never mind what for. Just whistle. I want him to know we are here and that we are pleased with his work. He's probably plowed twenty acres.

Yes sir.

I put the second and third fingers of each hand into my mouth and blew with all my might. It was good and loud. Nevertheless, it didn't seem as if Diego had heard me. He was pretty far away. We were walking toward him anyway, so I couldn't figure out why my uncle wanted me to whistle at him.

Once again, he said.

I whistled once again, but again Diego didn't hear.

Louder, please.

This next time I gave it all I had, and my uncle put his hands over his ears. My face got red, but this time the Mexican on the tractor heard the whistle. He slowed the tractor down, turned it around, and began plowing straight across the field toward us.

Do you want him to do that?

It doesn't matter.

In less than a minute and a half the tractor and the Mexican arrived. The Mexican was delighted. He wiped dirt and perspiration off his face and got down from the tractor.

Señor, he said, this is wonderful.

I'm glad you like it, my uncle said.

Would you like a ride?

My uncle was sure he didn't. He looked at me.

Go ahead, he said. Hop on. Have a little ride.

Diego got on the tractor and helped me on. He sat on the metal seat and I stood behind him, holding him. The tractor began to shake, then jumped, and then began to go. The Mexican drove around in a big circle and brought the tractor back to my uncle. I jumped off.

All right, my uncle said to the Mexican. Go back to your work.

The Mexican drove the tractor back to where he was plowing.

My uncle didn't get water out of the land until many months later. He had wells dug all over the place, but no water came out of them. He had motor pumps installed, but even then no water came out. A water specialist named Roy came out from Texas with his two younger brothers and they began to investigate the land. At last they told my uncle they'd get water for him. It took them three months, but the water was muddy and there wasn't much of it. The specialist told my uncle matters would improve with time and went back to Texas.

Now half the land was cleared and plowed and there was water, so the time had come to plant.

We planted pomegranate trees. They were of the finest quality and very expensive. Altogether we planted about seven hundred of them, and I myself planted a hundred, while my uncle planted eight or nine. We had a twenty-acre orchard of pomegranate trees away over in the middle of the dry desert, and my uncle was crazy about it. The only trouble was, his money was running out. Instead of going ahead and trying to make a garden of the whole six hundred and forty acres, he decided to devote his time and energy and money to the pomegranate trees alone.

Only for the time being, he said. Until we begin to sell the pomegranates and get our money back.

Yes sir.

I didn't know for sure, but it seemed to me we wouldn't be getting any pomegranates to speak of from the little trees for two or three years at least, but I didn't say anything. My uncle got rid of the Mexican workers and he and I took over the farm. We had the tractor and a lot of land, so every now and then we drove out to the land and drove the tractor around, plowing up cactus and turning over the soil between the pomegranate trees.

The water situation didn't improve with time, however. Every once in a while there would be a sudden generous spurt of water containing only a few pebbles and my uncle would be greatly pleased, but the next day the water would be muddy again and there would be only a little trickle. The trees took root and held fast, but they just weren't getting enough water.

There were blossoms after the second year. This was a great triumph for my uncle, but nothing much ever came of the blossoms. They were beautiful, but that was about all.

That year my uncle harvested three small pomegranates.

I ate one, he ate one, and we kept the other one up in his office.

The following year I was fourteen. A number of good things had happened to me: I had discovered writing, and I'd grown as tall as my uncle. The pomegranate trees were still our secret. They had cost my uncle a lot of money, but he was always under the impression that very soon he was going to start marketing a big crop and get his money back and go on with his plan to make a garden in the desert.

The trees grew a little, but it was hardly noticeable. Quite a few of them withered and died.

That's average, my uncle said. Twenty trees to an acre is only average. We won't plant new trees just now. We'll do that later.

He was still paying for the land, too.

The following year we harvested about two hundred pomegranates. We packed them in nice-looking boxes and my uncle shipped them to a wholesale produce house in Chicago. Eleven boxes.

We didn't hear from the wholesale produce house for a month, so one night my uncle made a long-distance phone call. The produce man, D'Agostino, told my uncle nobody wanted pomegranates.

How much are you asking per box? my uncle shouted over the phone.

One dollar, D'Agostino shouted back.

That's not enough, my uncle shouted. I won't take a nickel less than five dollars a box.

They don't want them at one dollar a box, D'Agostino shouted.

Why not? my uncle shouted.

They don't know what they are, D'Agostino shouted.

What kind of a business man are you? my uncle shouted. They're pomegranates. I want five dollars a box.

I can't sell them, the produce man shouted. I ate one myself and I don't see anything so wonderful about them.

You're crazy, my uncle shouted. There is no other fruit in the world like the pomegranate. Five dollars a box isn't half enough.

What shall I do with them? D'Agostino shouted. I can't sell them. I don't want them.

I see, my uncle whispered. Ship them back. Ship them back express collect.

So the eleven boxes came back.

All winter my uncle and I ate pomegranates in our spare time.

The following year my uncle couldn't make any more payments on the land. He gave the papers back to the man who had sold him the land. I was in the office at the time.

Mr. Griffith, my uncle said, I've got to give you back your property, but I would like to ask a little favor. I've planted twenty acres of pomegranate trees out there on that land and I'd appreciate it very much if you'd let me take care of those trees.

Take care of them? Mr. Griffith said. What in the world for?

My uncle tried to explain, but couldn't. It was too much to try to explain to a man who wasn't sympathetic.

So my uncle lost the land, and the trees, too.

A few years later he and I drove out to the land and walked out to the pomegranate orchard. The trees were all dead. The soil was heavy again with cactus and desert brush. Except for the small dead pomegranate trees the place was exactly the way it had been all the years of the world.

We walked around in the dead orchard for a while and then went back to the car.

We got into the car and drove back to town.

We didn't say anything because there was such an awful lot to say, and no language to say it in.

Five Poems

(from *San Joaquin*)

WILLIAM EVERSON

WINTER SUNDOWN

The fog, that nightlong and morning had lain to the fields,
Earth-loving, lifted at noon, broke to no wind,
Sheeted the sky blue-gray and deadened.
The sun somewhere over the dark height ran steeply down west;
And that hour, silence hanging the wide and naked vineyards,
The fog fell slowly with twilight, masking the land.

And alone at that falling, with earth and sky one mingle of color,
See how this moment yields sameness: December evening grayed and
    oppressive.
You have seen night come like this through all of your growing—
The trees screened, the air heavy and dead,
And life hushed down, this moment repeated,
The dusk and the fog all one.

OH FORTUNATE EARTH

Now afternoon's running.
There are men moving singly and slow, pruning dead growth.
In the cold south-falling light there are teams moving.
High up killdeer, crying, flash white from the breast as the sun takes
    them.

You can see from this hillock towns and their smoke on them, roads
    shining,
And miles under the thrusting sight the slumbrous earth.
That beauty shadows the heart,
Till evil and violence and the tragic splendor of the crashing world
Die on the mind, as thunder fades over a sleeper.
In islanded calmness, in the deep quiet, spirit nor blood will awake to
    the drum,
Perfectly tuned to the heavy mood that breeds in the valley.

"Oh fortunate earth, you must find someone to make you bitter
    music . . ."
No chanting of mine lures the talons down.
These places rare, and too dear.
The world is the plunder of hawks.

LINES FOR THE LAST OF A GOLD TOWN
MILLERTON, CALIFORNIA

When they rode that hawk-hearted Murietta down in the western hills,
They cut the head loose to prove the bounty,
And carried it here to this slope on the river's rim
Where the town sprawled, but no longer.
In a jar on the courthouse desk it lay for days,
While the wide-wheeled wagons swam in the dust,
And the word ran: upstate and down the folk heard it and sang;
And the head in the jar on the Millerton desk
Sneered through the glass at the faces.

Now the thick grass.
The willow fringe on the water's edge drinks the March sun and has
    peace,
Takes the deep sky, and bird-singing, the low mottled music, but heavy
    with peace.
On the low slope over the stream, with the roof of it thin and the
    windows gone.
The old courthouse alone on the meadow squats in the drag of the
    years;
Musty, floors fallen, the smell of dead time on it,
Of the killed moment, the stifling accumulation of sheer existence,
Thick in the air, and the wind takes it.

There can be heard over the earth,
Running in deep and vibrant gusts, the broken music;
Blowing, the reverberation of uttered sound,
Of bawd's talk and squaw's talk and the male-throated laughter,
Primal and harsh and brutely intense.
The mind's eye fashions the picture: glare on the night and the shacks
    crowded,
The congestion of flesh, of reeking animal flesh, blood burning, nerves
    blazing.

And one turns to the years,
Through the soft disintegration, thinking:
Where are the seekers and where are the whores?
What has come of the roaring, the lewd language, the riotous lusts and
     the acts? —
Here, where are only slow trees and the grass,
And this empty hulk and symbol of an order jeered at,
Spat at, hooted and scorned in the days of its birth?

Crumbles, the leaf; sags, the used stalk;
Softly, the alteration, the touch . . .
It has been said, often, tongues hating it.
It has been said.

SAN JOAQUIN

This valley after the storms can be beautiful beyond the telling,
Though our cityfolk scorn it, cursing heat in the summer and drabness
     in winter,
And flee it: Yosemite and the sea.
They seek splendor; who would touch them must stun them;
The nerve that is dying needs thunder to rouse it.

I in the vineyard, in green-time and dead-time, come to it dearly,
And take nature neither freaked nor amazing,
But the secret shining, the soft indeterminate wonder.
I watch it morning and noon, the unutterable sundowns,
And love as the leaf does the bough.

THE RAIN ON THAT MORNING

We on that morning, working, faced south and east where the sun was
     in winter at rising;
And looking up from the earth perceived the sky moving,
The sky that slid from behind without wind, and sank to the sun,
And drew on it darkly: an eye that was closing.
The rain on that morning came like a woman with love,
And touched us gently, and the earth gently, and closed down delicately
     in the morning,
So that all around were the subtle and intricate touchings.

The earth took them, the vines and the winter weeds;
But we fled them, and gaining the roof looked back a time
Where the rain without wind came slowly, and love in her touches.

The Wheatland Riot
(from *Factories in the Fields*)

CAREY McWILLIAMS

The erratic and violent development of agriculture in California has been paralleled by the sporadic turbulence which has characterized the history of farm labor in the State. The story of migratory labor is one of violence: harsh repression interrupted by occasional outbursts of indignation and protest. Nor is there much probability that the future will be one of peaceful adjustment to new social conditions; no one familiar with the dominant interests in California agriculture can have any illusions on this score. Violence, and more violence, is clearly indicated. It is indicated not only by the estabished patterns of industrialized agriculture, but, more explicitly, by the past record of violence in the industry. This record, it should be observed, stems from the early social behavior of the Californians. The history of the Vigilance Committees of 1850 and 1856 is well known and requires no repetition. While it is true that these early committees were organized to cope with crime, it is indisputable that they were largely representative of the "merchants and propertied" classes and that, at least in 1856, their activities were directed in part against organized labor. During the period when the vigilantes were in action, they completely usurped the functions of governmental officials, defied the Governor of the State, conducted their own trials, equipped and drilled an armed force, and operated in effect as an insurrectionary junta. The story of the vigilantes entered deeply into the consciousness of the merchants, businessmen, and industrialists of California. They never forgot the experience and their successors have never hesitated to constitute themselves "vigilantes" whenever the occasion has demanded "action." In 1934 "vigilante committees" appeared in practically every city, town, and rural district in California during the "Red" hysteria of that year. The significance of this deeply rooted tradition of violence must constantly be kept in mind. Insurrection was once sanctioned—violence was once glorified in the historical annals of the State—these facts have been remembered. Hence present-day industrialists are quick to drape themselves in the cloak of the vigilante tradition. Mining camps throughout the West, in Montana, Idaho, and Nevada, quickly improvised Vigilance Committees, on the San Francisco pattern, when they were first faced with a strong labor movement. Vigilantism, as such, had its origin in California.

The eruptions of farm labor have been at infrequent intervals and, in every instance, they have been violently suppressed, each incident provoking a long chain of prosecutions in the courts. No tearful glorification of the occasional protests of farm labor, however, is to be found in the official histories. Whatever theoretical considerations may be entertained concerning the use of violence in labor disputes, it is evident that, from a historical point of view, migratory labor has made gains in California when it has been militant. It has been potentially militant for a great many years, but, when strong protest movements have occurred, they have, in each instance, been directed by a clearly class-conscious leadership. One of the earliest instances of the stirring of deep-seated unrest in migratory labor was the Wheatland Riot, which occurred on the ranch of a large hop grower named Durst, near Wheatland, California, on August 3, 1913. Wheatland, clearly marked as one of the most significant episodes in the history of migratory labor in the West, also forms an important chapter in the social history of California. In the lurid illumination which the fires of the riot cast forth, the ugly facts about the condition of farm labor in California were, for the first time, thoroughly exposed. The riot and the subsequent trial attracted national attention.* It resulted in two important public documents bearing on the subject of farm labor (Report on the Wheatland Riot, issued June 1, 1914, and the Section titled "The Seasonal Labor Problem in Agriculture," Vol. V, Reports of the United States Commission on Industrial Relations), and one of the first serious studies of migratory labor (*The Casual Laborer,* 1920, by Carleton H. Parker).

The Wheatland affair marked the culmination of several years of agitational and organizational work on the part of the Industrial Workers of the World. To see the affair in proper perspective, therefore, it is necessary to indicate something of the background of these activities.

In the years between the Chicago convention at which the I. W. W. was formed in 1905, and 1913, the wobblies had been active in the fields, along the highways, on the trains, and in the jungle camps, with their spectacular propaganda and vivid agitation. The roots of the I. W. W. — if the organization may be said to have had any roots — were to be found among the migratory workers of the West. Not only were these workers unmercifully exploited — the conditions under which they worked making them highly susceptible to the inflammatory agitation of the wobblies — but they followed, in general, the routes pursued by the I. W. W. organizers. Organizers, coming from the timber camps of the Northwest, drifted south into the

* *Harper's Weekly,* April 4, June 20, 1914; *The Outlook,* May 16, 1914; *Technical World,* August, 1914.

agricultural fields. Always on the move, the wobblies, themselves essentially migratory, moved naturally into the currents of farm labor. Their organizational techniques — job action, organizing on the job, low dues or no dues at all — were well adapted to the circumstances under which farm labor was employed. They moved with the workers and organized them, so to speak, in transit.

During the years 1905– 1913, the wobblies had demonstrated considerable strength in California. They had, for example, conducted two sensational "free-speech" fights: in San Diego and in Fresno. The fight in Fresno was of particular importance, as Fresno has long been the nerve center of agricultural labor in California, located as it is in the heart of the San Joaquin Valley. In Fresno the wobblies fought for the right to maintain a headquarters, to distribute literature, and to hold public meetings. For six months, through one fall and winter in 1910, they battled the Fresno authorities. As often as they were crushed, they launched new campaigns, finally succeeding in winning a kind of tolerance for their activities. The courage and tenacity of the wobblies in Fresno attracted the attention of many migratory workers and made a deep impression throughout the State.

The San Diego fight was, if anything, even more sensational. Beginning in January, 1912, the San Diego authorities began to suppress wobbly meetings, the campaign culminating in a remarkable ordinance which outlawed free speech throughout the city (San Diego then had a population of about 40,000). The wobblies promptly sent out word for a "concentration" on San Diego, the idea being to crowd the jails and to raise such a fracas that the city fathers would despair of making arrests. Newspapers, at the time, carried scare headlines about "thousands" of workers converging on San Diego; in fact, only about 150 wobblies were involved. To cope with the situation, the authorities sponsored a local vigilance committee which established camps and posted armed guards along the highways leading to San Diego (one of the first California "border patrols"), turning back all transients. In San Diego itself the vigilantes rounded up all persons even remotely suspected of being wobblies and marched them, one night, to Sorrento. There the wobblies were made to mount an improvised platform, kiss the American flag and sing the national anthem, while hundreds of vigilantes stood about armed with revolvers, knives, clubs, blackjacks, and black snake whips. Then they were marched to San Onofre and driven into a cattle pen and systematically slugged and beaten. After a time, they were taken out of the pen and beaten with clubs and whips as, one at a time, they were made "to run the gantlet." One wobbly subsequently died in jail; scores received serious injuries. Not only was this performance sanctioned by the authorities, but the Merchants Association and the Chamber of Commerce passed resolutions praising the vigilantes.

Speaking on behalf of San Diego, the *San Diego Tribune,* in its issue of March 4, 1912, spoke of the wobblies as follows: "Hanging is none too good for them and they would be much better dead; for they are absolutely useless in the human economy; they are the waste material of creation and should be drained off into the sewer of oblivion there to rot in cold obstruction like any other excrement." When one local editor protested, the vigilantes attempted to lynch him. The facts, as I have given them, merely summarize the findings of Mr. Harris Weinstock who was appointed by Governor Hiram Johnson to investigate the incident.

After the San Diego free-speech fight, wobbly locals were established throughout California: in Fresno, Bakersfield, Los Angeles, San Diego, San Francisco and Sacramento. From these locals, camp delegates were sent into the fields to organize workers "on the job." Many "job strikes" were called and, frequently, they were successful. Largely because of the sensational character of their propaganda and the militancy of their free-speech fights, the wobblies built up a reputation in California out of all relation to their actual numerical strength. The I. W. W. had less than 5000 members in the State in 1913 and less than 8 per cent of the migratory farm workers were members. Nevertheless, the wobblies were a great influence. Whenever "labor trouble" occurred in the fields or in the construction camps, it was usually discovered that a "camp delegate" had been on the ground. The songs of the I. W. W. were frequently heard in the fields and in the jungle camps under the railroad bridges. To such an extent had this agitation permeated the mass of farm laborers that when the Wheatland incident occurred the I. W. W. was able to assume complete leadership of the workers. Conditions similar to those which existed on the Durst ranch in 1913 had existed in California for twenty years or longer, but militant action awaited the arrival of the wobblies.

1. The Riot

Immediately prior to August 3, 1913, some 2800 men, women and children were camped on a low, unshaded hill near the Durst hop ranch at Wheatland. Of this number, approximately 1500 were women and children. Over half the total number of workers in this miserable camp were aliens; at one of the subsequent mass meetings seven interpreters had to be used; and a field boss made note of twenty-seven nationalities represented in one working gang of 235 men on the ranch. Following the established practice of his fellow growers, Durst had advertised in newspapers throughout California and Nevada for workers. He had asked for 2700 workers when, as he subsequently admitted, he could only supply employment for about 1500. Within four days after his fanciful advertisements had appeared, this strange aggregation of workers had assembled. They came by every conceivable means of transportation; many of them had walked from near-by towns and cities. A great number had no blankets and slept on piles of straw thrown on tent floors. The tents, incidentally, were rented from Durst at seventy-five cents a week. Many slept in the fields. One group of 45 men, women and children slept packed closely together on a single pile of straw. There were nine outdoor toilets for 2800 people. The stench around the camp was nauseating, with children and women vomiting; dysentery was prevalent to an alarming degree. Between 200 and 300 children worked in the fields; and hundreds of children were seen around the camp "in an unspeakably filthy condition." The workers entered the fields at four o'clock in the morning, and by noon the heat was terrific, remaining, as it did, around 105 degrees. The water wells were "absolutely insufficient for the camp," with no means provided of bringing water to the fields. "Numerous instances of sickness and partial prostration among children from 5 to 10 years of age were mentioned in the testimony." One reason for Durst's chariness about providing water was that his cousin, Jim Durst, had a lemonade concession, selling lemonade to the workers at a nickel a glass. There was no organization for sanitation, no garbage disposal. Local Wheatland stores were forbidden to send delivery wagons to the camp, so that the workers were forced to buy what supplies they could afford from a "concession" store on the ranch.

The commission of inquiry which investigated the incident found that Durst had intentionally advertised for more workers than he needed in order to force wages down and that he purposely permitted the camp to remain in a filthy condition so that some of the workers would leave before the season was over, thereby forfeiting 10 per cent of their wages which he insisted on holding back. Carleton Parker stated that the amount paid, per hundred pounds of hops picked, fluctuated daily in relation to the number of workers on hand. Earnings varied between $1.00 and $.78 a day. Over half the workers were destitute and were forced to cash their checks each night. Throughout the season, at least a thousand workers, unable to secure employment, remained idle in the camp.

The foregoing is a very meager and abbreviated statement of the conditions which were found to have existed at the camp, on and prior to August third. Of the workers assembled, about a third came from California towns and cities; another third were "quasi-gypsies" from the Sierra foothills, with ramshackle wagons and carts; the remaining third were "hoboes," or their "California exemplars, the fruit tramps," with many foreigners among this group, including Japanese, Hindus, and Puerto Ricans. Of this strange assortment, about 100 men were I.W.W. "card men," i.e. they had, at one time or another, carried a wobbly card. Some of the wobblies had organized a loosely formed local in the camp in which some thirty workers had been enrolled. "It is a deeply suggestive fact," reads the official report, "that these thirty men, through their energy, technique and skill in organization, unified and dominated an unhomogeneous mass of 2,800 unskilled laborers" within two days. In was subsequently estimated that about 400 workers of those assembled knew, in a rough way, something of the philosophy of the I.W.W., and could sing some of its songs. Of the hundred card men, some had been in the San Diego fight, some had been soapboxers in Fresno. Among these men were Blackie Ford—an experienced I.W.W. organizer—and Herman Suhr.

Resentment had been steadily mounting in the camp for several days prior to August third. For the most part, the workers were indignant over living conditions; they were not primarily interested in wages. On August third, the wobblies called a mass meeting, Blackie Ford (he was unarmed) addressed the workers, and, among other remarks, told them to "knock the blocks off the scissor bills." He took a sick baby from its mother's arms and, holding it before the eyes of about 2000 workers, shouted: "It's for the kids we are doing this." The meeting had come to a close with the singing of "Mr. Block"—a wobbly song—when the sheriff and his posse arrived with the district attorney (who was, also, Durst's private attorney). The sheriff and a few of his men started through the crowd to arrest Ford. One deputy, on the fringe of the crowd, fired a shot in the air "to sober the mob," and, as he fired, the fighting started. The district attorney, a deputy sheriff, and two workers, a Puerto Rican and an English boy, were killed, and many more persons were injured, in the riot which followed. The posse, apparently astonished at the resistance they had encountered, fled the scene. Shocked beyond measure by reports of the riot, the State was immediately up in arms. The Governor dispatched four companies of the National Guard to Wheatland. The guardsmen marched to the workers' camp, surrounded it, and assisted the local officers in arresting about a hundred workers. Most of the workers had left the camp the night of august third, the "roads out of Wheatland being filled all that night with pickers leaving camp." The townspeople of Wheatland were so badly frightened by the incident that the National Guard remained on the scene for over a week.

Feeling that they had a revolutionary situation to cope with, the authorities were panicstricken and promptly launched a campaign of wild and irresponsible persecution. The Burns Detective Agency was called in and a hundred or more of its operatives were deputized. There followed one of the most amazing reigns of terror that California has ever witnessed. Wobblies were arrested literally in every part of the State. No one was ever able to make an accurate estimate of the number of arrests;

many cases were subsequently reported of men being arrested and held by local authorities incommunicado for seventy and eighty days. The total number of arrests ran well into the hundreds. Private detectives seized Suhr in Arizona (he was not even present when the riot occurred) and, without legal formalities, loaded him into a box car and brought him back to California. En route to Marysville, California, where the trial was held, Suhr was kept from consulting his attorney, being taken from hotel to hotel by night. Stool pigeons were placed with him to elicit confessions and he was beaten on an average of once a night with rubber bludgeons. It was several weeks after his "arrest" before his attorneys could even discover his whereabouts. Many other defendants were arrested and hurried from county to county in order to elude defense attorneys who were scurrying about trying to find their clients. So terrible was the treatment of these prisoners that one committed suicide and another went insane. An operative of the Burns Agency was, in fact, later convicted in Contra Costa County for a violent assault upon one of the men who was arrested but never tried. Eight months after the Wheatland riot occurred, Ford and Suhr were convicted of murder and sentenced to life imprisonment and this conviction was sustained on appeal, the first California labor *cause célèbre*. During the trial sixty or more wobblies rented a house in Marysville, which they used as headquarters. Every day of the trial, they marched from this house to the courtroom. When Austin Lewis, the defense attorney, needed a witness, he merely scribbled the name and address of the witness on a card and handed it to one of these men. Sympathetic brakemen and conductors on the trains invariably honored the cards as passenger tickets and allowed wobblies to travel about the State hunting witnesses.

People v. Ford, 25 Cal. App. 388.

Wheatland was not a strike, but a spontaneous revolt. It stands out as one of the significant episodes in the long and turgid history of migratory labor in California. For the first time, the people of California were made to realize, even if vaguely, the plight of its thousands of migratory workers. It had been customary to assume the existence of these laborers, but never to recognize the fact of their existence. The deplorable conditions under which they lived and worked were, also, brought to light for the first time. Although the immediate public reaction was one of horror over the I. W. W. menace, so-called, the incident made an impression. It created an opportunity for effective investigation by the Commission on Immigration and Housing in California which, under the distinguished chairmanship of Simon J. Lubin, did much to improve living and housing conditions among migratory workers in the State. As the annual reports of this commission began to appear after 1914, the Californians were given some interesting facts about labor conditions in the State's most important industry. It was discovered, for example, that, in 1914, there were about 75,000 migratory farm laborers in the State; and that, when employed, these people worked on ranches "devoid of the accommodations given horses." Sample studies indicated that about a fourth of them were suffering from one type of sickness or another and that about an equal percentage were feebleminded.

2. Kelley's Army

Following the Wheatland affair, and during the winter of 1914, an incident occurred which, for the first time, threw considerable light on the question of what happened to 75,000 migratory farm laborers during the winter months. The number of unemployed in San Francisco that winter was unusually large and the city authorities soon discovered that "General Kelley," a gentleman of mysterious antecedents, had organized an army of the unemployed. About two thousand men had enrolled in the army and were living in abandoned warehouses and store buildings; quite a number were camped in tents in the Mission district. Kelley had his men organized into companies and squads and put them through regular military maneuvers. As the size of the army increased, Kelley became more outspoken in his demands upon the authorities for relief, or "charitable assistance," as it was then called. The officials, and the business interests of the city, soon became alarmed over the situation, and, seizing upon Kelley's desire to stage a "march on the capitol," they escorted his army to the ferries and sent them across the bay to Oakland. The Mayor of Oakland, not at all delighted by this visitation of "rainsoaked, sick, and coughing" men, hurriedly arranged for their transportation to Sacramento. In Sacramento, they organized a "camp" and were preparing to march on the capitol building, 1500 strong, when a rival "army," of eight hundred special deputy sheriffs, arrived with pick handles and drove them across the river, burned their blankets and equipment, and mounted an armed guard along the bridge to keep them out. In the process of ousting the army, the deputies were none too gentle. E. Guy Talbott, a local clergyman, states that many of Kelley's men "were beaten into insensibility and the most atrocious and barbarous methods were used." Within three weeks the Army, 'rained on and starved out," melted away. For years afterwards, however, the story of Kelley's Army lingered in the social consciousness of the Californian as a grim portent of the days to come.

When the Industrial Relations Commission arrived in California in August, 1914, they took testimony both on the Wheatland affair and on the strange rise and fall of General Kelley's Army, and the connection between the two incidents was clearly indicated. "You can't analyze the Wheatland affair and the riot that took place," testified Carleton Parker, "or the problem of the unemployed in San Francisco last winter without bringing into the analysis the seasonal character of employment in California." Testifying further, he said: "The fact that San Francisco is said to have in winter thirty-five to forty thousand men lying up until the earlier season when the first agricultural demand for labor occurs, is explained by the fact that along in November and December, especially in November, agricultural work practically ceases. The State being fundamentally an agricultural State, the industrial life of the State not being of tremendous importance, and the fact that the State is geographically isolated, means that we have to nurse our own casual labor class through the winter." Witness after witness testified as to the instability of employment, the lack of co-ordination, and the refusal of the agricultural interests of the State to assume any measure of responsibility for the situation which they had created. It is interesting to note that one witness did suggest that if the growers continued to shirk their responsibility, it might be well for the State to condemn some of their holdings and settle the unemployed on the land so that they could earn a living. At about the same time, San Diego, faced with a serious unemployment problem, took over four thousand acres of "waste" land, and gave food and lodging to hundreds of unemployed, and paid them fifty cents a day, while they worked in improving and cultivating the tract. The experiment was quite successful and was continued until 1916, when, the demand for labor increasing, it was abandoned. August Vollmer, describing the operation of the plan in the *Christian Science Monitor*, advocated its extension throughout the State and claimed that there were approximately 11,000,000 acres of "waste" lands in the State that might be put to constructive social use in this manner.

The recognition of an acute social problem in migratory farm labor, a problem so serious as to shake the foundations of the State, which the Wheatland Riot and the appearance of General Kelley's Army had forced upon the people of California, was, unfortunately, destroyed by the World War. Both incidents passed into history. Even the beginning toward a solution of the problem, as indicated by the creation of the State Commission on Immigration and Housing, was soon nullified. Reactionary postwar administrations proceeded to undermine the work of the commission (Simon J. Lubin resigned in protest), and the blind chaos of former years once more prevailed.

I Never Knowed They Was Anything Like Her

(from *The Grapes of Wrath*)

JOHN STEINBECK

All night they bored through the hot darkness, and jack-rabbits scuttled into the lights and dashed away in long jolting leaps. And the dawn came up behind them when the lights of Mojave were ahead. And the dawn showed high mountains to the west. They filled with water and oil at Mojave and crawled into the mountains, and the dawn was about them.

Tom said, "Jesus, the desert's past! Pa, Al, for Christ sakes! The desert's past!"

"I'm too goddamned tired to care," said Al.

"Want me to drive?"

"No, wait awhile."

They drove through Tehachapi in the morning glow, and the sun came up behind them, and the — suddenly they saw the great valley below them. Al jammed on the brake and stopped in the middle of the road, and, "Jesus Christ! Look!" he said. The vineyards, the orchards, the great flat valley, green and beautiful, the trees set in rows, and the farm houses.

And Pa said, "God Almighty!" The distant cities, the little towns in the orchard land, and the morning sun, golden on the valley. A car honked behind them. Al pulled to the side of the road and parked.

"I want ta look at her." The grain fields golden in the morning, and the willow lines, the eucalyptus trees in rows.

Pa sighed, "I never knowed they was anything like her." The peach trees and the walnut groves, and the dark green patches of oranges. And red roofs among the trees, and barns — rich barns. Al got out and stretched his legs.

He called, "Ma—come look. We're there!"

Ruthie and Winfield scrambled down from the car, and then they stood, silent and awestruck, embarrassed before the great valley. The distance was thinned with haze, and the land grew softer and softer in the distance. A windmill flashed in the sun, and its turning blades were like a little heliograph, far away. Ruthie and Winfield looked at it, and Ruthie whispered, "It's California."

Winfield moved his lips silently over the syllables. "There's fruit," he said aloud.

Casy and Uncle John, Connie and Rose of Sharon climbed down. And they stood silently. Rose of Sharon had started to brush her hair back, when she caught sight of the valley and her hand dropped slowly to her side.

Tom said, "Where's Ma? I want Ma to see it. Look Ma! Come here, Ma." Ma was climbing slowly, stiffly, down the back board. Tom looked at her. "My God, Ma, you sick?" Her face was stiff and putty-like, and her eyes seemed to have sunk deep into her head, and the rims were red with weariness. Her feet touched the ground and she braced herself by holding the truck-side.

Her voice was a croak. "Ya say we're acrost?"

Tom pointed to the great valley. "Look!"

She turned her head, and her mouth opened a little. Her fingers went to her throat and gathered a little pinch of skin and twisted gently. "Thank God!" she said. "The fambly's here." Her knees buckled and she sat down on the running board.

"You sick, Ma?"

"No, jus' tar'd."

"Didn' you get no sleep?"

"No."

"Was Granma bad?"

Ma looked down at her hands, lying together like tired lovers in her lap. "I wisht I could wait an' not tell you. I wisht it could be all—nice."

Pa said, "Then Granma's bad."

Ma raised her eyes and looked over the valley. "Granma's dead."

They looked at her, all of them, and Pa asked, "When?"

"Before they stopped us las' night."

"I was afraid we wouldn' get acrost," she said. "I tol' Granma we couldn' he'p her. The fambly had ta get acrost. I tol' her, tol' her when she was a-dyin'. We couldn' stop in the desert. There was the young ones—an' Rosasharn's baby. I tol' her." She put up her hands and covered her face for a moment. "She can get buried in a nice green place," Ma said softly. "Trees aroun' an' a nice place. She got to lay her head down in California."

The family looked at Ma with a little terror at her strength.

Tom said, "Jesus Christ! You layin' there with her all night long!"

"The fambly hadda get acrost," Ma said miserably.

Tom moved close to put his hand on her shoulder.

"Don't touch me," she said. "I'll hol' up if you don't touch me. That'd get me."

Pa said, "We got to go on now. We got to go on down."

Ma looked up at him. "Can—can I set up front? I don' wanna go back there no more — I'm tar'd. I'm awful tar'd."

They climbed back on the load, and they avoided the long stiff figure covered and tucked in a comforter, even the head covered and tucked. They moved to their places and tried to keep their eyes from it — from the hump on the comfort that would be the nose, and the steep cliff that would be the jut of the chin. They tried to keep their eyes away, and they could not. Ruthie and Winfield, crowded in a forward corner as far away from the body as they could get, stared at the tucked figure.

And Ruthie whispered, "Tha's Granma, an' she's dead."

Winfield nodded solemnly. "She ain't breathin' at all. She's awful dead."

And Rose of Sharon said softly to Connie, "She was a-dyin' right when we —"

"How'd we know?" he reassured her.

Al climbed on the load to make room for Ma in the seat. And Al swaggered a little because he was sorry. He plumped down beside Casy and Uncle John. "Well, she was ol'. Guess her time was up," Al said. "Ever'body got to die." Casy and Uncle John turned eyes expressionlessly on him and looked at him as though he were a curious talking bush. "Well, ain't they?" he demanded. And the eyes looked away, leaving Al sullen and shaken.

Casy said in wonder, "All night long, an' she was alone." And he said, "John, there's a woman so great with love — she scares me. Makes me afraid an' mean."

John asked, "Was it a sin? Is they any part of it you might call a sin?"

Casy turned on him in astonishment, "A sin? No, there ain't no part of it that's a sin."

"I ain't never done nothin' that wasn't part sin," said John, and he looked at the long wrapped body.

Tom and Ma and Pa got into the front seat. Tom let the truck roll and started on compression. And the heavy truck moved, snorting and jerking and popping down the hill. The sun was behind them, and the valley golden and green before them. Ma shook her head slowly from side to side. "It's purty," she said. "I washt they could of saw it."

"I wisht so too," said Pa.

Tom patted the steering wheel under his hand. "They was too old," he said. "They wouldn't of saw' nothin' that's here. Grampa would a been a-seein' the Injuns an' the prairie country when he was a young fella. An' Granma would a remembered an' seen the first home she lived in. They was too ol'. Who's really seein' it is Ruthie an' Winfiel'."

Pa said, "Here's Tommy talkin' like a growed-up man, talkin' like a preacher almos'."

And Ma smiled sadly. "He is. Tommy's growed way up — way up so I can't get aholt of 'im sometimes."

They popped down the mountain, twisting and looping, losing the valley sometimes, and then finding it again. And the hot breath of the valley came up to them, with hot green smells on it, and with resinous sage and tarweed smells. The crickets crackled along the road. A rattlesnake crawled across the road and Tom hit it and broke it and left it squirming.

Tom said, "I guess we got to go to the coroner, wherever he is. We got to get her buried decent. How much money might be lef', Pa?"

"'Bout forty dollars," said Pa.

Tom laughed. "Jesus, are we gonna start clean! We sure ain't bringin' nothin with us." He chuckled a moment, and then his face straightened quickly. He pulled the visor of his cap down low over his eyes. And the truck rolled down the mountain into the great valley.

PART FOUR

Exploring

The suggestibility of the human organism in the direction of rhythmic response is so generous that the rhythmic forms to which the environment gives rise, seem to pass through the autonomic system, into and out of the subconscious without our having once become intellectually aware of them.

—*from The American Rhythm* (1930)
by MARY AUSTIN

W HEN THE FILM FAT CITY was released in 1972 it gave many Americans their first look at the Great Central Valley since the 1940 film version of THE GRAPES OF WRATH. Directed by John Huston, FAT CITY was based on Leonard Gardner's widely praised novel, which he set in and around his home town of Stockton. According to *The National Observer,*

Gardner's intimacy with boxing, harvesting, the subterrenean life of Californian cities festering in golden light, gives his book a denseness of fact, a humanity which plunges the reader into an immediate experience and punishes him with vivid rhythms and sensations.

This novel, published in 1969, has been the most visible example of a new generation of books, stories, poems and plays. It is a now-abundant body of writing which began to emerge in the early 1960s with works such as Gardner's story, "Jesus Christ Has Returned to Earth and Preaches Here Nightly," reprinted in *The Paris Review* after its initial appearance in a 1962 issue of the San Francisco State TRANSFER, and which continues to unfold in the works of younger writers like Selma's Nels Hanson, whose experimental novel, THE LONG SLOW DEATH OF JOE DAN MAR-TEN, won the James D. Phelan Award in 1973; and Fresno-born Gary Soto, winner of the International Poetry Forum's United States Award (1976) for his book, THE ELEMENTS OF SAN JOAQUIN; and dramatist/director Luis Valdez whose plays, most notably "Zoot Suit," which first gained prominence in Delano, have been performed and acclaimed in Los Angeles, in New York City, and in eight European countries as part of an official American Bicentennial Event.

The writers, for the most part, are native Californians exploring, re-discovering, sometimes leaving behind, the world their parents or grand-parents travelled to. Catching the region in the era of its most rapid change, these works often play the blur of the present against fixed images

85

from the recent past — scenes and images the writers tend to hold to with a classically Californian yearning for times and places that have too quickly slipped through our fingers.

Watching another day begin, Gary Soto writes,

> ... I saw the sun take
> Its first step
> Above the water tower at Sun
>   Maid Raisins
> And things separate from the dark
> And lean on their new shadows...

Today it is a valley of new shadows. Antelope are gone, wolves are gone, grizzly bears and beavers gone, elk and condors restricted to small reservations. All the major rivers have been dammed and much of the marshland drained. Most of the Indians are gone too, destroyed or absorbed or isolated — like the lone Washo making his way across the valley in the scene from Thomas Sanchez's epic novel, RABBIT BOSS — isolated by a culture they did not understand and could not successfully resist.

Almost everything has changed except the land's abundance, its energy.

Nearly a century-and-a-half of white settlement has altered the valley dramatically. Most notably, it has become the richest agricultural region in the world, greener than ever thanks to the irrigation of much previously desert land, and it supports a larger, more diverse population. Farming has not only been the major force of change in the region — social, economic, even geo-physical change — it has also molded the perceptions of many local writers. Art Cuelho, who toiled years on a Riverdale farm, remembers well the transition wrought by water on the valley's arid westside:

> There were no songs
> when scorpions did
> their dance to a
> whirlwind tune and
> a desert promise.
> No water wells then.
> A dry-farming stake
> was the way before
> canal hopes grew
> in the caterpillar dust.

Water also brought massive corporate farms, what Carey McWilliams called "factories in the fields," with their insatiable appetites for cheap labor. While the valley remains a land of chosen people with general prosperity, its riches are no longer shared as Indians once shared them, equally according to need. The region's haves and have-nots exist in starkly contrasting, yet symbiotic worlds. An experienced field worker, Amado Jesus Muro (Chester Seltzer), has depicted field life in numerous sketches, such as this one, taken from a 1968 issue of THE MEXICAN AMERICAN:

Another pea picker, spindly with a road-seared face, worked on his knees in the wet sand earth nearby. He filled his hamper until it could hold no more, and then straightened up grimacing from the strain on his back, calves and thighs.

"It's never popular to be poor — only in the Bible," he said. "A man must have invented stoop labor because a snake never would."

Along with land, sun and water, field labor has been a foundation of California agriculture for over a century, a base — however unrewarded — upon which great fortunes have been built.

The promise of abundant work, plus the lingering hope that one might somehow ascend the economic pyramid, has historically attracted migrants to the valley. California in general, the Heartland in particular, has been a region of the mind, a symbol of hope, a final westering destination.

A unique mixture of the Far West and the "Wide West," its reality is sometimes hidden by the reputations of Los Angeles and San Francisco. Range cattle still roam its bottomlands and hills, and valley people, though more live in towns than in the country nowadays, often remain rural in attitudes. In town or not, there is something of the rodeo, that ancient ritual, in the way folks see themselves and their relationship to nature. More is symbolically linked than mere roadways in Chico poet George Keithley's description:

> They arrive
> from all points in the valley —
> They travel the ranch roads that connect
> with paved roads feeding into the freeway
> to enter town by car or truck
> or on horseback, . . .

Southwestern life-styles pervade the valley; its cities seem more Lubbock than Los Angeles. Route 66, which enters the valley at Bakersfield, links this northernmost southwest with the old country, and has been a line of economic least resistance for many migrants seeking employment. The work of such writers as Leonard Gardner, James D. Houston, Nels Hanson, DeWayne Rail, Gerald Haslam and Wilma Elizabeth McDaniel strongly reflects transplanted southwestern themes and values.

Oil has attracted many a Texan or Oklahoman into the valley, and has itself been a major factor in valley life. The earthy good humor, the strict adherence to the work ethic, the direct, unsubtle worldview, even the twangy dialect and country music that have come to be identified with the region's oilfields have been tempered by white-only hiring policies that once characterized the petroleum business and reinforced southern racism moved west. Taft's William Rintoul, historian as well as fictionalist, reports that underlying the optimism and spirit of hustle that characterized valley oil towns "was one unwritten rule: not everyone could participate. . . . In oil towns . . . racial feelings were exaggerated to the point that these places became widely known as 'white man's towns' in which blacks were not permitted to remain overnight."

Most indigenous artists, no matter how deep their love for the Heartland, do not view valley life with blinders. In addition to racism, the region's historic economic inequities, its often-maimed landscape, its occasional xenophobia, and its tradition of anti-intellectualism all rankle writers to varying degrees. Criticism runs the gamut from snobbishness to heartfelt concern. Joan Didion, a Sacramento native, candidly reveals questions about her home place:

. . . Sacramento *is* California, and California is a place in which a boom mentality and a sense of Chekovian loss meet in uneasy suspension; in which the mind is troubled by some buried ineradicable suspicion that things had better work here, because here, beneath that immense bleached sky, is where we run out of continent.

For the forebears of Asian-American writers such as Alan Chong Lau and Lawson Inada, California was not continent's end, but a verdant east, an opening to new possibilities on a new land, a beginning. Many cultures — not exclusively westward-moving Europeans — have built valley life, physically constructed it and they have culturally influenced it. They are the valley; it is them. Writes Inada:

The Gomez family, the Inadas,
are exactly where they are,
where California starts from and goes out, and out, and out.

Like the Gomez family, the cultural ancestors of Luis Valdez, Luis Omar Salinas and Gary Soto moved into the far green reaches of what was then the northern provinces of Mexico, only to be surrounded by Americans surging toward the farthest limit of that continent they felt was theirs by right of manifest destiny.

Today, while many Chicanos are long-time residents, there exists a constantly renewed first-generation fresh from Mexico hoping to reap the valley's rich promise, and willing to toil desperately to do so. The ongoing Chicano struggle is the major theme in the highly symbolic dramas of Delano's Valdez. In the prologue to his bilingual play, EL FIN DEL MUNDO, a valley community is seen reacting to portents that could be signalling "the end of the world." Later, the central character, Mundo, seems to be betraying his own people, when he accepts a bribe from local growers. But he soon emerges as a kind of double agent, deliberately confusing the growers' scheme.

Another group that has distinguished itself with its hard work, its love of the land, and its rich literary heritage, Armenian-Americans, remain a prominent voice in valley writing. Their tradition which, transplanted, grew from the coffee houses of Fresno and was first nationally recognized in the flashing prose of William Saroyan, lives in the work of Khatchik Minasian and David Kherdian, among others. Kherdian finds his imagery in his mother's Armenian cooking, in the plowed earth that reclaimed his father, or right outside his window:

> Outside our bedroom window
>   the purple flowers
>   of the pomegranate tree,
>   whose buds caught the
>   hot sun of earlier day,
>   await the explosion
>   of birth.

Any discussion of the valley and its literature must begin and end with the land. Its broad fertile fields attracted the diverse population that has given the region so many voices and points of view. The struggle for shares of the land's produce has provided ongoing dramatic themes. And finally it is the details emerging from the landscape, or plucked from the atmosphere, that give so much of this writing its texturing and taste.

The surrounding mountains gave the Maidu their version of how the Sacramento River began. "Great Man," they said, "tore open the Coast Range and made the waters flow down to the ocean." Pomegranate trees gave shape to Saroyan's story and to poems by David Kherdian and Dennis Saleh. In *Delta Farm* the inrush of brine gives Dennis Schmitz a powerful image for measuring the ironies of nature's abundance:

> late November: a sixty-knot
> squall through Carquinez

Strait breaks
levees, backs salt water miles
inland to preserve
what it kills. . . .

The valley is a land of large gifts and large burdens. One of its gifts is this
body of writing — a perhaps unexpected form of produce — collected here
for the first time. It comes from writers who love the place or who reject
the place. It comes from natives and from passers-through. It comes from
those who have left it for good or who, as Selma's Larry Levis suggests in
his prose poem IN A COUNTRY, will forever be returning:

It looked like the land we had left, some smoke in the distance, but I
wasn't sure. There were birds calling. The creaking of our wheels. And
as we entered that country, it felt as if someone was touching our bare
shoulders, lightly, for the last time.

Two Poems
GEORGE KEITHLEY

THE RED BLUFF RODEO

They arrive
        from all points in the valley —
They travel the ranch roads that connect
with paved roads feeding into the freeway
to enter town by car or truck
or on horseback,
                            all morning
the main street so full of traffic
there isn't an empty seat
in a restaurant or bar and grill
for more than a mile around the fairgrounds.

"Let me have some coffee and three eggs."
"How do you like your eggs?"
"I like 'em fine!"

*

Clowns wearing costumes
of cowboys or ranch hands
perform, falling off
the back of a plow horse
too old to mind the jeers
of spectators. One clown
climbs a cow and flings
his feet in the air,
slaps her rear and lifts
his eyes to the sky as though
to ask why she won't buck —
But you hear little laughter
as people slide closer
on the wooden slats,
and settle for the serious show.

*

They roar for the first rider —
What's caught the eye of the crowd
is the swift stride of his horse
and the queer stiff legs of the calf.
His lasso loops over her neck
to stop her short.
He drops beside her in the dust
and ties her legs tight with one length
of rope, and one twisted sweep of his arm.
He throws his hands in the air to show he's done,
like a man who is surrounded and forced to surrender.

Applause rattles the grandstand from its full height,
as the man and horse trot toward the gate.

The clowns come for the calf and hurry off.

Another number is announced. The chute opens. Out
flies a fresh horse, a hat, and a pair of hands
too fast for the calf
who finds herself rolling helpless
in the grip of the rope.

*

Girls squirm in the sun.
Small boys see every event
with intent eyes
until the women unwrap
sandwiches, which the children eat.
But wives who worry
whether a man will earn
as much as his entry fee
turn to each other and talk,
to ignore the noise and nervous heat.

    "Did he come home sober last night?"
    "In the dark he tripped over a chair."
    "Well what did you do?"
    "I laughed so hard I fell out of bed."

        *

The last man in the saddle bronc competition
provokes a rough ride
to impress the judges.
His feet jab for flesh.

His spurs urge
the bronc to kick
three ways at once —

He flies from his mount
in mid-air, tossed
free. Falls
like a sack of meal in the dust.
The public disapproves and boos.
He crawls away from the hooves, on his hands and knees.

"Some sort of fun."

    " . . . I'm glad it's done.
All day I've been as dizzy as a squirrel."

    The crowd staggers out of the stands,
    pressing into the parking lot.

    Evening dresses the country in cool stars.

Far in the night a fitful line of light
searches the length of the valley,
where families follow one another home
beyond the lost barns and deserted fields.

AFTER HIS ASSASSINATION A PLACE OF PEACE

1

After his assassination a place of peace,
a church
impatient with piety,
pleas for Kennedy —
"Receive, receive, your servant Jack."
Long lines of mourners murmur and turn back.
St. John's belfry wheel winds, and unreels its chimes.

The amber lamps upon the roof
of the radio tower pulse on and off.
Throughout the hour
wire reports grow like fine steel vines.

Thru this electric speech a siren climbs
above the trees and screams
for the body borne away,
given to the grass.

Poor death, beggaring death
seeking a gift of us
that has our breath.

In our restless peace
what can my hand touch
that will bloom? Or our arms reach
that will bear?

2

Wind warps the shingled roofs slanting by the green
City Plaza where boughs storm;
winter oranges blaze like Christmas balls.

The green sign
of Christ will twine,
Love's wreath
cut from the tree of our wrath.

Everywhere we watch for this certainty.

The rain wells in the crotch
of a walnut tree.

3

Water slides off a purple rib of the foothills,
lifting silt;
washes west on the slow brush floor
and into the milling Sacramento
quietly spills.

4

Grief goes open in the street...
If we kill,
Sweet Christ,
who are free,
then where is our peace?

What burns my blood away
in my own flesh?

   Doves cower asleep
   dry in the crowns
   of green palms.

On the black airfield a radar cup waits.
Lights wink with power, clicking rise
along a low cloudbank, begin
their sweeping spin,
and death's found
day and night in each town;
O come under the drifting skies...

The valley rain chills your skin

and distracts and turns your dead
legs, and your spirit dead, growing into the winter of the war.

November carries cold across the land
an inconstant sun . . . the sand coasts gripped in ice.

5

Night nods beside the road but will not sleep.
A time to map the madness that destroys a man.

6

Dawn rises in the streets of our unrest.

Notes drop from the apartment of a pianist.
People in the plaza stop to listen,
caught by the cold strain
of music this morning,
as though memory might admire a deliberate refrain.

7

A raw rain pours and stains
the skinned sycamores.

The rain crawls in the street, it looks insane,
it sits there, at noon, unclean
licked by dogs.

South in the valley a late yield
is marginal. Water grass
eats the profits out of the rice field.

All of these things are so, this is the way
they are seen.

But there is a deep disorder now
between the eye and brain.

There is deep disorder, a ditch between
what you can see

and what you can reach, and touch:

the ordinary darkness
of human figures of men or women,
the company of others coming out on the river ground,

walking on a drying slope, overlooking the high water,
blades of wood awash in the mud-silt seeping
under a boat landing, and swelling down into the delta.

8

The wet air gleams. After the rain

the sunlight is planked by a blue shade
that moves. A human
figure, man or woman,
a shadow-shape the sun casts in the grass.

So my spirit's sorrow
returns to town, unable
to follow its friend further, as the shadow
of my flesh falls before me.

9

Jets cross the missile silos, and a bluff low
on the unchanneled salmon water,
and ride tandem, then divide

while the wind blooming the boughs
buries its breath in a pool.
After the rain all of these things are so —
on the road leaves spawn and litter and stream

in a flash chill like the first
frost on a ranch banked in blossoms;
late warnings are broadcast, the alert lamps smoke in the orchards.

Though disaster and death drive us out
of the solitary city
or town or prairie

we bring in our blood
all the joy and anguish which we see.

Our blest blood gains from the spirit the speed
of a child,
         grace in the veins,
the birds' timing—

A schoolboy fields a punt,
slips a tackler,
and he's free.

In the ranch air
and the deep farmland
the doves complain and hunt.

Notes from a Native Daughter

(from *Slouching Towards Bethlehem*)

JOAN DIDION

It is very easy to sit at the bar in, say, La Scala in Beverly Hills, or Ernie's in San Francisco, and to share in the pervasive delusion that California is only five hours from New York by air. The truth is that La Scala and Ernie's are only five hours from New York by air. California is somewhere else.

Many people in the East (or "back East," as they say in California, although not in La Scala or Ernie's) do not believe this. They have been to Los Angeles or to San Francisco, have driven through a giant redwood and have seen the Pacific glazed by the afternoon sun off Big Sur, and they naturally tend to believe that they have in fact been to California. They have not been, and they probably never will be, for it is a longer and in many ways a more difficult trip than they might want to undertake, one of those trips on which the destination flickers chimerically on the horizon, ever receding, ever diminishing. I happen to know about that trip because I come from California, come from a family, or a congeries of families, that has always been in the Sacramento Valley.

You might protest that no family has been in the Sacramento Valley for anything approaching "always." But it is characteristic of Californians to speak grandly of the past as if it had simultaneously begun, *tabula rasa*, and reached a happy ending on the day the wagons started west. *Eureka*—"I

Have Found It" — as the state motto has it. Such a view of history casts a certain melancholia over those who participate in it; my own childhood was suffused with the conviction that we had long outlived our finest hour. In fact that is what I want to tell you about: what it is like to come from a place like Sacramento. If I could make you understand that, I could make you understand California and perhaps something else besides, for Sacramento *is* California, and California is a place in which a boom mentality and a sense of Chekhovian loss meet in uneasy suspension; in which the mind is troubled by some buried but ineradicable suspicion that things had better work here, because here, beneath that immense bleached sky, is where we run out of continent.

In 1847 Sacramento was no more than an adobe enclosure, Sutter's Fort, standing alone on the prairie; cut off from San Francisco and the sea by the Coast Range and from the rest of the continent by the Sierra Nevada, the Sacramento Valley was then a true sea of grass, grass so high a man riding into it could tie it across his saddle. A year later gold was discovered in the Sierra foothills, and abruptly Sacramento was a town, a town any moviegoer could map tonight in his dreams — a dusty collage of assay offices and wagonmakers and saloons. Call that Phase Two. Then the settlers came — the farmers, the people who for two hundred years had been moving west on the frontier, the peculiar flawed strain who had cleared Virginia, Kentucky, Missouri; they made Sacramento a farm town. Because the land was rich, Sacramento became eventually a rich farm town, which meant houses in town, Cadillac dealers, a country club. In that gentle sleep Sacramento dreamed until perhaps 1950, when something happened. What happened was that Sacramento woke to the fact that the outside world was moving in, fast and hard. At the moment of its waking Sacramento lost, for better or for worse, its character, and that is part of what I want to tell you about.

But the change is not what I remember first. First I remember running a boxer dog of my brother's over the same flat fields that our great-great-grandfather had found virgin and had planted; I remember swimming (albeit nervously, for I was a nervous child, afraid of sinkholes and afraid of snakes, and perhaps that was the beginning of my error) the same rivers we had swum for a century: the Sacramento, so rich with silt that we could barely see our hands a few inches beneath the serface; the American, running clean and fast with melted Sierra snow until July, when it would slow down, and rattlesnakes would sun themselves on its newly exposed rocks. The Sacramento, the American, sometimes the Cosumnes, occasionally the Feather. Incautious children died every day in those rivers; we read about it in the paper, how they had miscalculated a current or stepped into a hole down where the American runs into the Sacramento, how the Berry Brothers had been called in from Yolo County to drag the river but how the bodies remained unrecovered. "They were from away," my grandmother would extrapolate from the newspaper stories. "Their parents had no *business* letting them in the river. They were visitors from Omaha." It was not a bad lesson, although a less than reliable one; children we knew died in the rivers too.

When summer ended — when the State Fair closed and the heat broke, when the last green hop vines had been torn down along the H Street road and the tule fog began rising off the low ground at night — we would go back to memorizing the Products of Our Latin American Neighbors and to visiting the great-aunts on Sunday, dozens of great-aunts, year after year of Sundays. When I think now of those winters I think of yellow elm leaves wadded in the gutters outside the Trinity Episcopal Pro-Cathedral on M Street. There are actually people in Sacramento now who call M Street Capitol Avenue, and Trinity has one of those featureless new buildings, but perhaps children still learn the same things there on Sunday mornings:

Q. In what way does the Holy Land resemble the Sacramento Valley?
A. In the type and diversity of its agricultural products.

And I think of the rivers rising, of listening to the radio to hear at what height they would crest and wondering if and when and where the levees would go. We did not have as many dams in those years. The bypasses would be full, and men would sandbag all night. Sometimes a levee would go in the night, somewhere upriver; in the morning the rumor would spread that the Army Engineers had dynamited it to relieve the pressure on the city.

After the rains came spring, for ten days or so; the drenched fields would dissolve into a brilliant ephemeral green (it would be yellow and dry as fire in two or three weeks) and the real-estate business would pick up. It was the time of year when people's grandmothers went to Carmel; it was the time of year when girls who could not even get into Stephens or Arizona or Oregon, let alone Stanford or Berkely, would be sent to Honolulu, on the *Lurline*. I have no recollection of anyone going to New York, with the exception of a cousin who visited there (I cannot imagine why) and reported that the shoe salesmen at Lord & Taylor were "intolerably rude." What happened in New York and Washington and abroad seemed to impinge not at all upon the Sacramento mind. I remember being taken to call upon a very old woman, a rancher's widow, who was reminiscing (the favored conversational mode in Sacramento) about the son of some contemporaries of hers. "That Johnston boy never did amount to much," she said. Desultorily, my mother protested: Alva Johnston, she said, had won the Pulitzer Prize, when he was working for *The New York Times*. Our hostess looked at us impassively. "He never amounted to anything in Sacramento," she said.

Hers was the true Sacramento voice, and, although I did not realize it then, one not long to be heard, for the war was over and the boom was on and the voice of the aerospace engineer would be heard in the land. VETS NO DOWN! EXECUTIVE LIVING ON LOW FHA!

Later, when I was living in New York, I would make the trip back to Sacramento four and five times a year (the more comfortable the flight, the more obscurely miserable I would be, for it weighs heavily upon my kind that we could perhaps not make it by wagon), trying to prove that I had not meant to leave at all, because in at least one respect California—the California we are talking about—resembles Eden: it is assumed that those who absent themselves from its blessings have been banished, exiled by some perversity of heart. Did not the Donner-Reed Party, after all, eat its own dead to reach Sacramento?

I have said that the trip back is difficult, and it is—difficult in a way that magnifies the ordinary ambiguities of sentimental journeys. Going back to California is not like going back to Vermont, or Chicago; Vermont and Chicago are relative constants, against which one measures one's own change. All that is constant about the California of my childhood is the rate at which it disappears. An instance: on Saint Patrick's Day of 1948 I was taken to see the legislature "in action," a dismal experience; a handful of florid assemblymen, wearing green hats, were reading Pat-and-Mike jokes into the record. I still think of the legislators that way—wearing green hats, or sitting around on the veranda of the Senator Hotel fanning themselves and being entertained by Artie Samish's emissaries. (Samish was the lobbyist who said, "Earl Warren may be the governor of the state, but I'm the governor of the legislature.") In fact there is no longer a veranda at the Senator Hotel—it was turned into an airline ticket office, if you want to embroider the point—and in any case the legislature has largely deserted the Senator for the flashy motels north of town, where the tiki torches flame and the steam rises off the heated swimming pools in the cold Valley night.

It is hard to *find* California now, unsettling to wonder how much of it was merely imagined or improvised; melancholy to realize how much of anyone's memory is no true memory at all but only the traces of someone else's memory, stories handed down on the family network. I have an indelibly vivid "memory," for example, of how Prohibition affected the hop growers around Sacramento: the sister of a grower my family knew brought home a mink coat from San Francisco, and was told to take it back, and sat on the floor of the parlor cradling that coat and crying. Although I was not born until a year after Repeal, that scene is more "real" to me than many I have played myself.

I remember one trip home, when I sat alone on a night jet from New York and read over and over some lines from a W. S. Merwin poem I had come across in a magazine, a poem about a man who had been a long time in another country and knew that he must go home:

> *. . . But it should be*
> *Soon. Already I defend hotly*
> *Certain of our indefensible faults,*
> *Resent being reminded; already in my mind*
> *Our language becomes freighted with a richness*
> *No common tongue could offer, while the mountains*
> *Are like nowhere on earth, and the wide rivers.*

You see the point. I want to tell you the truth, and already I have told you about the wide rivers.

It should be clear by now that the truth about the place is elusive, and must be tracked with caution. You might go to Sacramento tomorrow and someone (although no one I know) might take you out to Aerojet-general, which has, in the Sacramento phrase, "something to do with rockets." Fifteen thousand people work for Aerojet, almost all of them imported; a Sacramento lawyer's wife told me, as evidence of how Sacramento was opening up, that she believed she had met one of them, at an open house two Decembers ago. ("Couldn't have been nicer, actually," she added enthusiastically. "I think he and his wife bought the house next *door* to Mary and Al, something like that, which of course was how *they* met him.") So you might go to Aerojet and stand in the big vendors' lobby where a couple of thousand components salesmen try every week to sell their wares and you might look up at the electrical wallboard that lists Aerojet personnel, their projects and their location at any given time, and you might wonder if I have been in Sacramento lately. MINUTEMAN, POLARIS, TITAN, the lights flash, and all the coffee tables are littered with airline schedules, very now, very much in touch.

But I could take you a few miles from there into town where the banks still bear names like The Bank of Alex Brown, into town where the one hotel still has an octagonaltile floor in the dining room and dusty potted palms and big ceiling fans; into towns where everything—the seed business, the Harvester franchise, the hotel, the department store and the main street—carries a single name, the name of the man who built the town. A few Sundays ago I was in a town like that, a town smaller than that, really, no hotel, no Harvester franchise, the bank burned out, a river town. It was the golden anniversary of some of my relatives and it was 110° and the guests of honor sat on straight-backed chairs in front of a sheaf of gladioluses in the Rebekah Hall. I mentioned visiting Aerojet-General to a cousin I saw there, who listened to me with interested disbelief. Which is the true California? That is what we all wonder.

Let us try out a few irrefutable statements, on subjects not open to interpretation. Although Sacramento is in many ways the least typical of the Valley towns, it *is* a Valley town, and must be viewed in that context. When you say "the Valley" in Los Angeles, most people assume that you mean the San Fernando Valley (some people in fact assume that you mean Warner Brothers), but make no mistake: we are talking not about the valley of the sound stages and the ranchettes but about the real Valley, the Central Valley, the fifty thousand square miles drained by the Sacramento and the San Joaquin Rivers and further irrigated by a complex network of sloughs, cutoffs, ditches, and the Delta-Mendota and Friant-Kern Canals.

A hundred miles north of Los Angeles, at the moment when you drop from the Tehachapi Mountains into the outskirts of Bakersfield, you leave Southern California and enter the Valley. "You look up the highway and it is straight for miles, coming at you, with the black line down the center coming at you and at you . . . and the heat dazzles up from the white slab so that only the black line is clear, coming at you with the whine of the tires, and if you don't quit staring at that line and don't take a few deep breaths and slap yourself hard on the back of the neck you'll hypnotize yourself."

Robert Penn Warren wrote that about another road, but he might have been writing about the Valley road U.S. 99, three hundred miles from Bakersfield to Sacramento, a highway so straight that when one flies on the most direct pattern from Los Angeles to Sacramento one never loses sight of U.S. 99. The landscape it runs through never, to the untrained eye, varies. The Valley eye can discern the point where miles of cotton seedlings fade into miles of tomato seedlings, or where the great corporation ranches—Kern County Land, what is left of DiGiorgio—give way to private operations (somewhere on the horizon, if the place is private, one sees a house and a stand of scrub oaks), but such distinctions are in the long view irrelevant. All day long, all that moves is the sun, and the big Rainbird sprinklers.

Every so often along 99 between Bakersfield and Sacramento there is a town: Delano, Tulare, Fresno, Madera, Merced, Modesto, Stockton. Some of these town are pretty big now, but they are all the same at heart, one- and two and three-story buildings artlessly arranged, so that what appears to be the good dress shop stands beside a W. T. Grant store, so that the big Bank of America faces a Mexican movie house. *Dos Peliculas, Bingo Bingo Bingo.* Beyond the downtown (pronounced *downtown*, with the Okie accent that now pervades Valley speech patterns) lie blocks of old frame houses — paint peeling, sidewalks cracking, their occasional leaded amber windows overlooking a Foster's Freeze or a five-minute car wash or a State Farm Insurance office; beyond those spread the shopping centers and the miles of tract houses, pastel with redwood siding, the unmistakable signs of cheap building already blossoming on those houses which have survived the first rain. To a stranger driving 99 in an airconditioned car (he would be on business, I suppose, any stranger driving 99, for 99 would never get a tourist to Big Sur or San Simeon, never get him to the California he came to see), these towns must seem so flat, so impoverished, as to drain the imagination. They hint at evenings spent hanging around gas stations, and suicide pacts sealed in drive-ins.

But remember:

Q. In what way does the Holy Land resemble the Sacramento Valley?
A. In the type and diversity of its agricultural products.

U.S. 99 in fact passes through the richest and most intensely cultivated agricultural region in the world, a giant outdoor hothouse with a billion-dollar crop. It is when you remember the Valley's wealth that the mono-chromatic flatness of its towns takes on a curious meaning, suggests a habit of mind some would consider perverse. There is something in the Valley mind that reflects a real indifference to the stranger in his air-conditioned car, a failure to perceive even his presence, let alone his thoughts or wants. An implacable insularity is the seal of these towns. I once met a woman in Dallas, a most charming and attractive woman accustomed to the hospitality and social hypersensitivity of Texas, who told me that during the four war years her husband had been stationed in Modesto, she had never once been invited inside anyone's house. No one in Sacramento would find this story remarkable ("She probably had no *relatives* there," said someone to whom I told it), for the Valley towns understand one another, share a peculiar spirit. They think alike and they look alike. *I* can tell Modesto from Merced, but I have visited there, gone to dances there; besides, there is over the main street of Modesto an arched sign which reads:

WATER — WEALTH
CONTENTMENT — HEALTH

There is no such sign in Merced.

I said that Sacramento was the least typical of the Valley towns, and it is — but only because it is bigger and more diverse, only because it has had the rivers and the legislature; its true character remains the Valley character, its virtues the Valley virtues, its sadness the Valley sadness. It is just as hot in the summertime, so hot that the air shimmers and the grass bleaches white and the blinds stay drawn all day, so hot that August comes on not like a month but like an affliction; it is just as flat, so flat that a ranch of my family's with a slight rise on it, perhaps a foot, was known for the hundred-some years which preceded this year as "the hill ranch." (It is known this year as a subdivision in the making, but that is another part of the story.) Above all, in spite of its infusions from outside, Sacramento retains the Valley insularity.

To sense that insularity a visitor need do no more than pick up a copy of either of the two newspapers, the morning *Union* or the afternoon *Bee*. The *Union* happens to be Republican and impoverished and the *Bee* Democratic and powerful ("THE VALLEY OF THE BEES!" as the McClatchys, who own the Fresno, Modesto, and Sacramento *Bees*, used to headline their advertisements in the trade press. "ISOLATED FROM ALL OTHER MEDIA INFLUENCE!"), but they read a good deal alike, and the tone of their chief editorial concerns is strange and wonderful and instructive. The *Union*, in a county heavily and reliably Democratic, frets mainly about the possibility of a local takeover by the John Birch Society; the *Bee*, faithful to the letter of its founder's will, carries on overwrought crusades against phantoms it still calls "the power trusts." Shades of Hiram Johnson, whom the *Bee* helped elect governor in 1910. Shades of Robert La Follette, to whom the *Bee* delivered the Valley in 1924. There is something about the Sacramento papers that does not quite connect with the way Sacramento lives now, something pronouncedly beside the point. The aerospace engineers, one learns, read the San Francisco *Chronicle*.

The Sacramento papers, however, simply mirror the Sacramento peculiarity, the Valley fate, which is to be paralyzed by a past no longer relevant. Sacramento is a town which grew up on farming and discovered to its shock that land has more profitable uses. (The chamber of commerce will give you crop figures, but pay them no mind — what matters is the feeling, the knowledge that where the green hops once grew is now Larchmont Riviera, that what used to be the Whitney ranch is now Sunset City, thirty-three thousand houses and a country-club complex.) It is a town in which defense industry and its absentee owners are suddenly the most important facts; a town which has never had more people or more money, but has lost its *raison d'être*. It is a town many of whose most solid citizens sense about themselves a kind of functional obsolescence. The old families still see only one another, but they do not see even one another as much as they once did; they are closing ranks, preparing for the long night, selling their rights-of-way and living on the proceeds. Their children still marry one another, still play bridge and go into the real-estate business together. (There is no other business in Sacramento, no reality other than land — even I, when I was living and working in New York, felt impelled to take a University of California correspondence course in Urban Land Economics.) But late at night when the ice has melted there is always somebody now, some Julian English, whose heart is not quite in it. For out there on the outskirts of town are marshaled the legions of aerospace engineers, who talk their peculiar condescending language and tend their dichondra and plan to stay in the promised land; who are raising a new generation of native Sacramentans and who do not care, really do not care, that they are not asked to join the Sutter Club. It makes one wonder, late at night when the ice is gone; introduces some air into the womb, suggests that the Sutter Club is perhaps not, after all, the Pacific Union or the Bohemian; than Sacramento is not *the city*. In just such self-doubts do small town lose their character.

I want to tell you a Sacramento story. A few miles out of town is a place, six or seven thousand acres, which belonged in the beginning to a rancher with one daughter. That daughter went abroad and married a title, and when she brought the title home to live on the ranch, her father built them a vast house — music rooms, conservatories, a ballroom. They needed a ballroom because they entertained: people from abroad, people from San Francisco, house parties that lasted weeks and involved special trains. They are long dead, of course, but their only son, aging and unmarried, still lives on the place. He does not live in the house, for the house is no longer there. Over the years it burned, room by room, wing by wing. Only the chimneys of the great house are still standing, and its heir lives in their shadow, lives by himself on the charred site, in a house trailer.

That is a story my generation knows; I doubt that the next will know it, the children of the aerospace engineers. Who would tell it to them? Their grandmothers live in Scarsdale, and they have never met a great-aunt. "Old" Sacramento to them will be something colorful, something they read about in *Sunset*. They will probably think that the Redevelopment has always been there, that the Embarcadero, down along the river, with its amusing places to shop and its picturesque fire houses turned into bars, has about it the true flavor of the way it was. There will be no reason for them to know that in homelier days it was called Front Street (the town was not, after all, settled by the Spanish) and was a place of derelicts and missions and itinerant pickers in town for a Saturday-night druck: VICTORIOUS LIFE MISSION, JESUS SAVES, BEDS 25¢ A NIGHT, CROP INFORMATION HERE. They will have lost the real past and gained a manufactured one, and there will be no way for them to know, no way at all, why a house trailer should stand alone on seven thousand acres outside town.

But perhaps it is presumptuous of me to assume that they will be missing something. Perhaps in retrospect this has been a story not about Sacramento at all, but about the things we lose and the promises we break as we grow older; perhaps I have been playing out unawares the Margaret in the poem:

> *Margaret, are you grieving*
> *Over Goldengrove unleaving?* ...
> *It is the blight man was born for,*
> *It is Margaret you mourn for.*

Elements of San Joaquin

GARY SOTO

FIELD

The wind sprays pale dirt into my mouth,
The small, almost invisible scars
On my hands.

The pores in my throat and elbows
Have taken in a seed of dirt of their own.

After a day in the grape fields near Rolinda
A fine silt, washed by sweat,
Has settled into the lines
On my wrists and palms.

Already I am becoming the valley,
A soil that sprouts nothing
For any of us.

WIND

A dry wind over the valley
Peeled mountains, grain by grain,
To small slopes, loose dirt
Where red ants tunnel.

Gary Soto

The wind strokes
The skulls and spines of cattle
To white dust, to nothing,

Covers the spiked tracks of beetles,
Of tumbleweed, of sparrows
That pecked the ground for insects.

Evenings, when I am in the yard weeding,
The wind picks up the breath of my armpits
Like dust, swirls it
Miles away

And drops it
On the ear of a rabid dog,
And I take on another life.

WIND

When you got up this morning the sun
Blazed an hour in the sky,

A lizard hid
Under the curled leaves of manzanita
And winked its dark lids.

Later, the sky greyed,
And the cold wind you breathed
Was moving under your skin and already far
From the small hives of your lungs.

STARS

At dusk the first stars appear.
Not one eager finger points toward them.
A little later the stars spread with the night
And an orange moon rises
To lead them, like a shepherd, toward dawn.

SUN

In June the sun is a bonnet of light
Coming up,

Little by little,
From behind a skyline of pine.

The pastures sway with fiddleneck,
Tassels of foxtail.

At Piedra
A couple fish on the river's edge,
Their shadows deep against the water.
Above, in the stubbled slopes,
Cows climb down
As the heat rises
In a mist of blond locusts,
Returning to the valley.

RAIN

When autumn rains flatten sycamore leaves,
The tiny volcanos of dirt
Ants raised around their holes,
I should be out of work.

My silverware and stack of plates will go unused
Like the old, my two good slacks
Will smother under a growth of lint
And smell of the old dust
That rises
When the closet door opens or closes.

The skin of my belly will tighten like a belt
And there will be no reason for pockets.

FOG

If you go to your window
You will notice a fog drifting in.

The sun is no stronger than a flashlight.
Not all the sweaters
Hung in closets all summer

Could soak up this mist. The fig:

A mouth nibbling everything to its origin,
Pomegranate trees, stolen bicycles

The string of lights at a used car lot,
A pontiac with scorched valves.

In Fresno the fog is passing
The young thief prying a windowscreen,
Greying my hair that falls
And goes unfound, my fingerprints
Slowly growing a fur of dust —

One hundred years from now
There should be no reason to believe
I lived.

DAYBREAK

In this moment the light starts up
In the east and rubs
The horizon until it catches fire,

We enter the fields to hoe.
Row after row, among the small flags of onion,
Waving off the dragonflies
That ladder the air.

And tears the onions raise
Do not begin in your eyes but in ours,
In the salt blown
From one blister into another;

They begin in knowing
You will never waken to bear
The hour timed to a heart beat,
The wind pressing us closer to the ground.

When the season ends,
And the onions are unplugged from their sleep,
We won't forget what you failed to see,
And nothing will heal
Under the rain's broken fingers.

Fourth of July
(Woodson Bridge)
MICHAEL LOPES

We sinners gather by the river,
a living band of us, shoulder to shoulder,
from high on flat land, down the slope,
to the very edge of mud and moving water.

The long road stretches behind us, its
asphalt hot still with the heat of day,
lined with autos hot still with the heat
of their coming; the river glows with the
sun's going; expectation animates our flesh.

With whistle, flash, and boom the evening
shudders into life, and as the water darkens
we see the fiery hollow on the other bank
where, for an hour, stalk-like trajectories
spark up and burst into flaming, futile flower.

And then we straggle back along the road,
kids on our shoulders, lovers in our arms,
gangs of us, pairs of us, unsatisfied, still,
by anything less than death.

Christ Has Returned to Earth
and Preaches Here Nightly
LEONARD GARDNER

From the small, flat, hot valley town of Tracy, California — split by a
highway and surrounded by fields of sugar beets, alfalfa, and tomatoes —
an enormous pink car one day departed by the eastern end without
previously entering by the western end, this car being the property of a

permanent resident, Ernest Grubb, nineteen, who was in turn the property of a finance company. Ernest's fingernails were rimmed in black and there were black specks imbedded in the blemishes on his cheeks. Painted on the rear fenders of the car, though it was only a week out of the show room, were the words VALENTINO RETURNS.

Sunk in the passenger side of the front seat were the meager contours of Harry Ames, also nineteen, who had just been removed from unemployment insurance rolls in accordance with a code section under the heading "Failure to Seek Work." Harry was taking Ernest Grubb, with Ernest furnishing the car and gas, to a rendezvous with two divorcees in the neighboring town of Stockton. Until that day he had only mentioned one divorcee (and he mentioned her at every opportunity), but now it appeared there had always been two and that he divided his attentions equally between them, which made it sound as if there were only one. Ernest felt an innate caution around friends in need of chauffeurs, but as he had yet to score anything with his new car in a week of cruising, he could not decline Harry's proposition.

Once during that week he had almost been successful, but his passenger had passed out before he could take her anywhere. He had driven around as long as he could, waiting for her to revive, but as he had to drive a tractor early the next morning, he left her on the lawn in front of the library. Ernest had thought of leaving her in the car overnight to enjoy during his lunch hour in the fields; however, he had feared he might end up having to marry her, if she knew where he lived. Such things were known to happen in Tracy, as his father often warned him. His father himself had been discovered in front of his future in-laws' house one bright morning, asleep on the back seat of a model A Ford in only a pair of high-top shoes without socks (it was summer) beside the girl who was now the cranky, round-shouldered, doublechinned television fan for whom Ernest bought bubble-bath on Mother's Day. Divorcees were better risks; they were also anxious to regain lost delights.

When he had driven no farther than a hamburger stand at the edge of town, however, Ernest had already become skeptical.

"If we can't get hold of yours right away," Harry told him, "you just wait around till I'm through and we'll go find her. She's really fine looking, I swear it."

"I thought it was all fixed up."

"It's all set," Harry assured him. "Only her mother's dying in the hospital and maybe she had to go there for something, you know, to bid farewell. You wouldn't grudge her that, would you?"

"She won't be no fun coming from her mother's death bed," Ernest complained.

Harry answered that he had to have a hamburger, and Ernest felt obligated to stop. Having done so, he was likewise obligated to pay.

The girl behind the glass, who passed the hamburgers through an opening as small as the ticket hole in a box office, refused to speak to them, as it was generally known that certain advertisements penciled on local walls, involving her name and phone number and a very low sum of money, were the work of Harry Ames. Advertising ran in Harry's family; his father was the proprietor of *Neon Signs*.

As the two rode on placidly chewing, Harry said he wanted a donut, but Ernest stated they would stop no more until they picked up the divorcees. Harry alluded to loss of virility from malnutrition, then glumly stared at his tattoos. On one forearm beneath a dagger piercing his profusely bleeding skin was written DEATH BEFORE DISHONOR, and on the other, HARRY AMES and U.S.M.C. curved around the Marine Corps emblem — an anchor and the world with a boil in its northern hemisphere. He had obtained these in his thirteenth year from a Hawaiian who had come up from Stockton on a motor scooter with his needles in the tool box.

Farmers were still out irrigating, but the pickers had all come in. Butterflies and juicy bugs that had somehow eluded the divebombings of crop-dusters smacked against the windshield. Tomato lugs lay scattered between rows in the fields and Ernest, coming upon one in the road, attempted to swerve around it — without success, due to the immensity of his tires. He felt the bump and with a pounding heart heard a rush of air among the cracks and clatters under the car. With resignation he thumped off onto the shoulder.

Upon inspection of the trunk, Ernest discovered that the only accessory he had not been issued was a jack, and so he and Harry were forced to stand at the edge of the road waving at passing cars. Twilight was approaching and with it the opening of the drive-in movie. Ernest and Harry were rocked back on their heels, their clothes flapping like sails, as car after car raced by with a male head behind the steering wheel and a female head so close a two-headed monster appeared to be driving. Finally a low, dull-grey sedan with flames painted on the hood hurled by in a din of loose rods. Wobbling on and off the dusty shoulder, it screeched to a stop and began backing up. A dangling plaque with THE BLOWN GASKETS emblazoned across it identified the vehicle as Count Messner's, for his was the only car in that particular automobile club. The Count stepped out followed by Joe and Wallace Pucci, their hair sweeping upward on the sides in vast glistening arcs like the wings of birds of paradise, and curling down over their foreheads like the necks of swans, the ends in a beak over each of their noses. The Count succeeded in prying open the handleless trunk lid and threw a jack down in the dust. Then, his thumb hooked in the fly of his Levi's, he stood in a line with the others and watched Ernest flounder with his tire. Though it was a warm valley evening and the Count and the Puccis had lived their lives in Tracy, they wore red wool jackets with

"THE BLOWN GASKETS"
"OF"
"FRISCO"

on the backs in white letters. They were — the Count explained, as the jack began to lean under the sighing corpulence of the car — on their way to Manteca to pick up Sylvia Fuller, a girl who enjoyed considerable popularity despite an I. Q. uncoveted by her rivals. As her father, a Baptist egg producer, had archaic views on dating, it was necessary for the carloads of Sylvia's admirers to honk once when passing the farm house, then continue on to a dirt road leading to an irrigation ditch with grassy banks and the seclusion of willows where, a few minutes later, Sylvia would come stumbling to them over the clods.

Ernest bolting on the spare, was somewhat interested in this outing, but Harry assured him they had better things awaiting them. The car crashed back to earth, the Count and the Puccis returned to their flaming sedan, and when Ernest started his motor they roared away, spraying his windshield with gravel. He saw their derisive faces looking back, but as he had hundreds more miles of slow driving before his engine would be broken in, he had to watch the ash-colored car shrink away. While Harry sat in scornful silence, Ernest punched buttons on the radio until he got a good-music station to his liking. They were all good-music stations now, but some played better good-music than others.

A sawmill of electric guitars resounded in the car, and the abdomen of a large grasshopper, clinging desperately to a windshield-wiper blade, began to pulsate.

"She better not be no pig," Ernest threatened. "I won't take just anything."

"You won't be disappointed, I promise you. If she was a pig nobody would of married her in the first place, would they?"

Ernest was not dull. He had read Shakespeare in high school — "A Midsummer Night's Dream," in *Classic Comics* — and earned an A for his report on it. He told Harry he could hitch-hike back if things were not as represented. Harry slid down in the seat and stared out of the window with his nose on the sill.

They crossed the muddy San Joaquin River, where houseboats with smoking stovepipes and clusters of rowboats were tied among the tules, and they passed grain fields and orchards, fruit stands, and packs of erotic dogs. Though Stockton was less than twenty miles from Tracy, Ernest had to stop in French Camp for minor repairs; his sputtering car had consumed nearly a quarter-tank of gas. It died as he was attempting to cross to a station, settling in the center of the highway. After he had ground the starter several minutes with traffic swerving by on both sides, a man in a foreign sports car shouted something as he shot past.

"Come here and say that!" Ernest yelled, leaping out; then with a surge of indignant patriotism he strained against the door frame, as did Harry on the other side, until the car rolled a few inches and Ernest felt a hernia about to detonate. The station attendant, a young man with a sideburn on one side of his face and a small radio against the other, came out to assist.

In the station Ernest watched gloomily as the attendant worked under the hood with a dexterous right hand, his left still holding the radio to his ear.

"I bet you got to beat the women off it with a stick," the young man said when the hood was down again and he and Ernest were standing back gazing at the whole pink panorama, their eyes junping as if viewing a pinball machine where all the balls had been shot in one giant splurge.

"That's where we're going now," answered Ernest.

"Huh?"

Divorcees."

"I might of known it," the attendant said enviously. "Huh? I hope they come through for you."

"No hoping about it," replied Ernest.

He drove on, now very anxious to meet his divorcee. He felt so deserving of her it seemed unreasonable to doubt Harry's promises. Ernest Grubb had all the qualities necessary for the successful man about town and it would hardly make sense if they went unrewarded. Even on those occasions when he was outside his car his personal charm was magnetic, as he had once demonstrated in a truckbed full of supgar beets, where a young woman, Sylvia Fuller, had fallen hopelessly in love with him while his friends waited on the running board. He walked with his pants hung low, thumbs in his pockets, heel taps scraping, and when he spoke he mumbled just enough, with his head down and the hint of a sneer on his lips, to give him a suggestion of great suffering, of having a profound soul that had been misunderstood; and though he was swarthy and tended toward plumpness, he could nevertheless discern in his features a certain resemblance to the late James Dean.

"I'm going to make that divorcee cry for more," he said to Harry, who slipped his spine farther down the seat.

Nearing the city limits of Stockton, Ernest and Harry encountered several homemade signs—HAVE YOU BEEN CHOSEN? COULD YOU FACE JUDGMENT TODAY?—before approaching a large tent sagging next to a wrecking yard. Over the entrance of the tent a banner announced: CHRIST HAS RETURNED TO EARTH AND PREACHES HERE NIGHTLY.

Harry, a student of advertising, approved it as a good gimmick.

"I wonder how they got the guy rigged up," said Ernest, looking over at the tent where a few dilapidated cars and pickup trucks were parked.

"Let's stop and see," suggested Harry, "We don't have to put nothing in the plate."

When Ernest said they didn't have time, Harry assured him they were too early for their appointments. "You don't want to look eager, do you?"

"I'm not eager. I'm just in a hurry."

"But they won't be ready! You get what I mean? I'll have to call and say we're coming early."

"That's okay."

Harry ran his fingers down his face. "Turn in here then, and I'll use their phone."

"There wouldn't be no phone at a revival tent."

"Sure there would. Hurry up, turn! Turn!"

Flustered by Harry's urgency, Ernest turned with misgivings onto the dirt driveway.

"I don't see no phone booth.," Harry Ames said after they had climbed out. "I'll tell you what—I'll take the car into town and get the divorcees while you're watching the show, and we'll all come back here and pick you up. How's that?"

"I'll go with you," Ernest answered flatly.

"Well, hell, we might as well see what's going on then," Harry mumbled, kicking the dust.

As they entered the tent, a preacher under a string of dim light bulbs shouted to them in a ringing tenor. "He's not here yet, folks." Long strands of black hair, evidently combed across his bald spot before the sermon, hung down over one ear to his collar. The hair on the other side of his head was clipped short. "But just be patient. He's coming. I got the word from Christ himself that He's coming, and He won't let us down. No He won't. He told me definitely He would be here in this meeting tent tonight to talk to all you good people and come into your hearts, and I know He will, because He don't lie. No, friends, Jesus Christ don't lie—no He don't, no question about that—and He'll be here among us shortly to make us all singing saints in the sixties. I think I can feel Him coming now, folks; I think I can, and you'll feel Him, too—yes you will—if you'll just let yourselves. Won't you let yourselves feel Jesus?"

"Let's get out of here," whispered Ernest, who had at least expected someone in sandals from San Francisco. "There isn't going to be any guy, can't you see what he means? You're supposed to *feel* Him."

When Harry said they had better wait and see, Ernest knew it was a stall; if he waited until Christ came he never would find out about the divorcees.

As the preacher talked on, the rumble of an approaching motorcycle grew outside, finally coming to an idle near the tent flap, then flaring up into one last thunderous blast, and when the roar died away he was wailing: "O, I feel Him, He's coming, I hear Him, yes indeed I feel Him coming." As he rocked with closed eyes, saliva gleaming on his chin, the congregation turned toward the entrance.

A young man in a leather jacket, with a small goatee like armpit hair on the end of his chin, came in and walked unsteadily to the front. Across his back was painted BALLS O' FIRE.

"I feel Him coming," the preacher gasped. "To spread His gospel, yes, His blessed assurance."

The motorcyclist shambled up beside him. Then, spreading his arms, he addressed the congregation, "Verily I say unto you." Knees buckling, sighing, the preacher swooned backward. Women moaned and shrieked; one slumped in her chair speaking words unknown to mortal man.

"Let me talk," the motorcyclist interrupted, raising a hand, light sparkling off the chromium studs of his jacket. "Peace! Verily I am the Christ our Lord, let me tell you. And if none of you believe it you better read up on your Bible, because now I've come whether nobody expected me or not, and I can see by the size of our gathering that not too many did. Well, that's all right. Each man's salvation is up to him. But I could tell by your humble cars outside — all except one that's a vehicle of sin if I ever seen one — that you're the chosen ones. I know you lived clean and righteous lives by looking in your weary faces. And don't think you're going to be forgotten for your sacrifices, because right now, here in this tent tonight, is the Last Judgment. No need telling your friends and neighbors to come tomorrow. They're just out of luck. Only those that were here to greet me have earned them berths up in paradise."

There were cries of spiritual ecstasy. A woman fell on all fours, children wailed in confusion, and a gangling red-haired man was on his knees pleading: "Let me go home and get my daughter. My teen-age daughter, she's led a sinful life." Ernest, recognizing him as LeRoy Fuller, of Fuller's Eggs, Grad B Dirties, and the father of Sylvia, hunched down in his folding chair.

"We don't want no fallen women with us On High, man," replied the motorcyclist. "I bet you're the one that owns that big pink car out there, aren't you?"

"No sir, no, I don't," LeRoy Fuller protested. "No, no, just an old pickup. Won't you please wait while I get her?"

"Verily, like I said, only the people that happen to be here get in on the deal, out of all the peoples on the four corners of the earth, see? That's the way things go." He raised his hand to quiet the tumult. "Hark! I ask ye to be quiet, all right? I'll leave you now. Preaching can't do no more when you're as pure like unto a new born lamb. Go in peace to your eternal reward."

He strode out of the tent. Ernest left just as the motorcycle roared off. It was dark outside now, and he saw the single headlight rushing toward Stockton.

"You'd think they'd of dressed him up better than that," said Harry.

Others were leaving the tent. When the preacher came out holding the back of his neck and asking what had happened, everybody answered at once. "Are you sure?" he said in a cautious, puzzled tone, stroking the long sparse hairs back over his head. "You didn't just hear His words? What did He look like?"

"He had a beard."

"Had a *beard*?" he shouted, steadying himself on a tent rope. "What have I done, brothers and sisters? A *beard*! A materialization—God bless you—of the Holy Chost, amen, His most sacred heart, His lofty brow . . ."

"My daughter's been doing bad things," LeRoy Fuller interrupted, and Ernest crept toward his car.

"Bring her, that her wound may be healed, that she may never again tread the path of sin—no never—and bring a newspaper reporter. Dearly beloved friends, I'm on my way to bigger things—yes I am, I can see that—a great crusade to save Los Angeles, the juvenile delinquents, the moving picture industry . . ."

As LeRoy Fuller was trying to start his pickup truck, marked on the door with the name of his business, and on the hood and fenders with verifications by the hens themselves, Ernest and Harry departed.

LeRoy Fuller, and a covering of dust over the car, had depressed Ernest and when, at the edge of town, Harry returned from a phone booth with regrets that Ernest's divorcee was not home, Ernest mumbled that they were going right back to Tracy.

"No, no," protested Harry. "She left a message with her mother for you to meet her later at my divorcee's place. She said to be sure and wait for her."

Recalling that her mother was at the moment dying in the hospital, Ernest prepared to make a U-turn.

"Just give me an hour," Harry pleaded. "That's all I ask."

Harry Ames' appeal for women was famous. His legend could be found recorded in numerous lavatories with lists of mysterious names often included. Still his arsenal of charms lacked that major one Ernest had so recently acquired. And so Ernest decided to win the remaining divorcee for himself. As he continued into town, the folds subsided from Harry's forehead.

At a stop signal Ernest found himself between two choptop cars, one identified as HITLER'S REVENGE. The hunched drivers peered up at him through slot windows, shouting challenges above the eruptions of their mufflers. But Ernest had to let them, too, screech away without him. He proceeded with ardent limbs and just a trace of shame to the divorcee's residence—a room, in a transient hotel, that remained silent after five minutes of pounding. "Maybe she's not home," he suggested, but Harry, calling and kicking, shook the door until an old man with warts and slippers puffed up the stairs to request that Ernest and Harry go elsewhere.

They drove to the bar where the divorcee was employed, in case by some miscalculation she was working on her day off. Crowds of Filipino and Mexican farm workers milled on the sidewalks, and winos were against cars and walls and down in doorways. Ernest parked well away from the bottle-lined gutter, locked all the doors, walked around the car checking them, and then followed Harry into the *Club Aguascalientes*.

A crowd of men stood around a lone woman on a bar stool. Harry, out of the side of his mouth, requested that Ernest not mention the other divorcee, as his divorcee knew nothing about her. "I don't want to make her jealous," he explained, then pushed in among the crowd. Following, Ernest tripped over boots and was jabbed by the leather elbows of the BALLS O'FIRE motorcycle club.

"Hello, sweetie," Harry said. "Did you forget we had a date?"

The woman had orange hair, a bloodred dress, pink high heels with white bobbysocks, and a pallid face that had fallen into pouches. She squinted at him. "Who's that, anyhow?"

"It's me, sweetie—Harry."

"Harry who? Step over in the light, why don't you?"

"Harry Ames, your date and steady," he said in a rising voice as he shoved in closer.

"Watch it, man," somebody warned.

"Oh, it's you, honey. Why didn't you say so? Who's that with you?"

"Ernest Grubb, this is April Humphrey, the Georgia Peach."

"I got a brand new car outside," said Ernest. "You want to take a ride in it?"

The bartender demanded Ernest and Harry's identification, and as they slowly took out their wallets and went through the pantomine of searching for cards that must somehow have been misplaced, April Humphrey began necking with one of the motorcyclists.

"It's here somewhere," Harry said. "Come on, sweetie, let's get out of here."

"Let's you and me sneak off for a ride in my new car—alone," Ernest whispered in her ear, careful not to say it in the motorcyclist's.

Her lipless mouth, surrounded by a liberal red smear, puckered tenderly as she declined. "I'm sorry, honey, can't you see I'm working?" She held up a highball and began swallowing.

"How about afterwards?" Harry asked with a note of desperation, while the motorcyclist nibbled at her throat.

"Better make it some other time, honey."

A heel mashed down on Ernest's toes. When he squirmed to free himself he was cracked under the chin by a five-starred epaulet. "You better fade, man," somebody muttered beside him, and someone else in a loud voice said, "Minors." The bartender then ordered Ernest and Harry out, and as they hung their heads and stalled, mumbling about pickpockets, they were grasped around the shoulders and waists and hauled protesting to the doorway. Ernest felt a foot against his spine just before he was catapulted out into the night. As he rose to his hands and knees, the jukebox inside began to play.

Harry was sitting on the sidewalk with his pants leg pulled up examining his knee. Near him a woman in a black bonnet and dress, with a canvas satchel hanging from her shoulder, held up a magazine, *Awake!*

"There been signs and portents," she said. "A horse give birth to a chicken tonight, and Jesus Christ was seen just outside town in his flowing robes and crown of thorns. Are you ready for the end, young man?" She thrust the magazine at Ernest, and he yelled "No!" as he stumbled up against the car, trying to get the key in the lock. "Has your soul been purified?" He scrambled inside. Harry limped over and joined him, and Ernest started the motor with the woman's voice ringing in his ears. "Tomorrow's too late!"

A band was playing on the corner as Ernest stopped at the signal. Above the thuds and bleats, an old man jangling a tambourine was hysterically chanting that the world was coming to an end. Loiterers leaning against darkened store fronts gave no signs of caring, which seemed to make the man more desperate. He began to plead. Several BALLS O' FIRE motorcyclists parked by the curb were heckling, and one of them Ernest recognized. From his sneer, it also seemed he recognized Ernest's car as the one he had denounced at the revival.

"Didn't that thing get you there yet?" he yelled. Crouching for a fast start with his goatee jutting forward, he raced his motor. When the signal changed, Ernest bitterly roared off beside him with screaming tires. They buzzed up the block side by side, shot through the next intersection, then, as the motorcycle pulled ahead, a sudden great clamor of blacksmith banging commenced in Ernest's engine. He applied the brakes, his face going pale and his heart seeming to sink out of him.

Slumped over the wheel, too sick to speak, he drove slowly out of town. When the car passed the lot where the revival had been, the tent was already gone. A small gathering of patient people were still waiting by lantern light, their failing voices raised in song.

Banging and clattering, the car crept on, past fields, orchards, and lighted farm houses, over the black river, finally making it back to the glare of Tracy's neon. Ernest drove straight to his house and told Harry he could walk home. Leaving him complaining in the car, he trudged through the weeds to his back door.

But Ernest did not open it. In the night's immense emptiness the thought of his bed was more than he could bear. Instead, he crouched behind a shrub and peered through the leaves at the car. The interior light came on as Harry stepped out, then went off with a slam. Ernest remained among the twigs long after the horseshoe heels had faded off down the sidewalk. When he returned to the street it was with a desolation that frightened him.

He drove out of town, and as he neared Manteca the feeling seemed to lessen, and to his relief it lessened still more when, knocking past moonlit chicken pens, he gave his horn a short decorous honk. The feeling continued to grow less as he bounced over the ruts of a dirt road, and then, by the willows, as he watched the pajama-clad figure coming toward him across the field, it was gone altogether.

Two Poems

ALAN CHONG LAU

"SUMMER IS ALWAYS HERE"
(A Redneck Lullaby)

summer sunday afternoon
i am sitting in my car
my feet out the window
and the radio
turned on real loud

after the top twenty
the war comes on an usual
i run in the house
and get a sixpack
and drive to the river

i remember when my dad
caught a trout there
long as a rainbow

last week i caught
the clap
possibly from billy eckhardt's baby sister
it hasn't caught up with me yet

toying with the idea
of who gets it next
looms high on my list of priorities

i open the first can
the foam soaks my tee-shirt
filling my belly button
with cold relief

after the top twenty
the war comes on as usual
i take a leak under a tree
splashing ants out of their hole

asleep in my car
my feet out the window
i'm just waking up
crickets chirping up a storm

the moon sits fat
as a cat
on the rail

FATHER'S BAMBOO GROVE

those mexican kids
clothes pins clamped on the ears
to make me squeal

as a tagalong
one had to earn
rites of passage

we sat on haunches
drawing secret parts
of women

hidden away
in my father's bamboo grove
that grew back
after each cut

even after gravel
delicate green shoots
defined stones

they'd laugh
break off hollow stems
cop hits of bamboo smoke
satisfied only after
i'd coughed myself
red

came end of harvest
they left
their mother dead
after making a tamale pie

the bamboo too
no more
trampled over
still under a parking lot

only leaf patterns
cast in tar

with my father's chinese restaurant
we were the only ones
left in town

Three Poems
DeWAYNE RAIL

THE IDIOT

He would plow barefoot behind a mule
in a field at the edge of town,
the town kids said.

I remember how they first took me there
my first day after school, to show me,
and pestered him with questions:

Who cut your hair, Carl?
Do you sleep here?
Don't you ever wear shoes?

He didn't get mad.
He gave us some
ripe tomatoes from his patch

and stood grinning while we ate them,
glad we were there,
knee-deep in vegetables and kids.

THE FIELD

This field is the last refuge of squirrels,
jackrabbits, and mice. Deserted, left
to its own devices, it has taken years
to grow a thick cover of weeds that tangle

And arch over long tunnels. A dozen
kinds of birds feed here on sprays of seeds
that hang from dried stalks, and tracks lead
everywhere. At dark, the animals push up

From their holes and look cautiously out.

The hours between now and dawn belong to them.
They sniff the air, or nibble
at young shoots of grass, and each one moves

Slowly away from his den. They are free
to wander the length of the field,
never hunted, as each night rolls
easily into the next. Some stay on here

For years. Others die, drawn
to the highway that loops the edge of the field,
with its hiss of cars whose headlights
shine briefly into their lives, then flash on.

PICKERS

Scattered out like a handful of seeds across
The field, backs humped to the wind,
Faces like clumps of dirt in the white rows,
Their hands keep on eating cotton.
The long sacks fill and puff up tight,
Like dreams of money they're going to make
Or of what they'll have for supper.
They stagger with the weight to the wagon and scales,
Dragging their tracks out in the dust,
Faces bent close to the ground,
Their hands ragged from the cotton bolls.

Going Short
(Monologues)

AMADO JESUS MURO
(Chester Seltzer)

ANGLO MAN
(Bakersfield)
In the Sacramento Labor Office they asked if anyone wanted to milk rattlesnakes. One stiff asked if rattlesnakes had udders like cows. The boss man shook his head and said "You won't do."

— — —

ANGLO MAN
(Fresno)

I commissaried out of a starvation labor camp in Modesto. After that I jungled up in the woods near the Modesto Golf Course for a week. I picked up the golf balls that golfers sliced into the trees and sold them back to them. I got 25 cents for new ones. I was eating good and my cough was getting better, but now my throat's tickling again.

— — —

ANGLO MAN
(Bakersfield)

I'm poe-lice-minded. That's why I carry this lunch bucket. The laws don't bother me when I carry this lunch bucket. They don't think I'm a stiff. What would a stiff be doing with a lunch bucket. I walk where I want and the cops don't bother me.

— — —

BLACK MAN
(Bakersfield)

These mission preachers may be holy, but they damned sure ain't friendly. 'Come to God — you got nothing to lose,' that one said tonight. 'Now how many want to be saved?' Well now the way I see it you can save a man from a fire or drowning, but you can't save his soul. He got to do that himself. About a year ago they had that preacher called Brother Slick here. I'd heard him in Oklahoma City five years ago and I told him he'd been preaching that same sermon all the time — the one about how he was saved two years and six months ago. I said to him: 'Reverend, I heard that same sermon five years ago. 'cause that's how long you've been preaching it.' So he threw me out and cursed me.

— — —

ANGLO MAN
(Fresno)

After the altar service was over a man-catcher drove his truck up in front of the mission. He said: 'Any of you tramps want to pick cotton for Portagee Joe. It ain't no fancy tramp camp but he'll give you a bed and a mattress and you can sleep in your cotton sacks. They're eleven-foot pick sacks with good drag sides, and they are furnished — not rented. You don't have to turn them in until the Big Pick's over. If you want a jug he'll get it for you and charge the same price as the store. He's a errand boy to keep hands, but he ain't no wine doctor. I'm his cook and you know I wouldn't work for peanuts. Well, what do you say. It's better'n eating at mission and jungling out and sleeping with rattlesnakes and gophers ain't it?' Well, Sir, a bunch of us went out to Portagee Joe's camp. He charged $3 a day for Found, and it was mostly bologna. I didn't starve there, but I was always hungry. He charged 25 cents for a soda pop, and 12 cents for Durham and chewing gum, and if you didn't trade with him he'd tell you to hit the white line. He was a wine doctor, too. The wine lines formed there twice a day, and the Sweet Lucies was juggin' every night. You couldn't sleep with the fights and the arguing and there wasn't no blankets or mattress covers. He give the skin and bones winos their wine bills every Saturday. He called the bills 'love letters.' He made money off the wine he sold, the food we eat, and the cotton we picked. In other words he was just plain-hipped making money. I was streamlined when I white-lined. After I left Portagee Joe's starvation camp I went to L.A. and made three day hauls with Uncle Bill at Fifth and Wall every morning. I made three dollars a day topping carrots in the San Fernando Valley and I sat up all night in the triple-feature shows on Main Street. I'd rather nod and doze a little in a all-night show than stay in one of those flophouses on the Nickel Street Skid Row where they'll break into your 75-cent cage and rob you and won't nobody do nothing about it.

— — —

ANGLO MAN
(Delano)
In Stockton. I got a cup of coffee in a cafe just off the Center Street skid row. When I finished drinking it, a middle-aged waitress with marcelled hair asked if I wanted anything more. She was fat with one tooth out, and she walked on the sides of her feet like a tame bear. I said, "No ma'am, that was my last dime." I got up to go then but she said, "Wait young man," and brought me doughnuts and more coffee. When I thanked her, she said, "That's all right, young man. I know how it is to be broke."

— — —

ANGLO MAN
(Bakersfield)
I'm a hardtack tramp and I live slow and don't wear myself out. You don't see so many old-whiskered tramps like me sewing and resting around water tanks no more. All had on something patched, tied, hooked, or wired, and you could seen them wiring the splits and breaks in their shoes. They're mostly Gooseneckers and Bay Horse Riders now. I didn't use to worry about derails and washouts when I was a young tramp but I do now. I'd ride any kind of a load then. I rode them hot. The old-whiskers tramps used to

leave jungles clean and in order. Tramps didn't need to carry so many cans. I reckon I'll tramp for the rest of my life. I'm willing to go through any hardship to keep from settling down.

Everywhere To Run, Nowhere To Hide

(from *Rabbit Boss*)

THOMAS SANCHEZ

I am alone with you Christ. Our Spirits flow as two Fish in the same river. I have come down from the mountain to search your words. You have ridden the Ghost Pony the day the Sun died. Only you can dance our birth. If you dance the souls will come back. We sit here on this flat land. All around us the flat land goes out a distance further than a man's life. All around the flat land is covered by the white burden of snow. We sit alone. Two Blackbirds on a Cloud. The fire before you has grown cold. Only you can make the sacred Bird rise from its bed of ashes. Only you can sing the people up. The ring of rocks around the fire is the circle of our Ancestors. Only you can dance up the Sacred Piñon Tree of our family. Your song curling around the Tree. Sing your song oh Christ. I am too cold to die. My ears bleed. My tongue is bruised. Answer my soul. Uncover the sign.

The Sun was full over the Christ. His body sunk deep within his black clothes. He had no shadow. All around him the snow melted from the clumps of sage as he presented in his palm a black stone smoothed into a bowl. He screwed a hollow wooden stem into the notched stone bowl and made his Pipe. His other hand held the worn skin pouch that was the feed bag taken from the throat of the running Quail. The bag was not stuffed with wild seeds and nuts, it smelled strong of yellow medicine. The Christ filled the bowl with medicine, took off his boots and folded his legs beneath him, holding the Pipe carefully up in both hands as he offered it to my people so they may walk the Oneness Trail. He stretched the Pipe out in each sacred direction. To the north, *welmelti,* to the east, *pauwalu,* to the south, *haneleti,* to the west, *tangelelti.* To all Washo. He lit the Pipe. His breath sucking the flame through the bowl of tobacco until it glowed one strong bright red ember. The smoke of wildgrass sage came up from his body, its soft blue Spirit rising in the air. Traveling in all sacred directions to cover the Earth. He crossed the Pipe over to his left. I pushed my boots off and accepted, my legs folded beneath me with my head held high as I touched the wooden stem to my lips and filled my soul with sweet smoke. My lips sucked peacefully at the hot stem as my body rose to meet the

medicine. I smoked the root of the Earth, it did not go into my belly, it went
into my heart, ascending to the heavens. The yellow stonebacked ring on
my hand holding the sacred Pipe burned bright as a Bird against my flesh.
The wind goes by my head. The smoke is swirled over the face of the ring
and I see myself walking. I see myself walking way along down the road.
My Spirit catches up to my walking body and joins it. I walk with body and
soul, flesh and heart, way along down the black road toward the dying Sun.
I hear the horn honking behind me and turn to face the squareback car
popping and puffing up the hill. The horn honked at my back and I jumped
off the road, but the car stopped alongside me, its tin sides shaking and
engine steaming.

"Hey kid where you headed?"

I could see the driver high up on the seat, the shaking car chattering his
teeth away like a boxful of dice. I looked to see if there were any trees I
could run off into, but there was nothing, nothing but the bare brown roll of
hills. "Frisco Jeens."

"You mean San Francisco don't you kid?" he called out of the clattering
machine.

I looked back over the bald hills, there was everywhere to run, nowhere
to hide. "I guess so?"

He kicked the door open, "Get on in then. This here is Auburn we're
coming into. You've got a long haul ahead of you."

I jumped in and slammed the metal door shut. The car banged and
stuttered, then jolted back onto the road.

"Where you from kid?"

"Tahoe."

"Lake Tahoe! You mean you walked all the way from Lake Tahoe! That's
more'n one hundred miles of winding mountain road. Don't you have
folks?"

"They are all dead or dying."

He slammed the gear lever forward and put a funny look on me, "I don't
get your meaning." The funny look began to fade, like it saw something
coming in the distance it recognized so he smiled, "Hey, you're an Indian
aint you. You're so dark when I saw you walking along the road I thought
you was a nigger. I like to give a nigger a ride, they know all the best jokes.
Walked down from Lake Tahoe huh, that's something. I used to work up at
Lake Tahoe years ago when they had the commercial fishing. I was a
seine-rigger. You know what that is? It's a boatman who goes out setting
the long nets. We'd lug in a ton of fish a day. All Whitefish and Tahoe Trout.
I seen trout as long as your arm and weighing over fifty pounds, there was
no end to the fish in Lake Tahoe in those days, why that lake is so big they
still don't know how deep it really is. We took enough fish out of there to
ship them as far east as Kansas City. In one year the company I worked for

took seven hundred and forty thousand pounds out of that lake. Funny
thing about it though was whenever you'd have a thunderstorm the nets
would come up empty." He slammed the gear lever down again. "Well
there aint no big commercial fishing up there no more, been fished out,
these days a man needs a license just to throw a line and hook over the side
of his boat, hell, they just as well ought to give it back to you Indians is what
I say." He put his look back on me, "What's your business in San Francisco?"

"*Frisco Jeens.*"

"Walk do you mean, *Frisco Jeens.*" You're old enough to talk sensible,
you must be at least ninetcen. In two more years you can vote. Ah hell, no
you can't, Indians aint got the right to vote, Indians aint citizens of this
country. You can be damn good and sure you're better off not voting
anyway since it's Coolidge they'd get you to vote for. Somebody ought to
shoot that stuffed bird." He cocked his thumb and pointed it over the seat,
the back of the car was filled with boxes of apples, "All Coolidge ever gave
the farmer was worms in their apples. I have to cart these all the way to
Sacramento just to get a nickel a pound for them. Times is hard. You
Indians aint the only ones roughing it these days. Now you explain all this
stuff about *Frisco Jeens.*"

My fist covered the sock full of money in my pocket. I could feel the
sharp edges of the coins biting my flesh. "Mister Fixa. Mister Fixa told me
Frisco Jeens was in an iron bar cage where he can't hurt nobody. Mister
Fixa said someday I could go for myself to see if what he said was true.
Now I'm going. All the people are dead or dying. I'm going to see if *Frisco
Jeens* is behind bars." He put his look on me and screwed it down hard on
my eyes, "You're just talking Indian riddles. I can't make a nickel's worth of
sense out of you. Just what in hell is *Frisco Jeens?*"

I turned away from his look and saw through the window the brown
barren hills cover the Earth to the curve of the horizon, "A *Go-reel-ah.*"

His laughter banged out in the car, cutting through the heavy smell of
apples and pushing out the windows. "My God," he choked, slapping my
knee. "You Indians are funnier than a nigger!"

EATS! The high squarebacked car pulled off the road in among the
trucks parked around the small shack with the big sign soaring over its roof
EATS! I got down from the car among the trucks and the man leaned his
heat out of the window and shouted over the stuttering of his engine, "This
is your last truck stop before San Francisco. You just hook a ride here and
they'll roll you right into the big city." The car jerked out on the road,
"Hey," he called back. "Tell em about your Go-reel-ah. Hah. They'll love
that one so much they'll roll you right across the water to Hawaii!"

I could smell the food coming out the shack. Strong smells of potatoes and gravy. I felt my sock full of money. But I did not go in. I sat against one of the trucks, putting my back up the big wheel and closing my eyes to the world.

The boot nudged my leg. "Get on up. What do you think my truck is, the Cozy Cottage Motel?" The man stared down at me over the rise of his belly, the plastic sunvisor strapped over his eyes cast a money green glow on his entire face. I couldn't see his eyes. "Where do you think you're goin?"

"*Frisco Jeens.*"

"You'll never get to Frisco City in a truck, you can only go as far as the Oakland side across the bay from Frisco, then take the ferry boat over to Frisco City. You might as well get up in my truck then, I aint got all day to get to Oakland myself."

I climbed up and he swung the truck out into the highway, the rough surface bouncing his big body up and down on the hard seat, throwing the glow from the sunvisor over his face in different shades of green light. He turned to me as his hands held locked to the steering wheel. I couldn't see his eyes. "You know what I got in the back? You know what my load is? I'll tell you what I'm hauling since you asked. Lettuce. The worst job in California is picking lettuce. I wouldn't pick fucking lettuce in this State for no amount of pay, no how. Picking fucking lettuce is wetback work. It's my job to truck this fucking lettuce. I've been trucking lettuce up and down this haul seven years and I'll keep on trucking this fucking lettuce down this same road as long as people keep on eating like fucking rabbits."

I turned around in my seat and hung my head out the window, behind I could see the stacks of packed crates roped down tight on the flatbed of the truck, flapping green leaves poked out from between the wooden slats waving in the wind.

"Hey!" I could feel him poking me in the back. I turned around and looked at him, but I couldn't see his eyes. "Hey are you Mexican?"

"Washo."

"What is that? Indian or something? He rolled the window down and spit into the wind. "Aint too many of your kind left is there kid."

I saw the water, it went out big with the Sun slapping its face. It looked black. I tried to peer into it. It was thick with salt. It was heavy and secret. The boat scudded over its surface like a Turtle dragging itself through mud. I hid in among crates of lettuce, tomatoes and corn stacked high on the deck, drinking of their Earth fragrance and pressing my face to the green leaves as the OAKLAND TERMINAL sign on the far shore behind me seemed to sink in the water. Across the bay the white buildings of San Francisco leaned off the sharp hills into clouds. When the ferry bumped up along the dock I made a fist over the sock full of money in my pocket and jumped down into the City. I made my way off the docks and felt the hard ground beneath my feet. They had covered the Earth with stone.

Two Scenes from
El Fin Del Mundo
LUIS VALDEZ

UNO

Scene: A street in a pueblito del valle. Midnight. La raza esta roncando. Un perro starts barking y otro lo acompaña. Don Antonio, un winillo, comes staggering down the dirt sidewalk. Los perros hacen mas y mas bulla y la gente comienza a gritar de sus casas.

TAPON: Pinches perros, callense el hocico!

BOTELLA: (his wife) Que traen?

TAPON: La perra anda en brama.

BOTELLA: Tirales algo. Mi chancla no!

TAPON: Que, pues?

Los perros continue barking. Other people shout from inside their houses. Antonio howls with the dogs.

TAPON: Shut up Lobo!

VERA: Blackie, duermete!

UNAS: Brownie!

GUERITO: Whitie!

SUGAR: Nixon!

PRIETA: Dejen dormir!

ANTONIO: (on the street) Dejen ladrar!

TAPON: Quietos!

VERA: Shut up!

ANTONIO: No sean tan perros!

Los perros are in full swing. It sounds like all the dogs in town are barking.

PRIETA: (looking out the window) Oiga? Que se trae con el ruido? Tirele algo a esos perros!

ANTONIO: Son mis amigos.

PRIETA: Que amigos ni que su abuela. Callelos!

ANTONIO: Bueno, lo siento, pero . . . (he goes over and throws a rock) Tengan!

A dog howls and the others take off with him.

BOTELLA: Ahora si.

UNAS: Ya estubo.

TAPON: A dormir.

BOTELLA: Perros calientes.

PRIETA: Ahora vayase para su casa. (she goes)

ANTONIO: Ba? Y las gracias que? Que la chicharra, me babocio como un perro!

The winillo starts to leave, but the ground starts to tremble. Es un temblor, un terremoto, an earthquake.

BOTELLA: Viejito, viejito, wake up!

TAPON: Que pasa?

BOTELLA: The house is shaking.

VERA: Santo Dios!

UNAS: Es un temblor!

SUGAR: An earthquake!

GUERITO: 'Ama!

VERA: Stay where you are, mijo!

BOTELLA: Tapon!

TAPON: It's a strong one!

BOTELLA: We're going to die!

TAPON: Callate! Get the kids!

UNAS: Vamonos a la calle!

PRIETA: The building's gonna fall on us!

SUGAR: To the street. Everybody to the street!

The lights go out all over town.

BOTELLA: Dios mio, now the lights are out!

GUERITO: I can't see where I'm going!

VERA: Guerito, where are you?

TAPON: 'On ta la flashlight?

UNAS: A la calle, vamos a la calle!

VERA: Where's Flaco?

GUERITO: I got him here.

The people start to come out of their houses with flashlights.

SUGAR: Mira, all the lights in town are out.

TAPON: (con flashlight) This way, con cuidado.

BOTELLA: Bendito sea Dios.

TAPON: No hay heridos o golpeados?

PRIETA: Guera? Where are you?

TAPON: Everybody to the middle of the street.

FLACO: What's happening?

VERA: There was an earthquake.

TAPON: Who's that? (shines light on Flaco) Is he hurt?

UNAS: Chale, it's only Flaco.

TAPON: (shining light on Vera) Are you alright?

UNAS: Simon, he always looks like that.

VERA: Why don't you go to hell!

BOTELLA: (screams) Un muerto, aqui esta un muerto!

Lights shine on Don Antonio lying on the street.

SUGAR: It's only Don Tonio.

UNAS: Don Winillo!

ANTONIO: (rolling over) Apaga esa nacheta, babozo!

UNAS: Que pues? Le gusto el earthquake?

SEÑORA: Que tiene? Que tiene me hermano?

TAPON: Who's that?

SUGAR: Doña Cuca.

SEÑORA: Que tienes, Antonio?

ANTONIO: No tengo nada, hombre! Dejenme!

SEÑORA: Borracho! Sinverguenza!

ANTONIO: Vieja seca.

BOTELLA: This is really weird, you know? I was never in a temblor this strong before!

SUGAR: It made the whole town shake.

BOTELLA: I thought the roof was going to squash us.

UNAS: No hay pedo, we came out alright.

VERA: A thing like this makes you feel helpless.

BOTELLA: Verdad? I was really scared!

SEÑORA: Santo Dios de los Cielos!

TAPON: Que hay?

GUERITO: Look there!

TAPON: Donde?

GUERITO: Up there!

UNAS: Watcha! Que loco, man.

BOTELLA: What is that?

TAPON: Un cometa!

GUERITO: Hijola!

SUGAR: Look at that tail!

BOTELLA: Tapon, what's happening?

TAPON: Nada, vieja, no es nada. It's just a comet.

SEÑORA: Ya se llego el Fin del Mundo!

Silence. People look at each other.

UNAS: Fin del Mundo?

SUGAR: The end of the world?

UNAS: Chale!

The people laugh and scoff.

SEÑORA: Que tienen ustedes? Que no entienden las señas de Dios?

VERA: She's right. This is nothing to laugh about.

SEÑORA: Debemos de caernos de rodillas y pedirle perdon al ciel

BOTELLA: Pero como? How can the world come to an end?

PRIETA: That's not hard to figure out!

SEÑORA: La Santa Biblio nos dice. Viene la guerra, viene el hambre, viene la muerte.

ANTONIO: Viene la bomba atomica, y todos nos va dejar como chicharrones.

UÑAS: Not me.

SUGAR: How you going to escape?

UÑAS: Pos a correr, mano!

SUGAR: Chale! I'm staying right here. You think anybody's going to drop a bomba on this pueblito rasquachi?

BOTELLA: Verdad, we're safe here!

TAPON: No va pasar nada, hombre. If the comunistas start a guerra, los gringos les dan en la madre primero. Son muy matones, que no sabes?

BOTELLA: Tapon's right. This is los Estados Unidos.

UÑAS: Nothing's going to happen.

SUGAR: Nothing ever happens in this town.

GUERITO: Except earthquakes.

VERA: And cometas?

SEÑORA: Es una seña. Todos nos vamos a morir por pecadores. Recuerden mis palabras. (she goes)

SUGAR: Pecadores.

UÑAS: What does she mean?

SUGAR: She means you're a sinner, Uñas. Y el Señor is going to wipe you out.

UÑAS: Chale.

The lights come on.

ANTONIO: Ah, las luces.

TAPON: Mira, vieja, the lights.

BOTELLA: Gracias a Dios.

TAPON: Ves? Nothing to worry about.

PRIETA: That's what you think.

TAPON: What do you mean?

PRIETA: Y el jale mañana?

UÑAS: De veras. There's work tomorrow!

BOTELLA: What time is it?

TAPON: Time to go to sleep. A dormir todos.

BOTELLA: (looking up) That thing is still up there.

TAPON: Vieja.

BOTELLA: Maybe we should go to church sometime.
TAPON: Botella!
BOTELLA: I'm coming, Tapon, I'm coming. Que susto.
PRIETA: Que estraño.
VERA: Que raro.
ANTONIO: Pero no fue nada.
The raza goes back into their casas.

CINCO

A country road. Barnes and Mundo drive up in the sheriff's car.

BARNES: Okay, son, this is as far as we go. (stops the car) Aren't you curious about where we are?

MUNDO: Looks like a field.

BARNES: Well, God awmighty, you finally said something! We been driving for three quarters of an hour and you ain't said a single word. Not till now anyway. Quiet young fella, ain't ya? You ever do a lotta time?

MUNDO: You tell me.

BARNES: I couldn't find anything on you. Not in this county anyway. Maybe not even in the whole damn state. No record, clean bill of health! Found a few other Ray Matas, but I know they're somebody else. You sure that's your real name?

MUNDO: I don't know. Ask my mother.

BARNES: Born and raised in that little town, weren't you? Ever been in the service?

MUNDO: I was in the war.

BARNES: Vietnam?

MUNDO: World War II.

BARNES: Right. So was I. (stops) Just a minute, son. What the hell you take me for? Some kind of jackass? I'm trying to make conversation here. Why can't you have the decency to be human? First we drive all the way out there, with you sittin' there like a deaf mute. Now you can't answer a decent question!

MUNDO: Listen, Barnes —

BARNES: Just a minute.

MUNDO: You're the one who wanted to —

BARNES: Just a second!

MUNDO: Talk to me, man! I didn't —

BARNES: Hold it godammit! (Mundo stops)

MUNDO: (pause) Okay. Now you sound more like a pig, see?

BARNES: Is that what you think I am? A pig?

MUNDO: Well, where are we, ese? On the moon? Ain't this still the San
Joaquin Valley? Ain't that a field that some fat grower owns? Did the
world stop all of a sudden or what? I'm el Mundo, ese. El Mundo de
Burlap, Califas. And you're Deputy Sheriff Sam Barnes. 'Ora, if I'm still
a Chicano, un bato de aquellas tu sabes? Then you must still be a pig,
right? Makes sense.

BARNES: I don't think we're going to understand each other.

MUNDO: Oh, come on, man. What the fuck do you think this is, Chico and
the Man? You've been shitting me since we left town!

BARNES: I been trying—

MUNDO: You've been cagando la estaca!

BARNES: What's that supposed to mean?

MUNDO: It means, ese, that I know why you brought me out here, you
dig? El Mundo no es pendejo, marrano.

BARNES: I don't speak Spanish.

MUNDO: Why not? Sixty percent of the whole fucking county does. You're
a county Sheriff, que no? Why don't you speak the language of most of
the people in the county, carnal? Why are you my county Sheriff?

BARNES: Who else is going to do it? You?

MUNDO: Shit.

BARNES: I'm serious. You've got a clean record. I could recommend to the
Sheriff that you—

MUNDO: Toma. (le da un violin)

BARNES: What's that?

MUNDO: That's Spanish for this. (the finger)

BARNES: You're a very bitter young fellow.

MUNDO: Kiss my ass.

Mundo and Barnes sit in silence for a while.

MUNDO: Orale. Here they come.

BARNES: Who?

MUNDO: Your friends, Sheriff. Two growers called Gudunritch and Roddenberry. Que placas. I couldn't name 'em better myself.

ARNES: Well, I'll give you credit for that. You sure as hell know what's
going on in the world.

MUNDO: Simon, me caen huangos.

BARNES: Wait here.

MUNDO: Your ass.

The growers drive up in another car. Mundo and Barnes step out.

GUDUN: Sheriff Barnes?

BARNES: Right here, Bob.

GUDUN: Roddenberry's with me.

BARNES: Jack.

RODD: Sheriff.

BARNES: Gentlemen, this is the young fella you've heard so much about. Name's Mundo Mata.

GUDUN: Mundo Mata? Doesn't that mean the world kills?

MUNDO: Chale, puto. It means the world plants.

GUDUN: Y'don't say? Well, my Spanish is a little rusty, I'll admit. Look here, men, uh, why don't you sit in the back here and we'll, uh, talk. I think there's, uh, more room in my car.

BARNES: Get in.

MUNDO: You get in.

BARNES: Alright. We're all friends here, right?

He gets into the back and Mundo follows him cautiously.

BARNES: I should warn you guys that Mr. Mata is a very sharp young fella. We had a real int'resting conversation while we were waiting, ain't that right, son?

MUNDO: That's right, mother.

BARNES: See what I mean?

GUDUN: Great. Well, in that case, there's not much sense in the casual amenities. We'll proceed right to the point. Okay, Jack?

RODD: Shoot.

GUDUN: (turns with finger out at Mundo) Bang. (he laughs at his joke, but only makes an ass of himself, since Mundo doesn't twitch a muscle) Mr. Mata we've been led to believe according to highly reliable sources that our area is about to become the theater of operations for a calculated, highly organized, publically financed drive by subversive, leftwing interests with an eye toward controlling the agricultural labor pool as it exists in our area of the state.

RODD: Oh, fuck, Bob. Will you get to the point?

GUDUN: I'm trying.

RODD: Shit. Cesar Chavez is coming, okay?

GUDUN: That's the point.

RODD: The United Farm Workers Union is planning to put an office in your town.

GUDUN: Burlap is going to be the central organizing headquarters for the entire county.

RODD: They're going to petition every godamn ranch for union elections come next summer.

GUDUN: And we must comply.

RODD: The hell we do.

GUDUN: Unless, of course, our lobbyists in Sacramento achieve their mission of destroying the present farm labor law and turning the legislative tide.

RODD: How they gonna do that? It's hard enough to get them off their asses just to talk to the right people! They need expense accounts just to take a crap.

GUDUN: A new governor will stem the tide. If we're fortunate enough to find another Reagan.

RODD: Godammit, Bob, by that time we'll all be under union contract, you know that!

GUDUN: I'm merely saying there's hope for the future.

RODD: Screw the future. Talk about today. Right now! Chavez has 20,000 people in Sacramento at the drop of a hat. What the hell are we going to do?

GUDUN: I told you to consider the Teamsters.

RODD: The Teamsters are losing elections all over the frigging state, Bob. What the hell's the use of calling in the Mafia if they can't even win a godamned honest election?

GUDUN: Well, then, what's left?

RODD: Him! What the hell else are we doing out here in the middle of the night?

GUDUN: Mr. Mota—

MUNDO: Mah-ta, ese. Mota is something else.

GUDUN: You don't say?

MUNDO: Simon. Watcha. (pulls out a leño)

GUDUN: What's that?

MUNDO: Un leño of some of the most beautiful mota these fields have ever grown. Lemme lay it on you.

GUDUN: A joint. He gave me a joint.

BARNES: Marijuana!

MUNDO: Less than an ounce. (pause. all look at each other)

RODD: Well, what the hell you all waiting for? Gimme that shit. (takes the joint and lights it, sucks it in, holds his breath) Want some, Sheriff?

BARNES: What the hell, why not? Me and my wife, we do this once in a while in, uh, bed. It shore makes marriage a lot more inneresting. (tokes up)

GUDUN: Mr. Mata, I do believe we've struck a common chord. (tokes)

MUNDO: Sabes que? Why don't you call me Mundo?

GUDUN: (holding his breath) Mundo?

MUNDO: Right on. (tokes up)

RODD: Mundo, lemme tell it to you straight. We want you to work for us.

MUNDO: Us? Who's us?

RODD: Me and Gudunritch here.

GUDUN: And five or six other ranchers in the area.

RODD: We need to stop Chavez.

MUNDO: What do you want me to do, snuff him?

GUDUN: (they look at each other) Don't think the possibility hasn't been seriously entertained. And with the highest level of federal . . . encouragement, shall we call it?

RODD: Godammit, Mundo, we're fighting for our lives. Now we all know who's behind all this shit.

BARNES: The Russians.

RODD: No, shit, not the godamned Russians. That's a red horse of a whole different shade right now. Those bastards aren't only after our grain, they want our carrots, our tomatoes, our grapes. Christ, there's no end to it. But it's all good for agriculture here in America. What I'm talking about is our freedom right here. The freedom to grow, the freedom of choice! That's what's in danger. Used to be a man could plant his seeds in the ground and do whatever he godamned well pleased! Now with corporations moving in, and price controls, and unions, Shit, a man can't hardly breathe! You see? You see what Chavez is doing to our country? Now, Mundo, you're a redblooded American as much as I am, ain't that right? Weren't you born and raised right here in Burlap?

MUNDO: Simon.

RODD: I coulda sworn it! Wanna know somethin'? So was I! That's right. Old Jack Roddenberry was born in Burlap, California. Delivered right at home too. Used to be a great old doctor in town, name of William Crumb. Yep. Old Doc Crumb. Why, he delivered half the growers in this county you know that? Shit, life was different in those days. Burlap had its own judge, drugstore, barbershop, even a movie house with silent pictures and stage shows now and then. Minstrel Shows was my favorite. Christ, you shoulda seen those actors put on black face and come out like coons. It was a riot! Ain't none a that around no more. Hell, I bet there ain't even a doctor in town no more, right?

MUNDO: Right.

RODD: And we even had a dentist. Right above the drugstore. That's where they wanna put the union office now, right in the old drugstore. Shit. The whole town's a wreck. Nothing there no more. Nothing but wetbacks coming — well, I mean — (he fumbles for words)

MUNDO: What's that, ese?

RODD: Nothing. Forget it.

MUNDO: Oh. I thought you said something about wetbacks. (pause) You know who delivered me, ese? My mother. She took her scissors and snip, then she handed me to my sister Guera. You know the dike that owns the cantina there in town? That's my sister Guera. I think she never got over watching me be borned, you know?

Long pause.

GUDUN: (clears his throat) Gentlemen, why don't we come to some kind of agreement here, so that we can all get home to our perspective families, hm?

RODD: We'll pay you a hundred a week—

MUNDO: How much?

GUDUN: Two hundred a week—

MUNDO: How much?

RODD: Three hundred a week and that's it.

MUNDO: Fuck you.

GUDUN: How much do you want?

MUNDO::   I want a hundred a week from each grower in the deal.

RODD: Are you crazy?

GUDUN: That's about a thousand a week, in the round figures.

RODD: Shove it.

MUNDO: Look, man, what the hell you been so touchy about? If the union gets in, you sonuvabitches are going to pay through the mouth. All I'm asking is a hundred a week from you, and you, and everyone of your bloodsucking friends. What the hell is that? Mierda that's what it is. Shit! A hundred a week!

GUDUN: What are you prepared to do for this money?

MUNDO: Well, I'm not going to snuff Chavez, I'll tell you that.

RODD: We're not asking you to kill Chavez, okay! All we want is for you to screw up the election drive in any way you know how. Get in there and spy, bribe whoever you got to, threaten the hell out of whoever gets in your way, piss on the godamn ballots if you have to, but make them lose the frigging elections! Now, can you do that?

MUNDO: Man, in my town, I can do anything.

RODD: You're on. (sticks out his hand)

GUDUN: A thousand a week for how long?

RODD: As long as it takes.

GUDUN: You're going to be a very prosperous young man about town. The Sheriff here'll take care of paying you off—

BARNES: Do you have to put it that way?

GUDUN: Sheriff, come on. It will be cash, of course.

MUNDO: Of course.

GUDUN: Here's five hundred to start. We weren't prepared to go any higher. (gives him money) Next week we'll balance it off. And if you're ever caught. We don't even know you ever existed. Do I make myself clear?

MUNDO: I've never seen your ugly face in my whole life.

GUDUN: (slowly, deliberately) Fuck you.

MUNDO: In your mouth.

RODD: Come on, Bob, let's get out of here.

GUDUN: My pleasure.

Mundo and Barnes get out of the car.

BARNES: Jack, Bob? I'll see you.

The growers peel off without another word, not even a goodbye to Barnes.

BARNES: Those bastards. Come on, son, I'll drop you in town.

Mundo and Barnes get into the sheriff's car, drive back in silence. They pull into town.

BARNES: Where you wanna be dropped off?

MUNDO: Wherever, man.

BARNES: You didn't say nothing on the way back. (pause) That's okay. I understand. You probably got a whole lot on your mind. I would if I was you. (a man staggers across the path of the car) OH, Christ! What the hell is he—? (he hits him) Shit, I hit him! Did you see that? He just walked right out into the street!

MUNDO: (jumps out) It's Flaco.

BARNES: Who?

MUNDO: A friend of mine.

BARNES: I'll call an ambulance.

MUNDO: Wait a minute, ese. Hold on. Look, este, he's alright. You weren't going that fast, and he'll live.

BARNES: Are you sure? He looks kinda bad to me.

MUNDO: He's always this way, man. I know him. He's a . . . drunk. Ese, Flaco, you okay, carnal?

FLACO: Mundo.

MUNDO: Quihubo, ese? Que paso pues?

FLACO: Tu sabes.

MUNDO: He's going to be fine. You better leave him to me. It's better if nobody else saw us together tonight, you know what I mean?

BARNES: Oh. Right, sure, good thinking.

MUNDO: I'll see you in a week.

BARNES: Right. A week. Where shall I meet you?

MUNDO: Just drop the bread off at the bar, man. With my sister.

BARNES: Gotcha. (pause) Which one's your sister?

MUNDO: La Guera, man, the light one.

BARNES: Is that what Guera means? Well, I'll be, you learn something new every day don't you? Buenas noches.

MUNDO: Get lost. (Barnes drives off) Pinche Flaco. What you doing out in the streets so late, ese?

FLACO: I was looking for you, Mundo. Ya no aguanto, ese. I need some more shit.

MUNDO: Que bato.

FLACO: Please, Mundo. You can have my ruca again, man. Sabes que, I
   think she likes you, loco!

MUNDO: Chale, ese, Vera loves you.

FLACO: Did you go see her today?

MUNDO: She didn't want me, man. I tried, pero tu sabes. She gave me a
   hard time, y me aguite. So I left. I don't need that shit. Man, I got so
   many rucas in this town, I'm going to need a splint, tu sabes?

FLACO: (laughs) Simon.

MUNDO: Come on, I'll take you home and fix you up.

FLACO: Ese, I got no bread, carnal.

MUNDO: Man, who you with? Yo soy tu carnal, El Mundo. Y con el Mundo
   money is no fucking object! (takes him out)

She's My Rock

(from *Okies*)

GERALD HASLAM

Me and some other boys had stole us a case of Lucky from this truck that
was deliverin to the Tejon Club, and we was flat frog-eyed whenever we
drove into the Mohawk Serv-U-Self on Norris Road. I was a-fillin the tank
when old Clyde Mays he come back from the pisser a-gigglin and carrying
on; "There's a gal over in yonder van," he said, "that's hot for your body."
He pointed toward a U-haul gassin up at the next island.

Well, I believed him. Why shouldn't I? I mean I wasn't half-bad lookin,
and besides that, I was drunk, so I wandered over to that van, unbuttonin
my shirt and pullin my jeans down a bit so whoever the gal was could see
my built. Whenever I got to the van, I looked in the side door and seen
these skinny legs bendin over in a big mess of watermelons. I crinkled my
eyes up so I'd look like Ferlin Huskey, then I said, "Howdy."

The gal looked-up and Lordy! That's the ugliest gal I ever did see, and a
harelip to boot. "Nya wanna buy a wanermelon?" she asked me, and I
guess she was smilin, her lip all pulled up into her nose like someone
mended it on a footpedal sewing machine. That made me laugh, picturing
some fat old doctor puttin this ugly baby up on the machine, then whap-
whap-whap! sewin her mouth up while her skinny legs was a-kickin
a-round.

"Whan's vunny?" she asked, her eyes turnin sad all of a sudden. Well,
ugly or not, I couldn't let Clyde know he'd tricked me; sides, I could always
get me a flag to put over her face and screw for old glory. I wasn't gonna

crawfish on screwin this little old gal any more than I would on a fight, though I believe I'd rather've fought her; who wants to diddle a harelip gal anyways? "I'm just laughin at you in there with all them watermelons," I told her. "Looks to me like they ain't much room to set."

She smiled again. I think.

"Why don't you come over to my car and we can get comfortable in the back seat." I reached out and touched her hand real gentle, just kind of tickled it the way that drives em nuts, and she stayed bent over them watermelons, her eyes gettin big. That's when I realized she was real young; I wasn't but 17 myself, and I'll bet she wasn't no more than 14, but that ugly face surely aged her. Anyways, I don't believe she knew what I wanted.

"Hunh?" she asked.

I stepped closer, then touched her thigh, it all warm and smooth and not harelippy a-tall, and I felt her shudder. I was gettin hot all of a sudden myself, and I started wonderin if I really did have a flag in my car. Her eyes just sparked over that tore-up excuse for a mouth. Lord, she was one ugly girl! Ewe-gly! Double ugly! Still, them eyes and that way her thigh felt, I just figured tail's tail.

Then damned if somebody didn't sock me right on the shoulder, and I heard Clyde and the guys laugh. I spun around with my fists cocked, and there stood this good-lookin gal maybe 35-, 40 year-old; she just spit at me: "You keep your goddamn hands off Nola Sue or I'll kick your pimply butt clean back to Weedpatch!" She meant it.

Smack! She slapped my face. "Nola Sue," she ordered, "you close them doors. I'll deal with this punk," then damned if she didn't bust a watermellon right on my chest, the juice runnin down my jeans and all.

What could I do? That lady she had me by the short hairs. I mean I couldn't sock her. Besides, she's meaner than cat shit, and I didn't know for sure if I *could* whup her; some of them old honky tonk gals is mighty rough. So I just hustled back to my 40 Chevy, tryin to act like I thought it was a big joke, with that watermelon all over me and flies buzzin round, sticky melon juice drippin down into my drawers; I felt so damned stupid. I climbed into the car and drove us out to Kern County Park as fast as I could. Whenever we got there I kicked the livin shit out of Clyde Mays.

After we'd been there a hour or so, I barfed up all the beer I'd drunk. What a wasted day. Then a damned deputy he drove up just when Bobby Joe Hurd was pukin, and caught us with what was left of the beer we'd stole. We all got sent to juvie that time.

Next summer I was fishin in a canal out by Greenfield with a pole I'd swiped from Thriftys. Geneie Hicks was with me. We wasn't catchin nothin. There was one big colored lady up the bank from us, and she wasn't doin too good either.

Anyways, up drove this beat-lookin station wagon with old, cracked wood peelin off the sides. And guess who got out: the lady that busted the watermelon on me, and Nola Sue the harelip. They had these real long poles tied to one side of the wagon, and they commenced loosenin em. I pulled my cowboy hat down over my eyes and just set there a-hopin they wouldn't see me.

They finally got their poles untied, and come walkin up the bank. The mean lady she never even noticed me, but damned if that harelip gal didn't, her eyes lockin on me whenever she passed, then glancin back all the time after they got their rigs in the water up the canal. Geneie Hicks seen her and said: "Damn but that's a ugly girl yonder."

"You ain't shittin," I answered, not lookin up.

"Does she know you from somewheres? She's surely lookin you over."

"Let's get outta here," I told him. "We can drive up Kern Canyon and catch us some trout."

"Sounds good," said Geneie, so we packed up our gear and toted it back to my Chevy. Parked right next to me was the big old Caddy that the colored lady drove. It was unlocked, so I swiped some cigarettes and two of them wire seat cooler deals and a blanket from it; the glove compartment and the truck was locked, though. Just as I threw the stuff from the Caddy into my car, I heard a voice say: "I sneen nya."

I turned around and, ugly as a sinner's soul, there stood Nola Sue. "Mind yer own bee's wax," I snapped at her.

"I won' tnell on nya."

"Thanks a lot," I said real sarcastic, then climbed into my Chevy and got the hell away from there. She give me the creeps, and I didn't want her old lady seein me either.

We drove out Nile Street, through the last of the orange groves and the open hills then into the canyon. Up by Richbar, we seen a couple cop cars and a ambulance and a fire truck. We stopped and this here fat lady she run right up to my window and stuck her head in: "A Mexcan drownded," she hollered, "right in the river, and skindivers is lookin for im." The lady's eyes was all wide, and she kindly panted. Before I could answer her, another car pulled behind us, and she run back to it.

I parked the car and me and Geneie we walked over to where a crowd of folks was watchin them skin divers. Off to one side of us two Mexcans set on a log with their arms around this here Mexcan girl. None of em was cryin.

"It don't look half-bad," I heard one old boy say to his wife. "Hell, I could swim it easy." I poked Geneie in the ribs and whispered: "L.A." He laughed. Them bastards from down south thought they could do anything, but me, I knew about the river; pullin along lookin smooth and easy, it had one hell of a suck; I liked to got drownded there myownself back when I's fourteen.

Old Geneie he's real comical. He poked me back, and whispered out the corner of his mouth: "Well, hell, it looks like the Mexcans went and cinched the Kern River Sweepstakes for this summer. This here's about the twentieth one that drownded, and ain't but a dozen Okies done er. I sure hate losin to Mexcans. But at least we ain't last. Niggers ain't drownded but five or six, and I don't believe they's been a Chinaman or Jap or Flip done er yet." I like to split a gut tryin not to laugh out loud. Old Geneie he never even grinned: "I shore hate to lose," he said.

They had them one hell of a time findin that Mexcan's body, so me and Geneie we went back to where the cars was parked and rifled the open ones. Drowndins are pretty good, like wrecks, cause folks get excited and don't lock up whenever they park. We got all the junk we could pack into my Chevy's truck, cameras and everthing. And we found a full pint of sloe gin in a 59 Merc. It was a real good haul. We should of took off right then, but Geneie he said he'd never seen a dead Mexcan before, so we pulled two or three long times on the sloe gin and went back to the river.

Just about the time they found that Mexcan, a lady and a man came runnin up to a sheriff from where the cars was parked and they was yellin about how someone broke into their cars. Me and Geneie just looked at each other, then mozied back toward my Chevy and got the hell out of there before the cops got too curious.

We buzzed up to Hobo Hot Springs, and bought us burgers at the cafe. Afterward Geneie he went up to the campground to look for this girl he knew, so I broke out my pole and commenced fishin. When I got upstream I seen a campfire on a sandbar, but didn't think nothin of it except that it was near dark and the game warden might be out soon lookin for guys fishin late. I'd brought what was left of the sloe gin with me, so I reeled in and set myself on a log under this here big tree. It was real quiet up the canyon at night; all you heard was the river a-suckin past.

Then this voice said real soft like: "Hni."

I looked up and damned if that Nola Sue wasn't standin right in front of me in this here bikini, her body all outlined against that bonfire on the sandbar, her face hid in the dark; she'd filled out some. I started to leave, then thought better of it. "Hi," I said, "what're you doin here?"

"Ny Nomma an her bnoyfriend is cnookin not nogs yonder," she nodded toward the sandbar. "I sneen ya fishin."

I'd been pullin pretty good on that sloe gin, so I didn't think too straight, my head rememberin that ugly face, my pecker just seein that good body. "Set a spell," I finally said, and she come over to me, kinda slow and shy. I reached up for her hand, then pulled her down next to me, careful not to see her face. And, as it turned out, I never even had to kiss her.

After I come out of the county road camp in '65 and got me that job cleanin burlap sacks at the Sierra Bag Company, I commenced hangin out at this honky tonk, The Sad Sack. It was a real dark place out on Edison Highway where the cocktail waitresses went topless and they had this other gal that danced behind the bar stark neked. They charged a buck for a glass of beer.

What kept me goin there was this waitress named Penny who had the pinkest nipples I ever seen and pointed, and who had a face that liked to took my breath away; her mouth looked like a red flower. She got really friendly with me, cause I bought her lots of champagne to drink. It got to where I'd come in and she'd just smile at me, and all the other guys looked half-sore. They knew I was a-takin over.

Only thing was that my wages at the bag company couldn't stand them dollar beers and champagne at two-fifty a glass. Besides, I needed to buy Penny some presents, cause she wouldn't put out less I did. So I got in touch with some of the boys, and we commenced hittin gas stations pretty reg'lar, always late at night whenever there wasn't but one old boy workin. We never hurt nobody, and damned if we didn't scoop us up some money.

Penny she loved it. I told her what I was doin, and she laughed and said she was my gun moll. I bought her a new Dodge and moved us into a nice place over on Flower Street. She quit out at the Sad Sack and I had to step up my service station business, her buyin clothes and all, hittin one a week for a long spell, driving up above Fresno and clean down to San Diego so's the cops wouldn't know where to expect us guys next. In the back of my head I knew Penny was a hustler, but it wasn't my head I was listenin to. I even quit my job at the bag company, and maybe that was what really caused me to get caught.

I come home early one day after casin a gas station over in Arvin and caught Penny and this Mexcan makin out on the couch; she didn't have nothin on but her drawers, and she was doin somethin for him she hardly ever done for me. Jesus Christ! It was damn lucky I wasn't carryin my pistol, cause I'd of shot both of em. Still, I beat her bloody, and stomped that Mexcan.

I left em there on the floor and drove over to Oildale and found some of my partners at the Highland Club. There was this big strike of Mexcans goin on out at the grape fields north then, and most of us guys didn't like it a-tall. I mean, they wasn't just Mexcans, which is bad enough, but they was Commies too. I didn't have no trouble gatherin up a gang of boys to drive out to McFarland with me to whup us some goddamn Mexcans. I surely wanted to work over a few of them greasy bastards. I wanted to kill em and send em back to where they come from.

The first couple fields we seen had too many of em, and sheriffs too. But over by Cawelo there was a small field with mostly Flips workin in it and maybe half-a-dozen Mexcans carryin signs on a dirt road next to a irrigation ditch. We pulled up, two carloads of us, with some clubs we'd picked up on the way, and we pounded piss out of em and run em off. Them Fillipinos in the fields laughed, and some of the guys started to go after them, but I stopped em. "Them ain't Mexcans," I said, "they're on our side." Then this one Flip he come up to me and said there was another bunch of greasers down the dirt road a piece. "You kill kill," he said, and I liked to laughed at how funny he talked. Still, I wasn't through with goddamn Mexcans — the crooked, greasy bastards — not by a long shot. I needed to whup me a few more. I *needed* to, cause Penny and that spic kept flashin into my head.

Maybe some of them guys we'd beat up earlier had warned em, but the Mexcans at the next field was waitin for us. They fought like white men, and one guy, just when I's fixin to wallop him, he spun around and hit me across the bridge of my nose with a board. That's all I recollect. When I come to, I's in a hospital room. I could just barely see; my eyes had gone all fuzzy on me. They knocked me out and done a operation, but when they finally took the bandages off, I couldn't see no better; in fact, I believe it's worse. And it got worser.

If that ain't bad enough, Penny pressed charges for assault and rape (ain't *that* a kick in the ass!); that Mexcan was hurt bad and they got me for somethin called mayhem; one of my boys told about the gas stations; the only thing they didn't charge me with was whuppin them strikers, even the cops couldn't fault me there. The public defender told me I could get life for all the stuff they had on me what with my record and all. Then he said maybe a judge would go easy since I was blind.

When I heard that word I wanted to bawl. *Blind!* That meant I wasn't goin to get no better, and the goddamn doc never even told me. Blind, and goin to jail over that damned woman and her Mexcan. That night I tried to hang myself, but I couldn't even do that right.

The public defender knew what he's talkin about. I only got 5-to-20 years at Vacaville because I was blinded. And somethin funny happened after the judge passed sentence and the court adjourned. I heard the defender say "Alright," to someone, then this small hand touched my arm: "NI'm sorry," said a voice and I knew right then who it was. Ugly gals is hard to forget.

"I don't need nobody's fuckin sympathy," I kindly spit at her, jerkin my arm away. I tried to walk away but bumped into the goddam table.

"Cnan nI wrnite nya?"

"Leave me the hell alone," I said, then, damnit, I busted out cryin. "Dead people don't need no letters," I sobbed "NI'll wrnite," she said, touchin my arm. "Nyou ain' dnead."

Nola Sue did write, by God, and a couple months at Vacaville surely taught me to welcome anything I got. My folks was both dead by then, and I never had no mail cept from her. After a while, she asked in a letter if she could come up and visit me. That was hard, cause there she was just a-sendin me letters and stuff, and willin to drive clean up to Vacaville but, to tell the truth, I just didn't want none of the guys up there to see me with a harelip, so I wrote her no.

Then she sent me this here tape recorder so I could send her letters without having to dictate to some other guy, and that really helped. She sent me lots of presents — Christmas, birthday, and just for the hell of it too — so I made her a leather wallet and key case, and had this other ol boy tool it all fancy. Then she wrote and asked again if she could come up; she had vacation, and she'd surely like to visit me.

I couldn't tell her no again, good as she'd been to me. So up she come, me really dreadin the whole thing. When I heard her talkin all funny, I just wanted to crawl away, but damned if I didn't forget all about the way she sounded once she was tellin all about how things was at home. And it felt mighty nice to have a woman's hand reach over and squeeze mine. It felt damned good.

I was all mixed up between being happy and sad whenever I headed back to my job at the hospital laundry. I enjoyed havin Nola Sue to talk to, but it made me feel sadder bein inside. Then I heard this one old boy kindly whistle through his teeth while I was passin, and he said to whoever was next to him: "I just seen the ugliest woman in the world. Gaw-awd damn but she was enough to gag a maggot." The other guy laughed.

"Shut your fuckin trap!" I hollered at em.

They didn't say nothin for a second, then the guy doin all the talkin he said, "What's wrong with you, pard, you're the lucky one. You didn't have to see her."

I started swingin but only messed my hands up.

I spent nearly three years inside that time, and I determined that I'd never go inside again. It just wasn't worth it. On the day they let me go, Nola Sue was there to pick me up. We never discussed it or nothin, but I just naturally moved in with her whenever we got back to Oildale.

She'd helped me find a job sandin paddles at this here new canoe factory out on North Chester, and I went right to work when I got home. The job wasn't that much, but between the both of us—Nola Sue worked as a beauty operator—we ate regular and even snuck in a little in savins. Three nights a week Nola Sue drove me to school so's I could finish my high school diploma. She helped me avoid the boys, and she seen to it I never missed no meetins with my parole officer either.

One afternoon I stopped after work with some fellers from the factory for a beer. I no sooner'n set, and I heard this familiar voice call out: "Damn if that ain't a squirrely-lookin Okie sittin yonder!" It was that crazy Clyde Mays, and even if the parole officer wouldn't like it, he surely sounded good to me. "Come over here you skinny fart," I hollered, and directly he was sittin next to me a-pumpin my hand. "You ol sack a shit," he said, "damned if you don't look fat and sassy."

Well, we had lots of old times to talk about, and he filled me in on where everone was now. We had us a few more beers than I'd planned and I stayed later. Finally, I said to him, "Wait a minute, Clyde. I got to call home so my ol lady don't get too worried."

"What?" he asked. "You pussy-whipped by a harelip gal? Shit, I can almost see screwin her and lettin her donate a little money, but I sure as hell didn't think you'd be pussy-whipped."

That pissed me. "I ain't pussy whipped!"

"You act like you really give a shit for that ugly harelip gal," he laughed, just eggin me on.

"Talk sense!" I snapped. "Tail's tail, and blind guys don't get much choice."

"I 'precciate that," Clyde went on, "but don't let no woman get aholt to you, bo, or you'll damn sure take a pussy-whippin."

"Well I don't give a shit for her, so shut up about it!" He did, and we talked a while longer, but the fun was gone.

Whenever I got home that night, Nola Sue asked if I'd eat and when I said I hadn't she went into the kitchen. Me, I set in the livin room and turned on the radio so I could listen to some good country music. I didn't feel too hot and it wasn't just the beer I'd drunk. Directly, she come in and put a T.V. tray in front of me and told me where things was on it. I didn't like the sound of how she talked, all n-sounds, so I just said "Shut up and leave me be!"

She did, takin herself back into the kitchen, then I heard her cryin, snortin in that funny way harelips do. Old Stoney Edwards come on the radio and went to singing about how his woman was his rock. Well, I set there awhile, that beer a-workin in me, and I heard Nola Sue had quit cryin in the kitchen. Somethin in me wanted to apologize, but I couldn't be pussy whipped by no harelip, so I rared up and hollered for her to come out from the kitchen, me puffin like a ol bull I's gettin myself so shook.

Soon as I heard her shuffle kinda close I raged at her: "I don't need no goddam harelip!" But I no sooner'n got the words out than somethin wet and hot salted my cheeks. "I don't need no goddam harelip," I said again, my lower lip commencin to shiver so bad I couldn't hardly talk.

I waited for her to bawl some, but she never, and my own face just wouldn't get under control. She never said nothin, and I could only hear my own breath snortin, makin me wonder in my darkness if the whole thing wasn't just a beer dream, and maybe I's alone, stuck in a cell somewheres, or maybe just inside myself. Then I felt her hand, cool and real, on my face. I wanted to slap it away, but I couldn't move, so I blubbered one more time: "I don't no goddamn harelip."

She had both hands on my face then, cradlin it, and she answered: "No, but nyou need a woman."

She was right.

Three Poems

Gary Thompson

LESSONS FOR FISHING THE SIERRAS

for Tom Crawford

wake up alone.
find breakfast and eat from the plate
of the earth.
look east for the sun and warm
yourself.
then carry the gear
in for miles and find a spot
with a lake.

drink from the fastest and coldest mountain
stream.
leave your fingers
in
until they turn red.
try now to understand yourself
as a stranger.
hold the line steady and deep.
disown your wife,
debts,
and small favors. forget your name.

now empty yourself first.
grasp the fish
firmly.
use a sharp knife and clean up
in cold water.
afterwards, throw back the eyes

which are not yours.

IN THE WILD RICE

in the wild.rice fields two rivers
meet;
one river from the north bears soil
so fertile that the dead
grow
in their graves.
the other carries the cleaned bones
and empty skin
of animals that once lived
inside the mountain snows. when the sun fades
these old friends stay outside
and exchange
stories of the past and the silent days
when being a river
was something to be proud of.
for warmth, they drink up their own gifts.

now because they are drunk and tired
of the journey
they lie down in their deep beds.
friendship falls through the heavy water of sleep
like a stone:
some people would say this is home.

HARDPAN

six inches
below this city is another world
protected by hardpan.
the trees here live on the surface.

only a few brave houses
have basements: their owners store
half their memories
in another, deeper life.

at least here the earth
is solid. people born in this city
are very sure of themselves;
we could not dig up our dead if we wanted.

Three Poems

DAVID KHERDIAN

THE FAST

Trying to discipline myself
    to eat less,
a moral lesson I'm badly
            in need of—
I savor the *rojik* my mother
has sent all the way from
    California

            western walnuts
            coated in a shell
            of jellied grape
            juice & rolled in
            a coating of pow-
                dered sugar

an Armenian delicacy from which
    deliverence
            is not easy/
and so
      then,
            the first small bite is
easy
      but the restraint sends an
avalanche of saliva
                down
and drops a message on the head

of my animal
which has suddenly opened
    my mouth
    (making a sound I notice)
and before I can get my *rojik*
  out of the way
    it lunges and
  bites my hand with my teeth

OUTSIDE OUR BEDROOM WINDOW

Outside our bedroom window
    the purple flowers
    of the pomegranate tree,
      whose buds caught the
      hot sun of earlier day,
    await the explosion
    of birth.

My wife and I lie naked after love
    and watch the setting
    sun turn the yellow window
    shade to gold.

A lonely bird comes to our tree
    and makes a shadow
    we can watch—
      and in the stillness that
      gathers to await dusk

I reach for her upturned hand in a
    gesture of peace
      that in the reaching
      turns to sleep.

ON THE DEATH OF MY FATHER

Dead now, and forever,
ceremony release him to the the ground,
where once he played in tales that
have been handed down.

Cupped upturned hands
lower thru your spreading fingers
this soil-splashed man.
You knew him first that touch him last.
His circling fading time
hovers over my head,
his life my own to lose or live again.

Take him earth
in final release.
Toss him and catch him
in your cloudy hands.
He'll know your touch, his
feet, when he comes to you
are sure to be bare.

Three Poems
KHATCHIK MINASIAN

VALLEY DITCH

In our ditch
    there are water skaters,
    frogs,
    tall reeds,
    mud bugs,
    apple cores and plum seeds,

    and little naked children.

RULE 449

boy with blackspider
on hat,
and four June bugs
on new red sweater,
parades before student body
holding bull-frog high.

principal summons boy
to office,
begins with rule 173 —
(not to molest fellow student)
   eye on spider;
ends with rule 449 —
(becomes property of school)
   hand on bull-frog.

AWAKENING

He went to sleep a lad
in the late years of promise,
and when they thought he'd overslept,
he rose up like a giant
in monolithic fury
and made his resurrection epic,
pounding deep prints on the land
like the spoors of pachyderms
indelibly shod.

Comeback

William Rintoul

On a summer evening in the mid-1930's, my older brother, whom we called Jing, and I set out from our home in Wilson in the oilfields of California's central valley for the arena in Carverville, thirty-eight miles away. Bugs were so thick by irrigated fields where cotton and alfalfa grew that Jing stopped at Station One, a pumping plant seventeen miles out, to clean the windshield.

Wiping it reasonably clean, he looked sadly at the stained grill. He had bought the car second-hand several weeks before and was inordinately proud of it. I could tell he had misgivings.

"I'll wash it tomorrow," I said.

It had been generous of him to offer to drive me to Carverville to see Rulon fight, particularly since he himself wasn't interested in the fight game. I knew he would rather have been on Center Street, driving slowly up and down, looking at boys like himself who passed in other cars and at

girls who found an excuse to walk along the sidewalk in the evening.
Dragging Center, that particular pastime was called.

"Suppose Rulon loses?" Jing said.

I smiled. I was confident that was the last thing that was going to happen.
A man didn't fight main events in Madison Square Garden just to come back
to Carverville's corrugated tin arena to get licked by the kind of guy Rulon
was fighting. The only reason he'd agreed to fight the Mexican was to help
the promoter.

"But supposing he gets whipped?" Since Jing had finished his freshman
year at the University of California, he had come home with all kinds of talk
about premises and probabilities and laws of averages.

"He won't."

The way I had it figured, Rulon would knock out the Mexican. He'd have
another tune-up or two, then start fighting in big arenas again, like the
Olympic in Los Angeles and Dreamland in San Francisco and, sooner or
later, Madison Square Garden. Soon he'd back in the top ten. They'd
dropped him after he got hurt. He'd beat the other challengers, some of
whom he'd already beaten, and the champion would have to fight him. The
champion's manager wouldn't be able to pull the deal he'd pulled before,
making it a condition that Rulon's manager sign away half Rulon's contract
if Rulon won. Rulon's manager hadn't signed, and Rulon, to keep busy, had
had to make a trip around the world, fighting in Australia, where
featherweights were a popular class, and also in Europe.

"What if his heel acts up?"

"It didn't bother him in training."

It had been a freak accident. Rulon had been irrigating on his folks' ranch
near Carverville, swinging a shovel. Somebody shouted. He had turned,
still swinging, and the blade of the shovel cut through the Achilles' tendon
above his right heel. He'd hobbled on crutches and hopped on one leg until
the muscle in it was more pronounced than its mate, and there was still a
lump above the heel with marks where the doctor had taken stitches.

"Don't misunderstand," Jing said. "I hope he wins."

"He will."

If it had not been for the accident, I probably would not have gotten
acquainted with Rulon. There had been an article in the Carverville newspaper about how Rulon Culp, who'd gotten his start in the fight game in
Carverville, had been injured while visiting his folks on the ranch he'd
bought with money earned in the ring. It was the first I'd known that
anyone as famous as Rulon Culp, whose name often appeared in The Ring
magazine, came from Carverville. (Actually, he didn't. He'd lived in Texas,
coming to California when he was nineteen.) I had been writing to fighters
for more than a year asking for autographed pictures, and I quickly wrote

to Rulon Culp, expressing regret for the accident and wishing him a speedy recovery, also asking for an autographed picture.

Sometime afterward on a rainy Sunday afternoon I was sitting in what we called the middle room of our house, memorizing the axioms and theorems of plane geometry, when a strange car pulled up outside. The car was long and black like the one my father's boss drove.

I watched as the driver backed in close to the curb and parked. Two men in raincoats got out. One was short, the other tall. The short man limped toward our door; the tall man matched his pace.

My father, who had been sitting in the front room with my mother, alternately reading the Sunday newspaper and listening to the afternoon radio programs, answered the door. I heard him talk for a moment, then he opened my door and, looking perplexed, said there were two men to see me.

The short man was Rulon Culp. His nose was almost flat, except where it flared for the nostrils, and his ears in places where they were not puffed looked as if they had retained their identity only after the severest ordeal. The taller man was Joe Armendariz, a middleweight from San Francisco, who was unranked but regarded as a comer. He was managed by the same man as Rulon, and he and Rulon were friends. He was visiting at the ranch. Rulon, not having anything to do, had decided to come over and see me. He had brought a picture, which he autographed later.

It was only with great effort that I pulled myself together to introduce my two visitors to my father and mother. Then, not knowing what to do or say, having had no experience in entertaining dignitaries, I invited the two men to see my collection of autographed pictures.

With my parents still trying to recover from their surprise, I took my guests through our kitchen and out onto the back porch, then up the narrow flight of stairs that led to the sleeping room my brothers and I called upstairs. In the corner where I had my bed, I had covered the wall with pictures and these I proceeded to show to my guests.

They looked with interest.

"Say," Joe Armendariz said once to Rulon Culp, "this kid's all right." He said it as if there might have been some doubt.

Rulon looked at the pictures for some time.

"How come I don't see a picture of the greatest one of them all?" he said finally.

"Who's that?"

"Mickey Walker."

I told him I had written to Mickey Walker several times but never gotten an answer.

"Mickey's like that," Rulon said. "If he had a picture handy, he'd send it right away. But if he didn't, he'd put your letter aside and mean to send you a picture later and forget all about it."

We talked awhile, and I apologized for the coldness upstairs.

"Fine for sleeping," Rulon said. "I always sleep with lots of fresh air." He breathed deeply of the cold air. "It's good for you."

We went back downstairs. I was in a quandary over what to do with my guests. I supposed our visit would be over when we got downstairs and that they would leave. I walked through the front room and they looked surprised when I went to the door as if to open it and show them out.

My father saved the day by asking them to sit down and visit. My mother was polite, but not unbending until we had talked awhile. Rulon told interesting stories about such things as boxing a charity exhibition in a cage of lions in Melbourne and having a brief audience with Adolph Hitler in Germany.

After awhile, my mother asked if they would care for a piece of cake. They politely accepted, though Rulon asked that his piece be particularly small. He said he had to be very careful of his weight.

Mother had baked a banana nut cake that morning and frosted it with a rich whipped cream frosting that was thick and good-looking.

Joe Armendariz ate his cake, frosting and all. Rulon ate sparingly, first carefully scraping off the frosting. As he ate, he told how he normally ate only two meals a day and how careful he had to be of drinking too much water when he was in training and of how he never chewed gum or smoked cigarettes, which he said would make him just as drunk as beer.

My mother told him how my younger brother, Monty, ate his breakfast one thing at a time, that is, he ate all his egg, then all his bacon, then all his potatoes, never skipping from one to the other, and Rulon said there might be some merit to eating your food that way as it could be that it made digestion easier.

When the two fighters left, my father watched them through the window. "They were driving a Cadillac," he said to my mother, who was carrying Rulon's cake dish with its accusing pile of frosting to the kitchen. "They seemed nice," my mother said.

The Sunday visit was the first of many for Rulon. On several occasions, my mother invited him for dinner, making it a point to cook an especially large number of vegetables, which Rulon seemed to appreciate.

My brother Monty let Rulon read his books of poetry, and Rulon surprised us by reciting several verses of a poem called "Lasca," which was about a cowboy and his sweetheart on the plains of Texas. There was one poem Rulon said he'd particularly like to memorize. He thought it was called "The Kid's Last Fight." Monty found it in a book titled "My Pious Friends and Drunken Companions," and he typed a copy for Rulon.

When Jing came home for Easter vacation, he drove me to the ranch, and Rulon showed us some of his souvenirs. He kept them in a trunk that looked as if it had been picked up and dropped many times. He let me put on a jeweled belt they had given him for beating the Australian champion, and he even let me read the typewritten pages of a play he had started in Australia while waiting for a bone in his hand to knit. The play was about a fighter named "The Kid" who was fighting for the title, and it contained many misspelled words.

Rulon loaned me a huge scrapbook. There were clippings in the book of Rulon's fights and pictures of Rulon in many places: striking a fighting pose on the ship that took him from Australia to England; standing with one arm around a half-naked native woman on Pago-Pago, surrounded by a score of barefooted children; shaking hands with Jack Dempsey in New York. I showed the scrapbook to my friends. I could not have been more proud if it had been my own.

In time, the Achilles' tendon healed, and Rulon's visits became infrequent as he began training to fight again.

Rulon climbed into the ring before his opponent, going directly to the resin box to wipe his feet. He wore a faded bathrobe. On the back, white letters spelled out "Rulon" in a semicircle over "Culp." He took off the robe to shadow-box, not seeming to look at anyone. He returned to his corner, placed his gloved hands on the upper strand of rope, and looked casually at the audience. He saw Jing and me and waved. I wondered if the men sitting near us noticed.

Rulon's opponent came into the ring. He was a tall, thin Mexican named Gomo Ybarra. He came from Denver, Colorado, and he had fought in preliminaries around Hollywood and Los Angeles for more than a year, winning often enough to work his way into an occasional main event in places like Stockton and Sacramento. His face, in contrast to Rulon's, was unmarked. He had none of the square-shouldered powerfulness. I felt sorry for him.

Introductions did not cause as much stir as I expected, considering the fact Rulon had been a main eventer at Carverville ten years ago and gone on to become famous. The referee gave the instructions, lights went out except for those over the ring, and the fight began.

Rulon came out with both hands low, moving almost flatfooted so that it looked as if he were shuffling. The Mexican danced, moving to the right, then the left. He flicked his left hand in Rulon's face, which seemed no great trick for he had the reach and Rulon kept no particular guard. Rulon shuffled forward, swinging short, sharp blows when he came in close. He seemed content to take his time.

Between rounds, a sallow-faced man with gray hair held a bottle of water for Rulon, who washed out his mouth. I assumed the man to be a second Rulon had picked up in absence of his manager, who was in Chicago training a heavyweight for an important fight. Ybarra's manager was a lean man with monocle and thin, waxed mustache. He was known as the Baron, though in one write-up it was stated he'd been a night clerk in a hotel before he began managing boxers. He spoke in a confidential manner to Ybarra, who leaned back, resting.

In the second round, Rulon came out faster. The Mexican moved away, poking his left in Rulon's face. Rulon crouched, bobbing and weaving to confuse the Mexican. There was a brief exchange before the bell sounded.

The third round was repetition.

In the fourth, Rulon came out fast enough to catch the Mexican in his corner. He moved in close, throwing punches with both hands, landing the majority. I expected the Mexican to go down. He got away. When Rulon tried to corner him, the Mexican stuck out his left and kept away. I wondered when Rulon would land the right he'd knocked out more than forty men with. Before the round ended, it was the Mexican who began to land, jolting Rulon's head back, causing a shower of perspiration to fly.

In the fifth round, I realized Rulon was losing. He threw flurries of punches, but he could not get set for the solid ones he apparently needed. The Mexican kept moving, dancing, darting, flicking.

The crowd, which had been noisy during the preliminaries, when there were three knockouts, was quiet. At first, there had been a shout or two advising Rulon to finish it, but those were absent now. There was an occasional call in Spanish, but these seemed subdued.

The sixth, seventh, and eight rounds passed. There was no question the Mexican won them all. In the ninth, he grew bolder, setting up Rulon with his left, making him take looping blows from his right. Though Rulon had begun to make an effort to get away from the left, he kept coming forward, apparently not shaken. It dawned on me the Mexican, though he would win, could not knock Rulon down, let alone knock him out. Rulon wouldn't even have the satisfaction of making a courageous last stand.

In the tenth round Rulon ran out of his corner. The Mexican dodged without difficulty and resumed flicking his left. Rulon chased him, throwing blows when he had no target, missing most of them. Once he lost his balance and slipped to the canvas springing to his feet again. The movement apparently overtaxed his trunks. When he turned, I saw he had ripped them across the back. If he was aware, he paid no attention, and the crowd, after a nervous laugh, ignored them too. The bell rang. Rulon returned to his corner, accepted the faded bathrobe over his shoulders, and stood looking straight ahead.

The referee raised Gomo Ybarra's hand.

Rulon walked over shook hands, and climbed out of the ring.

There was no applause, for the crowd had gotten to its feet before the decision and was concerning itself with getting out of the arena. I wondered if anyone remembered the nights Rulon had won, but the only comment I heard was about one of the preliminaries in which a light-heavyweight had knocked out his opponent with a single blow. "He's a comer," one man said to another. There were no complaints about Rulon. It had been obvious he was trying. And the preliminaries had been good. Nobody felt cheated. Now it seemed to be time to go home and get a night's sleep so everyone could go to work the following day.

Jing and I paused in the emptying arena. Someone had thrown a paper cup into the center of the ring; there were two empty beer bottles on the apron.

"Let's see Rulon," Jing said.

It had not occurred to me that we might be able to see him. I'd gotten the impression from reading sports pages that dressing rooms were barred to everyone except fighters, their handlers and important people. On the other hand, it occurred to me I'd also gotten the impression from the same source that there was something glamorous about the fight game.

We walked toward the dressing rooms. I wondered what to say to Rulon. I remembered a poem I had read, a line of which went something like: "... it matters not whether we win or lose but only how we played the game."

I tried to recall more of the poem as Jing and I approached the aisle that led to the dressing rooms. A uniformed policeman blocked the way, his arms folded, a firm look on his face. If I had been alone, I would have turned back.

Jing did not pause.

"Which is Culp's dressing room?"

Jing spoke with a tone he had begun to use in service stations and stores when he was paying for what he had bought. It was a deep tone, full of authority.

The policeman unfolded his arms. "First door to the left. sir," he said, standing straighter than before.

"Thank you," Jing said sharply.

In the dressing room, Rulon, still in trunks and bathrobe stood counting out dollar bills while the man who had seconded him watched. The room was silent except for the sound of shuffling feet and unintelligible voices outside. On a bench lay a pair of scissors, a disorderly layering of bandage, and an open kit that looked like a doctor's bag. When Rulon reached a given number, he handed the money to the second, who put it in his wallet. The second picked up the scissors, put them in the kit, and closed the kit.

"Glad to seen you again," he said to Rulon. He looked at Jing and me. "Got to catch a bus," he said defensively, turning toward the door.

"Thanks, Dink," Rulon said.

"See you around the gym."

"Sure."

Rulon's face was more marked than had been apparent. There were places where his skin looked as if something had been dragged across it, scraping off an outer layer, and one eye was swollen. I forgot about reciting poetry. It didn't seem appropriate.

Rulon shook hands. I was careful not to squeeze hard because he had told me once, off-handedly, how painful it is for a fighter to endure a hearty handshake.

"How's your mother and daddy?" he said.

I told him they were just fine when we left and that they'd been pulling for him even if they were not able to come to the fight.

Rulon sat down wearily. It seemed like time to say something. I wondered what to say.

"Before we came," I said impulsively, "Mother said she'd like to have you come over for dinner. Could you make it Sunday?" I figured I could always talk Mother into having Rulon as a guest.

Jing looked startled. "Monty's got a new book of poems," he said, recovering quickly.

"You won't have to dress up," I said, encouraged by the grin that began to spread over Rulon's face. "It won't be anything fancy. Just a family dinner."

Three Poems

Wilma Elizabeth McDaniel

LETTER TO CLEOTIS

Dear Cleotis
    I don't mean to be a gossip
not this time, anyway
    and crying, to boot
    but
    if you had seen poor Harley
    carrying his baby
in one arm

and sobbing like a child himself
you would have cried
when the taxi came
and jerked the diaper bag
    and baby from him
    you are that brave
and run away with them
    you are that swift

    before the cab door opened
and a social worker claimed the baby
don't ask me
    for I don't know
how crying will help
    but I am
    and you must cry with me in Sausalito
    and call Marvin Mandel
    who knows all the mourners
and certified
where he hangs out
    we will cry buckets for Harley
every freckle on his face
must be accounted for

CLOTHES DRYER

Monday used to be
the day after Sunday
it meant washday to most women
on Persimmon Road
but seance to Ardella Pitts
who always hung her dead husband up
            with wooden pins
beside a yellow trousseau gown
and allowed the wind
to whip him with daffodil might
while she washed his shirts
and put away each week
until a man in overalls
            who had no right
broke Ardella's contact with the
            great beyond
by installing a dryer

now we never see Mr. Pitts
and Ardella moans
that he doesn't love her any longer

LEFTOVERS
Table scraps are useful
and prophets
there is one in my family
who noticed a half jar of jelly
    left on the table
    after a tornado felled Clifford
    on a day so quiet
we could hear him breathing happily
    about a girl
who lived down in Bowlegs

The prophet said
a half jar of jelly
is only a life half spent
there will be other loaves of bread
other knives as sharp as Clifford's
    that will slice
the days as thick
    and spread the nights as lavishly
until we reach the sugar crystals
in the bottom of the jar

Hill People

BILL HOTCHKISS

In the meadow below me
a tarpaper shack is huddled
Beneath a huge liveoak,
Grown there like a mushroom.

A pencil line of smoke
From the stovepipe on the roof
Sketches its way down through the meadow
Toward Bear River.

The sky is gray and the grass
Is withered and broken with November;
The air is rank with the smell
Of loneliness.

And yet outside the cabin,
In the brown dust by an old green truck,
Three children are playing.

Two Poems

OMAR SALINAS

TOLUSA OF THE VALLEY
I saw you
in the garden
whispering
to roses,
fourteen year old
daughter
of this valley's sunlight/
my nineteen year old
hands
blossoming in the night
air you exhaled;
handling your very
chubby stoic breasts
seemed I thought
the very gawky essence
of a dream
I carelessly played with
and crudely left
damning the oxygen of life.
Expecting
ruffled sunburned hair
to pull me by the arms
out of the tripe.

AZTEC ANGEL
          I
I am an Aztec angel
     criminal
          of a scholarly
               society
     I do favors
          for whimsical
               magicians
     where I pawn
          my heart
               for truth
          and find
               my way
     through obscure
               streets
          of soft spoken
               hara-kiris

          II
I am an Aztec angel
     forlorn passenger
          on a train
     of chicken farmers
               and happy children

          III
I am the Aztec angel
     fraternal partner
          of an orthodox
               society
     where pachuco children
          hurl stones
     through poetry rooms
and end up in a cop car
     their bones itching
          and their hearts
     busted from malnutrition

          IV
I am the Aztec angel

who frequents bars
   spends evenings
      with literary circles
and socializes
      with spiks
niggers and wops
   and collapses on his way
      to funerals

      V

Drunk
   lonely
      bespectacled
  the sky
         opens my veins
           like rain
        clouds go berserk
          around me
        my Mexican ancestors
            chew my fingernails
I am an Aztec angel
   offspring
  of a woman
     who was beautiful

Sanchez

RICHARD DOKEY

That summer the son of Juan Sánchez went to work for the Flotill Cannery in Stockton. Juan drove with him to the valley in the old Ford.

While they drove, the boy, whose name was Jesús, told him of the greatness of the cannery, of the great aluminum buildings, the marvelous machines, and the belts of cans that never stopped running. He told him of the building on one side of the road where the cans were made and how the cans ran in a metal tube across the road to the cannery. He described the food machines, the sanitary precautions. He laughed when he spoke of the labeling. His voice was serious about the money.

When they got to Stockton, Jesús directed him to the central district of town, the skidrow where the boy was to live while he worked for the Flotill. It was a cheap hotel on Center Street. The room smelled. There was a table with one chair. The floor was stained like the floor of a public urinal and the bed was soiled, as were the walls. There were no drapes on the windows. A pall spread out from the single light bulb overhead that was worked with a length of grimy string.

"I will not stay much in the room," Jesús said, seeing his father's face. "It is only for sleep. I will be working overtime too. There is also the entertainment."

Jesús led him from the room and they went out into the street. Next to the hotel there was a vacant lot where a building had stood. The hole which was left had that recent, peculiar look of uprootedness. There were the remains of the foundation, the broken flooring, and the cracked bricks of tired red to which the gray blotches of mortar clung like dried phlegm. But the ground had not yet taken on the opaqueness of wear that the air and sun give it. It gleamed dully in the light and held to itself where it had been torn, as earth does behind a plow. Juan studied the hole for a time; then they walked up Center Street to Main, passing other empty lots, and then moved east toward Hunter Street. At the corner of Hunter and Main a wrecking crew was at work. An iron ball was suspended from the end of a cable and a tall machine swung the ball up and back and then whipped it forward against the building. The ball was very thick-looking, and when it struck the wall the building trembled, spurted dust, and seemed to cringe inward. The vertical lines of the building had gone awry. Juan shook each time the iron struck the wall.

"They are tearing down the old buildings," Jesus explained. "Redevelopment," he pronounced. "Even my building is to go someday."

Juan looked at his son. "And what of the men?" he asked. "Where do the men go when there are no buildings?"

Jesús, who was a head taller than his father, looked down at him and then shrugged in that Mexican way, the head descending and cocking while the shoulders rise as though on puppet strings. *"Quién sabe?"*

"And the large building there?" Juan said, looking across the rows of parked cars in Hunter Square. "The one whose roof rubs the sky. Of what significance?"

"That is the new courthouse," Jesús said.

"There are no curtains on the windows."

"They do not put curtains on such windows," Jesús explained.

"No," Juan sighed, "that is true."

They walked north on Hunter past the new Bank of America and entered an old building. They stood to one side of the entrance. Jesús smiled proudly and inhaled the stale air.

"This is the entertainment," he said.

Juan looked about. A bar was at his immediate left and a bald man in a soiled apron stood behind it. Beyond the bar there were many thick-wooded tables covered with green material. Men crouched over them and cone-shaped lights hung low from the ceiling casting broadening cones of light downward upon the men and tables. Smoke drifted and rolled in the light and pursued the men when they moved quickly. There was the breaking noise of balls striking together, the hard wooden rattle of the cues in the racks upon the wall, the hum slither of the scoring disks along the loose wires overhead, the explosive cursing of the men. The room was warm and dirty. Juan shook his head.

"I have become proficient at the game," Jesús said.

"This is the entertainment," Juan said, still moving his head.

Jesús turned and walked outside. Juan followed. The boy pointed across the parked cars past the courthouse to a marquee on Main Street. "There are also motion pictures," Jesús said.

Juan had seen one movie as a young man working in the fields near Fresno. He had understood no English then. He sat with his friends in the leather seats that had gum under the arms and watched the images move upon the white canvas. The images were dressed in expensive clothes. There was laughing and dancing. One of the men did kissing with two very beautiful women, taking turns with each when the other was absent. This had embarrassed Juan, the embracing and unhesitating submission of the women with so many unfamiliar people to watch. Juan loved his wife, was very tender and gentle with her before she died. He never went to another motion picture, even after he had learned English, and this kept him from the Spanish films as well.

"We will go to the cannery now," Jesús said, taking his father's arm. "I will show you the machines."

Juan permitted himself to be led away, and they moved back past the bank to where the men were destroying the building. A ragged hole, like a wound, had been opened in the wall. Juan stopped and watched. The iron ball came forward tearing at the hole, enlarging it, exposing the empty interior space that had once been a room. The floor of the room teetered at a precarious angle. The wood was splintered and very dry in the noon light.

"I do not think I will go to the cannery," Juan said.

The boy looked at his father like a child who has made a toy out of string and bottle caps only to have it ignored.

"But it is honorable work," Jesús said, suspecting his father. "And it pays well."

"Honor," Juan said. "Honor is a serious matter. It is not a question of honor. You are a man now. All that is needed is a room and a job at the Flotill. Your father is tired, that is all."

"You are disappointed," Jesús said, hanging his head.

"No," Juan said. "I am beyond disappointment. You are my son. Now you have a place in the world. You have the Flotill."

Nothing more was said, and they walked to the car. Juan got in behind the wheel. Jesús stood beside the door, his arms at his sides, the fingers spread. Juan looked up at him. The boy's eyes were big.

"You are my son," Juan said, "and I love you. Do not have disappointment. I am not of the Flotill. Seeing the machines would make it worse. You understand, *niño?*"

"*Si, Papa,*" Jesús said. He put a hand on his father's shoulder.

'It is a strange world, *niñito,*" Juan said.

"I will earn money. I will buy a red car and visit you. All in Twin Pines will be envious of the son of Sánchez, and they will say that Juan Sánchez has a son of purpose."

"Of course, *Jesús mio,*" Juan said. He bent and placed his lips against the boy's hand. "I will look for the bright car. I will write regardless." He smiled, showing yellowish teeth. "Goodbye, *querido,*" he said. He started the car, raced the engine once too high, and drove off up the street.

When Juan Sánchez returned to Twin Pines, he drove the old Ford to the top of Bear Mountain and pushed it over. He then proceeded systematically to burn all that was of importance to him, all that was of nostalgic value, and all else that meant nothing in itself, like the extra chest of drawers he had kept after his wife's death, the small table in the bedroom, and the faded mahogany stand in which he kept his pipe and tobacco and which sat next to the stuffed chair in the front room. He broke all the dishes, cups, plates, discarded all the cooking and eating utensils in the same way. The fire rose in the blue wind carrying dust wafers of ash in quick, breathless spirals and then released them in a panoply of diluted smoke, from which they drifted and spun and fell like burnt snow. The forks, knives, and spoons became very black with a flaky crust of oxidized metal. Then Juan burned his clothing, all that was unnecessary, and the smoke dampened and took on a thick smell. Finally he threw his wife's rosary into the flames. It was a cheap one, made of wood, and disappeared immediately. He went into his house then and lay down on the bed. He went to sleep.

When he woke, it was dark and cool. He stepped outside, urinated, and then returned, shutting the door. The darkness was like a mammoth held breath, and he felt very awake listening to the beating of his heart. He would not be able to sleep now, and so he lay awake thinking.

He thought of his village in Mexico, the baked white clay of the small houses spread like little forts against the stillness of the bare mountains, the men with their great wide hats, their wide, white pants, and their naked, brown-skinned feet, splayed against the fine dust of the road. He saw the village cistern and the women all so big and slow, always with child, enervated by the earth and the unbearable sun, the enervation passing into their very wombs like the heat from the yellow sun so that the wombs themselves bred quiet acceptance, slow, silent blood. The men walked bent as though carrying the air of sky, slept against the buildings in the shade like old dogs, ate dry, hot food that dried them inside and seemed to bake the moisture from the flesh, so that the men and women while still young had faces like eroded fields and fingers like stringy, empty stream beds. It was a hard land. It took the life of his father and mother before he was twelve and the life of his aunt, with whom he then lived, before he was sixteen.

When he was seventeen he went to Mexicali because he had heard much of America and the money to be obtained there. They took him in a truck with other men to work in the fields around Bakersfield, then in the fields near Fresno. On his return to Mexicali he met La Belleza, as he came to call her: loveliness. He married her when he was ninteen and she only fifteen. The following year she had a baby girl. It was stillborn and the birth almost killed her, for the doctor said the passage was oversmall. The doctor cautioned him (warned him, really) La Belleza could not have children and live, and he went outside into the moonlight and wept.

He had heard much of the loveliness of the Sierra Nevada above what was called the Mother Lode, and because he feared the land, believed almost that it possessed the power to kill him — as it had killed his mother and father, his aunt, was, in fact, slowly killing so many of his people — he wanted to run away from it to the high white cold of the California mountains, where he believed his heart would grow, his blood run and, perhaps, the passage of La Belleza might open. Two years later he was taken in the trucks to Stockton in the San Joaquin Valley to pick tomatoes and he saw the Sierra Nevada above the Mother Lode.

It was from a distance, of course, and in the summer, so that there was no snow. But when he returned he told La Belleza about the blueness of the mountains in the warm, still dawn, the extension of them, the aristocracy of their unmoving height, and that they were only fifty miles away from where he had stood.

He worked very hard now and saved his money. He took La Belleza back to his village, where he owned the white clay house of his father. It was cheaper to live there while he waited, fearing the sun, the dust, and the dry, airless silence, for the money to accumulate. That fall La Belleza became pregnant again by an accident of passion and the pregnancy was very difficult. In the fifth month the doctor — who was an atheist — said the baby would have to be taken or else the mother would die. The village priest, a very loud, dramatic man — an educated man who took pleasure in striking a pose — proclaimed the wrath of God in the face of such sacrilege.

It was the child who must live, the priest cried. The pregnancy must go on. There was the immortal soul of the child to consider. But Juan decided for the atheist doctor, who did take the child. La Belleza lost much blood. At one point her heart had stopped beating. When the child was torn from its mother and Juan saw that it was a boy, he ran out of the clay house of his father and up the dusty road straight into a hideous red moon. He cursed the earth, the sky. He cursed his village, himself, the soulless indifference of the burnt mountains. He cursed God.

Juan was very afraid now, and though it cost more money he had himself tied by the atheist doctor so that he could never again put the life of La Belleza in danger, for the next time, he knew with certainty, would kill her.

The following summer he went again on the trucks to the San Joaquin Valley. The mountains were still there, high and blue in the quiet dawn, turned to a milky pastel by the heat swirls and haze of midday. Sometimes at night he stepped outside the shacks in which the men were housed and faced the darkness. It was tragic to be so close to what you wanted, he would think, and be unable to possess it. So strong was the feeling in him, particularly during the hot, windless evenings, that he sometimes went with the other men into Stockton, where he stood on the street corners of skidrow and talked, though he did not get drunk on cheap wine or go to the whores, as did the other men. Nor did he fight.

They rode in old tilted trucks covered with canvas and sat on rude benches staring out over the slats of the tail gate. The white glare of headlights crawled up and lay upon them, waiting to pass. They stared over the whiteness. When the lights swept out and by, the glass of the side windows shone. Behind the windows sometimes there would be the ghost flash of an upturned face, before the darkness clamped shut. Also, if one of the men had a relative who lived in the area, there was the opportunity to ride in a car.

He had done so once. He had watched the headlights of the car pale then whiten the back of one of the trucks. He saw the faces of the men turned outward and the looks on the faces that seemed to float upon the whiteness of the light. The men sat forward, arms on knees, and looked over the glare into the darkness. After that he always rode in the trucks.

When he returned to his village after that season's harvest, he knew they could wait no longer. He purchased a dress of silk for La Belleza and in a secondhand store bought an American suit for himself. He had worked hard, sold his father's house, saved all his money, and on a bright day in early September they crossed the border at Mexicali and caught the Greyhound for Fresno.

Juan got up from his bed to go outside. He stood looking up at the stars.

The stars were pinned to the darkness, uttering little flickering cries of light, and as always he was moved by the nearness and profusion of their agony. His mother had told him the stars were a kind of purgatory in which souls burned in cold, silent repentance. He had wondered after her death if the earth too were not a star burning in loneliness, and he could never look at them later without thinking this and believing that the earth must be the brightest of all stars. He walked over to the remains of the fire. A dull heat came from the ashes and a column of limp smoke rose and then bent against the night wind. He studied the ashes for a time and then looked over the tall pine shapes to the southern sky. It was there all right. He could feel the dry char of its heat, that deeper, dryer burning. He imagined it, of course. But it was there nevertheless. He went back into the cabin and lay down, but now his thoughts were only of La Belleza and the beautiful Sierra Nevada.

From Fresno all the way up the long valley to Stockton they had been full with pride and expectation. They had purchased oranges and chocolate bars and they ate them laughing. The other people on the bus looked at them, shook their heads, and slept or read magazines. He and La Belleza gazed out the window at the land.

In Stockton they were helped by a man named Eugenio Méndez. Juan had met him while picking tomatoes in the delta. Eugenio had eight children and a very fat but very kind and tolerant wife named Anilla. He helped them find a cheap room off Center Street, where they stayed while determining their next course of action. Eugenio had access to a car, and it was he who drove them finally to the mountains.

It was a day like no other day in his life: to be sitting in the car with La Belleza, to be in this moving car with his Belleza heading straight toward the high, lovely mountains. The car traveled from the flatness of the valley into the rolling brown swells of the foothills. where hundreds of deciduous and evergreen oaks grew, their puffball shapes like still pictures of exploding holiday rockets, only green, but spreading up and out and then around and down in nearly perfect canopies. At Jackson the road turned and began an immediate, constant climb upward.

It was as though his dream about it had materialized. He had never seen so many trees, great with dignity: pines that had bark gray twisted and stringy like hemp; others whose bark resembled dry, flat ginger cookies fastened with black glue about a drum, and others whose bark pulled easily away; and those called redwoods, standing stiff and tall, amber-hued with straight rolls of bark as thick as his fist, flinging out high above great arms of green. And the earth, rich red, as though the blood of scores of Indians had just flowed there and dried. Dark patches of shadow stunned with light, blue flowers, orange flowers, birds, even deer. They saw them all on that first day.

"Adónde vamos?" Eugenio had asked. "Where are we going?"

"Bellísima," Juan replied. "Into much loveliness."

They did not reach Twin Pines that day. But on their return a week later they inquired in Jackson about the opportunity of buying land or a house in the mountains. The man, though surprised, told them of the sawmill town of Twin Pines, where there were houses for sale.

Their continued luck on that day precipitated the feeling in Juan that it was indeed the materialization of a dream. He had been able in all those years to save two thousand dollars and a man had a small shack for sale at the far edge of town. He looked carefully at Juan, at La Belleza and Eugenio and said, "One thousand dollars," believing they could never begin to possess such a sum. When Juan handed him the money, the man was so struck that he made out a bill of sale. Juan Sánchez and his wife had their home in the Sierra.

When Juan saw the cabin close up, he knew the man had stolen their money. It was small, the roof slanted to one side, the door would not close evenly. The cabin was gradually falling downhill. But it was theirs and he could, with work, repair it. Hurriedly they drove back to Jackson, rented a truck, bought some cheap furniture and hauled it back to the cabin. When they had moved in, Juan brought forth a bottle of whiskey and for the first time in his life proceeded to get truly drunk.

Juan was very happy with La Belleza. She accepted his philosophy completely, understood his need, made it her own. In spite of the people of the town, they created a peculiar kind of joy. And anyway Juan had knowledge about the people.

Twin Pines had been founded, he learned, by one Benjamin Carter, who lived with his daughter in a magnificent house on the hill overlooking town. This Benjamin Carter was a very wealthy man. He had come to the mountains thirty years before to save his marriage, for he had been poor once and loved when he was poor, but then he grew very rich because of oil discovered on his father's Ohio farm and he went away to the city and became incapable of love in the pursuit of money and power. When he at last married the woman whom he had loved, a barrier had grown between them, for Ben Carter had changed but the woman had not. Then the woman became ill and Ben Carter promised her he would take her West, all the way West away from the city so that it could be as it had been in the beginning of their love. But the woman was with child. And so Ben Carter rushed to the California mountains, bought a thousand acres of land, and hurried to build his house before the rain and snows came. He hired many men and the house was completed, except for the interior work and the furnishings. All that winter men he had hired worked in the snow to finish the house while Ben Carter waited with his wife in the city. When it was early spring they set out for California, Ben Carter, his wife, and the doctor, who strongly advised against the rough train trip and the still rougher climb by horse and wagon from Jackson to the house. But the woman wanted the child born properly, so they went. The baby came the evening of their arrival at the house, and the woman died all night having it. It was this Ben Carter who lived with that daughter now in the great house on the hill, possessing her to the point, it was said about his madness, that he had murdered a young man who had shown interest in her.

Juan learned all this from a Mexican servant who had worked at the great house from the beginning, and when he told the story to La Belleza she wept because of its sadness. It was a tragedy of love, she explained, and Juan — soaring to the heights of his imagination — believed that the town, all one hundred souls, had somehow been infected with the tragedy, as they were touched by the shadow of the house itself, which crept directly up the highway each night when the sun set. This was why they left dead chickens and fish on the porch of the cabin or dumped garbage into the yard. He believed he understood something profound and so did nothing about these incidents, which, after all, might have been the pranks of boys. He did not want the infection to touch him, nor the deeper infection of their prejudice because he was Mexican. He was not indifferent. He was simply too much in love with La Belleza and the Sierra Nevada. Finally the incidents stopped.

Now the life of Juan Sánchez entered its most beautiful time. When the first snows fell he became delirious, running through the pines, shouting, rolling on the ground, catching the flakes in his open mouth, bringing them in his cupped hands to rub in the hair of La Belleza, who stood in the doorway of their cabin laughing at him. He danced, made up a song about snowflakes falling on a desert and then a prayer which he addressed to the Virgin of Snowflakes. That night while the snow fluttered like wings against the bedroom window, he celebrated the coming of the whiteness with La Belleza.

He understood that first year in the mountains that love was an enlargement of himself, that it enabled him to be somehow more than he had ever been before, as though certain pores of his senses had only just been opened. Whereas before he had desired the Sierra Nevada for its beauty and contrast to his harsh fatherland, now he came to acquire a love for it, and he loved it as he loved La Belleza; he loved it as a woman. Also in that year he came to realize that there was a fear or dread about such love. It was more a feeling than anything else, something which reached thought now and then, particularly in those last moments before sleep. It was an absolutely minor thing. The primary knowledge was of the manner in which this love seemed to assimilate everything, rejecting all that would not yield. This love was a kind of blindness.

That summer Juan left La Belleza at times to pick the crops of the San Joaquin Valley. He had become good friends with the servant of the big house and this man had access to the owner's car, which he always drove down the mountain in a reckless but confident manner. After that summer Juan planned also to buy a car, not out of material desire, but simply because he believed this man would one day kill himself, and also because he did not wish to be dependent.

He worked in the walnuts near the town of Linden and again in the tomatoes of the rich delta. He wanted very much to have La Belleza with him, but that would have meant more money and a hotel room in the skidrow, and that was impossible because of the pimps and whores, the drunks and criminals and the general despair, which the police always tapped at periodic intervals, as one does a vat of fermenting wine. The skidrow was a place his love could not assimilate, but he could not ignore it because so many of his people were lost there. He stayed in the labor camps, which were also bad because of what the men did with themselves, but they were tolerable. He worked hard and as often as he could and gazed at the mountains, which he could always see clearly in the morning light. When tomato season was over he returned to La Belleza.

Though the town would never accept them as equals, it came that summer to tolerate their presence. La Belleza made straw baskets which she sold to the townspeople and which were desired for their beauty and intricacy of design. Juan carved animals, a skill he had acquired from his father, and these were also sold. The activity succeeded so well that Juan took a box of their things to Jackson, where they were readily purchased. The following spring he was able to buy the Ford.

Juan acquired another understanding that second year in the mountains. It was, he believed, that love, his love, was the single greatness of which he was capable, the thing which ennobled him and gave him honor. Love, he became convinced, was his only ability, the one success he had accomplished in a world of insignificance. It was a simple thing, after all, made so painfully simple each time he went to the valley to work with his face toward the ground, every time he saw the men in the fields and listened to their talk and watched them drive off to the skidrow at night. After he had acquired this knowledge, the nights he had to spend away from La Belleza were occupied by a new kind of loneliness, as though a part of his body had been separated from the whole. He began also to understand something more of the fear or dread that seemed to trail behind love.

It happened late in the sixth year of their marriage. It was impossible, of course, and he spent many hours at the fire in their cabin telling La Belleza of the impossibility, for the doctor had assured him that all had been well tied. He had conducted himself on the basis of that assumption. But doctors can be wrong. Doctors can make mistakes. La Belleza was with child.

For the first five months the pregnancy was not difficult, and he came almost to believe that indeed the passage of La Belleza would open. He prayed to God. He prayed to the earth and sky. He prayed to the soul of his mother. But after the fifth month the true sickness began and he discarded prayer completely in favor of blasphemy. There was no god and never could be God in the face of such sickness, such unbelievable human sickness. Even when he had her removed to the hospital in Stockton, the doctors could not stop it, but it continued so terribly that he believed that La Belleza carried sickness itself in her womb.

After seven months the doctors decided to take the child. they brought La Belleza into a room with lights and instruments, they worked on her for a long time and she died there under the lights with the doctors cursing and perspiring above the large wound of her pain. They did not tell him of the child, which they had cleaned and placed in an incubator, until the next day. That night he sat in the Ford and tried to see it all, but he could only remember the eyes of La Belleza in the vortex of pain. They were of an almost eerie calmness. They had possessed calmness, as one possesses the truth. Toward morning he slumped sideways on the seat and went to sleep.

He put her body away in the red earth of the town cemetery beyond the cabin. The pines came together overhead and in the heat of midday a shadow sprinkled with spires of light lay upon the ground so that the earth was cool and clean to smell. He did not even think of taking her back to Mexico, since, from the very beginning, she had always been part of that dream he had dreamed. Now she would be always in the Sierra Nevada, with the orange and blue flowers, the quiet, deep whiteness of winter, and all that he ever was or could be was with her.

But he did not think these last thoughts then, as he did now. He had simply performed them out of instinct for their necessity, as he had performed the years of labor while waiting for the infant Jesús to grow to manhood. Jesús. Why had he named the boy Jesús? That, perhaps, had been instinct too. He had stayed after La Belleza's death for the boy, to be with him until manhood, to show him the loveliness of the Sierra Nevada, to instruct him toward true manhood. But Jesús. Ah, Jesús. Jesús the American. Jesús of the Flotill. Jesús understood nothing. Jesús, he believed, was forever lost to knowledge. That day with Jesús had been his own liberation.

For a truth had come upon him after the years of waiting, the ultimate truth that he understood only because La Belleza had passed through his life. Love was beauty, La Belleza and the Sierra Nevada, a kind of created or made thing. But there was another kind of love, a very profound, embracing love that he had felt of late blowing across the mountains, from the south and that, he knew now, had always been there from the beginning of his life, disguised in the sun and wind. In this love there was blood and earth and, yes, even God, some kind of god, at least the power of a god. This love wanted him for its own. He understood it, that it had permitted him to have La Belleza and that without it there could have been no Belleza.

Juan placed an arm over his eyes and turned to face the wall. The old bed sighed. An image went off in his head and he remembered vividly the lovely body of La Belleza. In that instant the sound that loving had produced with the bed was alive in him like a forgotten melody, and his body seemed to swell and press against the ceiling. It was particularly cruel because it was so sudden, so intense, and came from so deep within him that he knew it must all still be alive somewhere, and that was the cruelest part of all. He wept softly and held the arm across his eyes.

In the dark morning the people of the town were awakened by the blaze of fire that was the house of Juan Sánchez. Believing that he had perished in the flames, several of the townspeople placed a marker next to the grave of his wife with his name on it. But, of course, on that score they were mistaken. Juan Sánchez had simply gone home.

Two Poems

ART CUELHO

DANNY, MY MAN

They all thought I was lucky
getting the inheritance, but
it just brought out what I had
held in check for so long.
When I was working steady
and tending to the fields
with barley checks to water
I didn't have any extra time
to go into Tiny's and let
loose at some wild spree,
or let my eyes roll over some
of the hotter broads in town.

Before I knew it Jenny
said she's gonna leave me
and take away the kids
if I didn't quit making
a fool out of myself while
running down the family name.

I guess some of the devil's horns
rubbed off on me because
I said damn what people say —
I only want a stab at a good time.
As long as I could order a round
for the whole house and
hear the crack of the pool balls
and a lonesome tearjerker
throbbing away in the night
with the whiskey making me loud.
And old Rhyming Fast Lil
making it all seem right,
as if she she could lift every cloud.

When I had to stumble back home
and look into Jenny's eyes
I'd repeat one of
Lil's rhymes to ease
my guilt and shame.
"Com'on Danny, my man —
you're a young wild stud,
take my fun-loving hand.
Ain't nothing like a fiddle
to play up an old dance band."

THOSE COOK SHACK DAYS
Before the sun had a voice
in the morning with
the grey sagebrush rooted
in a horned toad's alkali swale,
a man, a Westside farmer,
took a deep breath and got
a good whiff of adobe mud,
of topsoil once threaded
with crumbling antelope bones.

He rubbed his eyes.
Not by any clock
did he know it was time.
Some measure of the fields
told him with the rising scent
of furrow beds to the calluses
layered thick in his hands.
Sleep was only a nuisance.
His dream had rounds to make.
He knew it deep down
like the mottled
valley pigeons swarming
the open barn door.
And like a favorite horse
the pickup found its way
in the dark to the
threshold of the farm.

There were no songs
when scorpions did
their dance to a
whirlwind tune and
a desert promise.
No water wells then.
A dry-farming stake
was the way before
canal hopes grew
in the caterpillar dust.

No deed in a
county clerk's office
can take away those
cook shack days with
the ruts of wheels
lit by the full moon.

None of it was
won in the office
where a perfect-lined
ledger combed for
row crop profits.
All of it was gained

in the open sun;
a ball of fire that
gave sunstrokes like
gobs of halloween candy.

A dove feeding
in the shade of
a sunflower ditchbank
will crack through memory
with longing and suspend
a lifetime of sweat.

Now the purple tops of alfalfa
invite the diamond dew charm,
but somewhere between drinking out
of a rain puddle with centipedes
and waiting for dawn to remove
the cut and bleeding rattlers
from the disc blades was
the answer to a dreamer's dream.

Two Poems

DENNIS SALEH

BELLADONNA NIGHTSHADE

In the wet of early spring
kinds of belladonna and nightshade

in the waste ground
at the bottom of trees

For a week it breaks the surface
uncoils, loosening in the earth

then hangs the miniature folded bells
of its first blossoms in the sun

The cup petals shake out silence
dust in the wind

bells, the sound of dark earth

bells, the ringing toll of nothing

The dull flowers
are almost mistakes

first tries early in the year
still clouded with winter

The first roll of color is faint red
then purple, like the hood of dusk

the first black berries
are like drops of night

when the stalks and branches thicken
black pearls

swollen, almost glittering
like ornaments of a deadly lady

The flowers are in a hall
the flowers are in a grave

the blossoms sway and lift
offering like hands

they touch the lips with sleep
they lead back into darkness

they remind the spring of death
dying planned and carried out

POMEGRANATE
Walking in alleys after October
with two children my own
in the old neighborhoods
Brando gives directions

In banking light
from an aisle of palms
down two streets
shadows play over the alley

A tide of wind rolls too
and a child's painting
blows in the alley
swollen suns like eggs

thick rays shooting out
blue clouds
We see a woman in a yard
calling to shirts on a line

A lawn hums dully
The little blades are Zs
air picks its way through
they saw the wind

The sun comes around the
corner of a garage
A line goes down the alley
like it follows it

Brando says inside the sun
are pink stars purple enemies
enough for an army
purple enemies soldiers

A bark and a dog slide by
a newspaper boy
A man comes out of a door
We are the Pomegranate Gang

Along the backs of yards
you find them tucked away
hanging out over fences
upside-down like they're stupid

Almost accomplices
they fit the hand so
Pomegranates make you
take them swollen so

Precious gems to eat
all of one afternoon

little gorged beads of wine
in a leather pouch

The tree's hung with balloons
tied off knotted rising
but held in the branches
to decorate

Ornamental even royal
with its purple chambers
veil upon veil
and the dynasties

Lineage age old like chins
When the seeds bleed
in your hands
a hundred years gone

It is the heart
of an old statue
Ventricle aorta
sun rusting authority

The brick wall
and the tree make
a court and shade
The balls are goblets

Brando scrapes
and straddles the wall
the ears of the scissors
alert to the air

Take the pomegranate
We should take one
The ground will
put it back

Little Bree tears her knee
deep kidney red
The tree awards purple hearts
to the air

Five Poems

DON THOMPSON

WINTER EVENING AT METTLER
The sun has gone down, its glow
clouding
like breath in the chill air.

A lamp snaps on
in the window behind me.

Far off, across plowed fields:
black smoke,
as if night were rising
from a crack in the earth.

MOVIE STREET
(Old Kernville, Beneath Lake Isabella)

Only the drowned ever go there,
to that street, deeper now
than anyone can think.
Photos show a hard sky, a steeple,
cottonwoods poised for
the next hanged man
who'd ask for a raise when they cut him down.
Store fronts shimmer like fans
in the long afternoon:
siesta,
no one dreaming of water. Dust
never settled in that town,
nor those lost men drifting through old movies
to whom the street said Saloon,
Hotel, Hot Bath,
but meant something deeper.

ON THE GLENNVILLE ROAD
Oaks on the hillside,
like hoboes

in their ragged bark,
refuse to move on.

Stones slump to the ground,
exhausted.
no one knows how
they made it so far.

This is where creeks
go dry and
the wind runs out of breath.
This is where you stop.

1936
The years beneath me
ribbon like fish sperm
slowly toward the surface,
then flow uselessly
into a once ripe sun.

Drifting belly up
in the pond my father dug,
I hear the old windmill
ache in the still air.

It is that year again:
my blood swirls like dust
and blows me west.

VALLEY OAK
Fist of a crippled wizard
shaken in rage against limits,
I am with you.

I too grow crookedly
and stobbornly
toward an impossible stance.

Almost Persuaded

(from *A Native Son of the Golden West*)

JAMES D. HOUSTON

Two years after the Second World War Andrew and Hooper sit side by side for the drive to church. Hooper's as tall as his father now. Their faces echo, the way son's and father's do, similar, yet opposite, something in the straightness of the nose, the chin knobs, Andrew's face rusty, his blue eyes finely coated with rust, Hooper's tan and smooth, his eyes brown, Cherokee shadows at the cheek.

A heavy silence hangs between them. Andrew is counting his blessings, a weekly habit that gets him in the mood for worship service: good health, a solid house, plenty to eat, and this is their last Sunday in the '38 Dodge. Next week it's a brand-new four-door.

Counting his blessings he glances at Hooper, who stares moodily at passing houses. Andrew begins to count his misfortunes, part two of this Sunday meditation, taking the bad with the good, so that inevitably he enters church wearing the creased face the congregation expects of its leaders.

Fourth son in a family of nine, with generations of vast families behind him, child-rich brothers and sisters spread clear back to Tennessee, and Andrew went and married a woman with a weak womb, who bore him one son and had to quit. It's hard facing those brothers of his when the families meet every five years or ten, in Albuquerque or Salt Lake, and stand their broods together for the crowd-scene photo. It isn't Andrew's fault. Nor Naomi's. She would if she could. She didn't order the weakness. Not even God's fault, since all things created by him were perfect once. If anything's to blame it's the species itself. Riddled with flaws. Trials. Burdens. And one son is better than none at all. So the least you can do is pass on the comforts that you, growing up, scarcely dreamed of, comforts of the flesh of course, but more important, those eternal ones, comforts of the afterlife, available to any man who can learn to behave himself these seventy years or so. And the first step toward that afterlife, well, that is what's on Andrew's mind this morning, that act of faith which any man who loves his son would encourage at the earliest opportunity. Witnessing that one act would reduce all these other blessings and misfortunes to sounding brass and tinkling cymbals.

"Hooper, I sent your mother on ahead with Sister Winslow because I want to talk to you about something I been meaning to talk to you about for a long time now."

Hooper stares out the window, closes his eyes.

"Boy reaches a certain age, it gets time for him to start doing the work of the church." Pause. "Know what I mean?"

"I guess so."

"There's work to be done and you can only put off doin' it so long. There's prayers to lead. There's communion table to wait on. There's ushering to do when people are coming in to the service."

He glances at Hooper, who sighs with boredom.

"Now nobody can do the work of the church until he is baptized. That's what it comes down to. You are fourteen years of age, Hooper. It's about time you started thinking about these things."

"What about Jesse Bullington?"

"What *about* Jesse Bullington?"

"Jesse didn't get baptized till he was *eighteen*."

"Jesse Bullington had only been coming to our church a year when he got baptized. Before that he went to the Methodists. Fact *is*, Jesse Bullington is a convert."

"Then what about Jesus?"

"Jesus?"

"Jesus didn't get baptized till he was thirty."

Andrew feels his face turn to rhubarb. "That's a special situation. Jesus was the first man to ever get baptized."

"But if we're supposed to follow his example. . ."

"Your great-grandfather, David Dunlap, was baptized when he was twelve and devoted his whole life to the Lord's work. By the time any boy reaches fourteen and knows right from wrong. . ."

Andrew is disgusted with himself. Raising his voice when he wants to sound benevolent and Christ-like. This isn't the way it was supposed to go. He looks at Hooper, whose face is still averted. Andrew searches for some phrase to end this, to change the mood, to reconcile. Can't find it. Lets the sentence hang.

In Sunday School Hooper is wishing his mother came along for that ride. She never allows the frontal attack. She comes in from the side, and likes everyone else to and never really say what's on his mind. Like this morning's breakfast, looking sideways over the toaster: "Brother Dailey won't be with us no more after today, Hooper. He's moving up to Fresno to a new congregation. He's a mighty good man, and we sure will miss him. I guess he's been preaching here as long as anybody you can remember, hasn't he? I know he thinks an awful lot of *you*. It's sure nice having a preacher you've known awhile when things come up you want a preacher to do."

With his mother he can answer from the side and evade her. But his father comes right ahead, corraling him.

In Sunday School they study The Acts of The Apostles, the teacher now reading from Chapter 26. "Then Agrippa said unto Paul, Almost thou persuadest me to be a Christian." Hooper has heard it many times but never listened to this verse before. Today the words sound ominous, the words themselves. A premonition. He reviews his father's words. He starts to shiver. Something is closing in.

He feels like yelling, "I don't want to be baptized." Tries it a couple of times, silently. The blasphemy scares him. Add "today" and try it again, louder. "I don't want to be baptized today!" Yes, that is exactly how he feels.

Jo Ann Babcock, sitting behind him, touches his shoulder, whispers, "Hooper, are you all right?" Jo Ann has the biggest chest of any girl in church, impossible to hide even though her mother makes her wear a thick green overcoat to Sunday service, winter and summer. He turns, eyes burning into her bosom. Flames rise to his cheeks. He feels feverish. A victim and a martyr. He will rest his head there on the highest curve.

Worship service opens with communion. From a crisp white tablecloth trays spread out through the congregation. Toward Hooper one is passed along the pew, glinting below the skylight, stopping as each hand raises a small ruby glass and returns it half empty to its padded hole. Andrew sips, passes the tray to Hooper, then bows to dwell solemnly on Jesus. Hooper passes it on, quickly. The touch of it unnerves him, reminds him that Deacon Andrew Dunlap here assigns the weekly duties. Hooper *knows* the first time he waits on communion table he'll drop the tray of glasses. He can hear the crash, tinkle of their rolling underneath pews down the sloped floor toward the stage. He hears himself laughing, cursing his luck.

During two songs and a long prayer the hall is strangely dark. Through the frosted skylight a gray layer of overhanging cloud encourages his dark and fearful, martyr's mood. But now Brother Dailey is starting for the stage, and a glow replaces the darkness. He mounts four stairs, crosses to the rostrum, grips its rim and gazes sadly into the crowd, a long, bony man, Abraham Lincoln without a beard. The crown of his head is bald. All that remains of his hair is a gray wreath around the side and back, and while he stands there a sudden gush of sunlight streams down upon him, a band of brilliance brightest in the center where his polished dome glows.

Whenever this happens a fine chill grips Hooper, at the coincidence that cannot be explained. He wouldn't call it a signal of divine approval. He knows such things aren't possible. Yet on cloudy days he always watches the light, to see which parts of the service are illuminated, which overcast. He can't help connecting this sunburst to Brother Dailey's final sermon, can't help thinking some spirit moves within, around this shiny-headed man.

The preacher's palms lift slowly into whiteness, making two more brights. Hooper hears the deep voice when it starts to speak. But not the words. He doesn't want to listen to the words. The sounds will be enough. The sound and the sunlight. It's just a farewell sermon. He'd rather dazzle his eyes in the light. Upthrust of beckoning arms mesmerizes him, and sun rushing down to fill void when the voice dies.

Hooper stares, and lets his mind go blank, and half the sermon's gone before the words penetrate. He has been trying to get a glimpse of Jo Ann Babcock's chest, between the shifting shoulders of two elderly women. A loud silence catches his ear. Then out of the light a white sword runs through, pins him to the pew.

The preacher shouts, "One Lord, one faith, one baptism! Ephesians four and five!"

Hand slap on Brother Dailey's Bible.

I don't want to be baptized today!

"The one Lord, brethren, is Jesus Christ. The one faith is faith in Him. The one baptism is what God tells us about time and time again right here in the New Testament."

Gilt-edged pages flapping in the sunlight, and Hooper wants out of here. He knows what's coming next. He dreads it. And he knows it's already too late. This is no farewell sermon, it's salvation talk. Each of these verses is tied to every other verse like an enormous fisherman's net, and he is already caught inside it, caught too behind these poles and sheets of brilliance, and caught by the very jerking of the long body on the stage, like a life-size puppet strung from who knows how high above, sudden pops of knee and elbow, legs snapping, arms darting into the shine.

"Now let us think what that one baptism means. It does not mean to sprinkle water over a little baby's head. It does not mean to pour half a gallon of water from a pitcher over a young child's face and arms. If we look at the original meaning of this word, if we go back to the language of these scriptures, the Greek of the apostles' day, we find the Greek word was *baptizein*, which literally meant to plunge, to immerse in water. If we go a little farther and explore the word *immerse* we find it comes from the same Latin root that gives us *merge*, which means to be combined or absorbed or swallowed up. Which is why the scriptures tell us we are *buried* with Christ by baptism, and like Christ was raised from the dead by the glory of his father, even so we also should walk in newness of life."

Back of his hand again on the open page, "Romans six and four."

Slap shut the book, sudden quiet. White dome bends out the light, hands clutch the rostrum edge as he leans toward Hooper, kind and grizzled patriarchal face, the voice going low and gutteral for the waiting crowd.

"Now isn't that a wonderful concept, friends, to be *immersed* with Christ, to become one with him, and then to *emerge* in newness of life? It is God's gift to each of us. And wouldn't you rather take that gift than walk through life alone, in darkness, stumbling down the steps to hell. Look into your hearts, and ask yourself where you stand with Jesus. The Lord himself tells us, in Mark 16:16, He that believeth and is baptized shall be saved; he that believeth not shall be damned."

The white sword twists, carving Hooper's bowels. This is the part he hates. He doesn't have to look into his own heart. He knows he's in the darkness. He doesn't enjoy it there. He didn't understand hell until he was sick once with flu, four hours of violent stomach cramps and sure then that damnation must be the same torment but a thousand times more agony and lasting forever. He doesn't want to go through that. Yet he risks it. He flirts with the chance that he could be swallowed up unsaved while they're driving home from church, because he fears even worse losing his chance for washing away all such darkness from his soul. As it is, he never worries long about his sins. They can pile up, darkness can accumulate toward the time when it'll all be washed away. How comforting to know that no matter what he does or thinks, all will be purified later on. It's an ace he doesn't want to play until he has to.

So he flirts with the darkness. And he flirts, as Brother Dailey just described it, alone. No doubt about that. In this crowd of two hundred he sits the object of their communal gaze. Every eye is piercing the back of his neck. A hail of holy arrows. Every eye except his father's.

Hooper happens to glance at Andrew, and Andrew is watching Brother Dailey, and while he observes the side of Andrew's ruddy face he sees something appalling, yet, once witnessed, entirely predictable. He sees, at least he thinks he sees his father winking at the preacher.

Hooper leans back, breathing deep. Could that explain it? The way things are closing in? Not coincidence at all, but an actual conspiracy? The light, the sermon, the prologue in Sunday School—a plot hatched between preacher, teacher and Deacon Dunlap who knows, though Hooper has never confessed it, how the sunshine weakens his resistance.

He's thankful Brother Dailey doesn't wink back. Too holy for that— weary eye rings, the knees back-snapping as some thread of light yanks upward—holiest man Hooper has ever seen, and somehow this plot is all his father's. Yes, and going on a long time, the looks, the interrogations, launched among holy arrows from all these hovering eyes, a circle of spikes pressing him ever closer to the pool.

It is likely Andrew bribed the preacher to deliver this exhortation, instead of the soothing farewell he probably planned; and bribed the teacher too; and arranged for the clouds to draw back, and stay back, for sunlight to edge the passion of this climax:

"Look into your heart, friend, and if you're not yet one with Christ, and if you want to be, then do not hesitate. Come forward this very day. Repent of your sins, express belief in Jesus, join your life to His by being buried in holy baptism. Look into your heart, step out of the darkness that can only lead to damnation, and step forward this morning to stand in the light with Jesus, as together we all stand and sing."

He bounces down four stairs to stand below the rostrum, right in front of the center aisle, and Andrew fills the stage in his place, catching sun on his straight black slab of hair. With a lift of arms he brings the crowd to its feet, flipping for page 342.

Andrew looks a little frightened up there in the floodlight of Sunday morning, announces the number with a voice too loud. Hooper is embarrassed by the look, by the coffee-colored double breasted suit and hard white collar bunching neck skin over the edges. He is embarrassed until his father begins to sing. Then, even if the building were half full and that half fumbling with some unfamiliar verse, as long as Andrew's leading, it sounds as if the church is jammed with choristers.

His suspicions dwindle as Andrew sings. He likes to let his father's voice swallow his, make his low notes just as round and full and thrilling, especially when two hundred voices well into a song like this. It is one of Hooper's favorites. The bass line pleases him, and he knows the lyrics by heart, doesn't need a book. Smug, superior to all the page-rustlers, he is that much closer to his father's song. Andrew sings from memory too, coffee arms waving in the sunshine:

> *Almost persuaded, Christ to believe,*
> *Almost persuaded, Christ to receive.*

Brother Dailey sings from memory, and sings bass, and before the first verse is done, Hooper finds himself in a trio with the preacher and his father, shivering when they all hit the same note, pulling in his chin for the low ones, belting loud bars in transcendental unison. Other singers are muted background chorus. Hooper hears only the trio and, concentrating on its overtones, hears some new resonance in its other two voices, a quiver as each note lifts through the pouring light with a plea, a vibration of voices arcing toward his. He feels it rising through the floorboards, and those notes bring to his eyes sudden water. Brother Dailey's eyes are shining, Andrew's too, with the same water. For the first time Hooper hears and understands the words.

Almost does not avail, almost is but to fail.
Sad, sad, that bitter wail—Almost but lost.

He hears it, and a rage starts to boil. His father *chose* this song. A final stake in Sunday's fence. He stops singing.

But with his own voice silent he only hears more clearly, as Andrew, on the last line, drags his arm through the air to retard the crowd. That final word, *lost*, spreads into the most hopeless moan he has ever heard, a dirge for his own hopeless soul staggering toward some remote, unlivable catacomb where he will spend eternity weak with flu and convulsed by Satan's stomach cramps.

Arms soar into the sunlight, two hundred voices swoop into the second verse. Hooper is singing again, trying to lose himself in the music.

He can't keep his throat from thickening. He feels so sorry now. For everything. For his father, who has to plot to get his only son baptized. And for the congregation, all water-eyed, warning Hooper about that bitter wail. Sorry then for Brother Dailey's saintly face so lonely and his arms spread to welcome the world, elbows jerking out the tempo on this last Sunday and no one answering his call. But sorriest of all for Hooper, who now wants to be up there bathing with them in that ever pouring light. He thinks of the Transfiguration, Jesus, Moses and Elijah in their reunion on the mountain top, *his raiment became shining, exceeding white as snow*. It could be like that. And he knows if he doesn't join them now he doesn't know when he'll feel this close again. Although if not now, then not much later. Only a matter of time, after all, a matter of choosing the time. He wants to save this moment of washing. But here's the sun still cataracting down on Brother Dailey's dome, and Hooper's eyes are wet in a hall of waiting eyes, and he almost talks himself into it then. He just can't cut loose from the pew to walk in front of everyone. He breathes deep, sings louder, afraid to think, his voice lost in his father's.

Head expanding where round notes tingle, he imagines it's his own voice filling the hall and he never decides to step into the aisle. Later he can't remember walking down. One moment he's singing, the next the light is blinding him, the stage is cracked and tilted bending through the wet he tries to blink away.

Brother Dailey's old face is right in front of Hooper's, tears streaming, smiling, broken-voiced. He takes Hooper's hand in both of his and whispers, "Are you coming forward to be baptized?"

Scarlet nod.

"God bless you, boy."

He asks Hooper to sit. The last notes fade. Brother Dailey announces, eyes brimming, that someone has come forward. Hooper's face is feverish again. The preacher takes his hand, helps him stand.

"Do you believe with all your heart that Jesus Christ is the son of God?"

Hooper had forgotten about that. The main reason he waited this long in the first place, and he'd forgotten it entirely. He doesn't see how anyone his age can believe that. The all your heart part bothers him most. He needs more time to think. He just isn't ready. *I don't want to be baptized today.* But here is Brother Dailey tall in front of him, smile devoutly waiting to spread as wide as heaven. Hooper know what the answer has to be. "Yes. . . I do."

"God bless you for that confession," the preacher declares for the back rows to hear, then softly, "You come along with me now."

He beckons Hooper to follow him up onto the stage, through a door behind the pulpit. Hooper hesitates, doesn't want to walk up there. Motionless blue curtains conceal the bapistry. He has watched them open many times, watched the penitent sink into that blue tank, rise dripping, and different. Something happens back there, some weird transformation. People get buried there, Brother Dailey always says the water is warm. That's a comfort. But not enough. Hooper has examined those arisen from the tank. It still baffles him, whatever happens. He doesn't want to change until he's ready.

Too late. His life's in other hands. Behind the baptistry now and he hears his father calling out the page for "Up From the Grave He Arose." Jo Ann's father is back there too. He shows Hooper into a little cubicle, leaves him with a big set of white coveralls made of thin rubber. Hooper takes off his coat and trousers, climbs into the coveralls, looks at himself in the mirror. He's a deepsea diver. He thinks of Brother Babcock's daughter. He has always wanted Jo Ann to get baptized so he can see the wet gown sticking when she emerges. Now Jo Ann will be watching *him*, in this ridiculous deepsea rig.

A knock. Brother Dailey opens the door, wearing waist-high rubber wading pants, his coat and tie. He explains how they'll stand for the immersion and assures him the water is warm. Then they're waiting at the top stair, gazing into blue water. Brother Babcock holds the curtain cords.

The song ends. He pulls the curtains open with a swish. Brother Dailey wades down, turns, extends the bony hand that will dip him into the cleansing tank. Hooper, the same way he stepped into the aisle, mind blank and feet propelled by hidden forces, follows. Blue water is always warm, it slaps against the tile and plaster, spit spat.

One arm around his shoulder, the other hand, flat, raised, "I now baptize you in the name of the Father, and the Son, and the Holy Ghost. Amen."

Nose pinched, fall back, falling down, into blackness, silence, no more spats or drones or fences. Dark and easy. Hold it. Aaaaaaahh. Plink. The sound of water past his ears. Shreds of blackness fall away. Hooper opens his eyes blinking gray trickles back.

No time to look at the audience. Curtains swish. The crowd breaks into "Only in Thee." Brother Dailey guides him up the stairs, water slapping as they slosh, back to the cubicle, dazed, blind, jelly-legged, stepping out of coveralls and no sense of what to do next, where to go, how to stand or speak. Sit. Listen to the song.

Knock on his door. It opens. In the hallway Brother Dailey stands, head bowed. Someone is praying the benediction.

"We are grateful, O Lord, that this young brother has seen fit in his heart to come forward today to confess the name of our saviour, Jesus Christ, to be buried with him in baptism and to arise again in newness of life. As he goes forth now in his new raiment to do thy work, Lord, we pray that you will bless him and be with him, and be with us all, Lord, until we meet again. Amen."

Newness. Of life. It finally hits Hooper who they're praying about. The way you slap your pockets searching for a pencil, he feels around inside for signs of newness. Next to Brother Dailey, bowing his head at the same angle, staring at the same floorboard, same rubber smell in their coats, he does feel a warmth, a giddiness, a fine bulge of well-being. Detachment. A balloon in the shape of a young man will at any moment simply decide to float away. Is that it? He wants to laugh, grab the preacher's hand, tell him how fine he feels, and how infantile seem all those fears that cluttered his already hazy, disintegrating past.

Like the last glimpse of a man departing into a heavy fog, he sees those long-ago Sundays he prowled these gloomy halls and rooms behind the baptistry, dark stairways, to the second floor, corridors lined with frosted glass leading from the church office toward the classrooms. While his parents chatted he explored the labyrinth, crept along, lightly touched the mottled glass, knew every songbook, flimsy testament, map of the Mediterranean, chalk-dusty blackboard, shapeless rostrum, murky rug. Yet each time he longed to find something different, new, and each time his explorations left him unrewarded. At last, back here with Brother Dailey, he sees this corridor behind the baptistry with clear eyes. The tank too. The blue water's mystery is solved. Everything glows with new meaning. He has been blind. Now he can see.

The prayer ends. Shoes scrape. Pages rustle. Voices purr and crackle. Brother Dailey takes his hand. Hooper squeezes, hoping his grip will transmit the wonder of all this newness.

The preacher's eyes are dry now. Hooper's are brimming.

"You've just done the finest thing a man can ever do. You're pure.

Beginning again. Believe in the lord and do his work, son, and don't do anything to stain that purity. It's your most precious possession."

Holy eyes probe his, and Hooper doesn't want this gaze to end. As long as they can stand here, man to man, hand to hand, eye to eye, this giddy elation, this clear vision might never leave him.

The preacher says. "I guess we'd better join the others."

He opens the door. Crowd noises swell in, suck them out onto the stage. The first thing Hooper sees is his father shaking hands with Brother Babcock. The look on both their faces — an oddly conspiratorial smugness, as of some bargain settled — this punctures whatever it is Hooper has been feeling. It begins to leak away. He wants to step over there and read the signals passing between them. But they turn toward him, Andrew red-eyed, his stiff collar pushing at the rhubarb skin. He grabs Hooper's hand.

"Mighty proud a you, boy. Mighty proud."

Brother Babcock turns his tight Texas face into a leathery sideways smile. "We're *mighty* proud, son."

"Thank ya, thank ya," Hooper says, affecting a slight drawl that seems the easiest way to reply.

These two escort him up the aisle to the rear where a crowd of well-wishers wait to congratulate the clebrity. Among them stands Jo Ann, watching him with a look he recognizes. It is the way he used to stare at those arisen from the tank, the look of the as-yet-unsaved wondering, trying to discover what has changed. His sense of newness swells again. He regards her with superior eyes. It is so warm she has removed her coat and hat, revealing silky hair, white rayon blouse, and Hooper is shaking hands with someone else but aching to use on Jo Ann this new power he wields. He thinks about what he'd do if he could ever get her back to the church kitchen some night after service, help her off with the overcoat. He has never touched a girl's blouse, a girl's skin.

As quickly as it forms, this fantasy dissolves, taking with it all his blood, leaving him hollow veined.

Whatsoever think ye in your hearts, so do ye.

His first sin. Not five minutes since brother Dailey instructed him about purity, and it's already tarnished. He wasn't ready. Goddam it, he knew he wasn't ready. His chance spent, and now he yearns for it back, if only till he finds the nerve to corner Jo Ann. His baptism squandered, and through the crowd around him he see Brother Dailey's lean silhouette at the distant doorway, shaking hands, such a holy man, and how disappointed he'll be to learn that Hooper's brand new spotlessness didn't even make it to the vestibule.

Next to Hooper someone shakes his father's hand, saying, "We're all mighty proud, Brother Dunlap. Hooper's gonna make a fine Christian, make a deacon just like his daddy, one a these days." Turning then to Hooper, who has to smile, and shake the hand, and keep blinking to hold back the tears that now begin to well.

Something's wrong, terribly wrong. Perhaps he wasn't completely immersed. Perhaps some unwashed, unsaved thumb or nose or knee survived to taint the rest. Or did some essential current low in the pool fail to swirl up and touch him? How long was he under there? Not nearly long enough. Can you baptize someone again, if the first one didn't take?

"Sure be nice if Hooper could lead a prayer at the service this evenin', don't you think so, Andrew?"

"I think that'd be mighty nice, Brother Newcomb. How about it, Hoop?"

Strong mechanic's hand still clutches his arm, compels him to look into his father's eyes, sees a fresh shine of water to match Hooper's. But what is *he* crying about? What has been taken from him? Nothing. Those are tears of joy. The deacon in charge of manning the services has gained himself a prayer leader and a passer of communion plates. The songs they sang, the farewell sermon, the plunging sunlight — Hooper lives through all of it again, and this moment siphons off whatever residue of triumph or achievement or sanctity of lightheadedness he felt. He hates his father for conspiring and betraying him. And that's another sin. His hate bulges. And yet, if Andrew did launch all the holy arrows, Hooper failed to evade them. The circle of spikes, he should have found a path through them, or under, or around.

He wants to excuse himself from the small knot of handshakers still clustering, get outside where he can shout in the street, heap blasphemy on blasphemy till the asphalt cracks and swallows him.

One last tug at his arm. "How about it, Hooper boy?"

I DON'T WANT TO BE BAPTIZED TODAY!

Delta Farm

DENNIS SCHMITZ

a friend weighs little a wife
makes the body heavy
as she swims away in the marriage
sheets — she seems more
strange than my mother's

face surfacing
in memory. yet the drowned displace
the living. not my wife's but
mother's thirst dries the sweaty

fingerprints
from the handle of the short-hoe
or cutter
bar skimming the overflow
our salty bodies deposit between
windrows. together we pressed

drool from the sugar
beets & threw
or wished to throw our bodies
like pulp to the few
hogs we kept for meat on the tufted
mud of an upstream
island. this is the sweetness we refused
one another

        * * * *

this neighbor is married
to solitude
another whose bridal sheets still smell
fresh drinks
greenish mouthsful from the cistern
children won't grow
up their roots churn in
the cultivated
zones fractured by a hundred
canal reflections. when women come

or even visit
maybe they fix cots in fallen
down coolie shacks below
the town produce
sheds now abandoned & shifting
with the sun's weight.
when they always leave boys

will lie restlessly
fishing in the narrow
beds skiffs make, between the pilings
hear the sheet
metal pop nails to trail
in a swifter river.

     * * * *

late November: a sixty-knot
squall through Carquinez

Strait breaks
levees, backs salt water miles
inland to preserve
what it kills. animal features
wake on the bedroom
windows—buck deer the flood
divorced; our cow sewn with scars
bawls, against the dawn rubs
her painful ballast

of milk. my wife by instinct
washes her own
breasts before our daughter
feeds. birds in refugee dozens
scatter as I walk
a smaller yard. for days only boats

define the horizon. only the doctor
salt-stained
like us in boots & overalls
scares us. our daughter crawls
through fever one week
then her mother the week after

dies. my wife,
still my wife, what I have
of you, this residue, this love-

salt, will not let me cross private
places in my body

anymore. without you
I can only continue a snail inside
my shell of sleep trailing sticky
dreams. nowhere to walk I go
away from you.

    * * * *

I am forty-two, my body
twenty-five.
my skin recopies over
& over my small daughter's

hand barely
holding against its current.
once I wanted to be still
water, a puddle the sky
fell in or halo
my forehead molds from the saturated
marsh when I bend

my face to the first
unconfirmed rice shoot.
now I wait for the March-fed
river to clean
the delta, knead our thought —
out acres of orchard high
ground where picking ladders descend

legless into their own
reflections. the bottomland rice
is lost but these trees
reach deeper. rings of salt show
each step back the sea
takes. swaying from tree
to tree at last my daughter learns

to walk.

Three Poems

LARRY LEVIS

IN A COUNTRY

My love and I are inventing a country, which we can
already see taking shape, as if wheels were passing
through yellow mud. But there is a problem: if we
put a river in the country, it will thaw and begin
flooding. If we put the river on the border, there
will be trouble. If we forget about the river, there
will be no way out. There is already a sky over that
country, waiting for clouds or smoke. Birds have
flown into it, too. Each evening more trees fill with
their eyes, and what they see we can never erase.

One day it was snowing heavily, and again we were lying
in bed, watching our country: we could make out the
wide river for the first time, blue and moving. We
seemed to be getting closer; we saw our wheel tracks
leading into it and curving out of sight behind us.
It looked like the land we had left, some smoke in the
distance, but I wasn't sure. And as we entered that
country, it felt as if someone was touching our bare
shoulders, lightly, for the last time.

THE CRIMES OF THE SHADE TREES

Today everyone forgave me.
No one mentioned the felony
Of my back against the oak,
Or the air I was breathing, earlier.
So it is possible I am not Levis.

I smoke and think possibly
I am the smoke —
Drifting through Omaha as smoke does,
Past the new sofas on sale.
Past the south view of the slaughter house,
And the shade trees flushing with light.

And it doesn't matter.
For example, if I am really
Something ordinary, a doorstep,
Or the gleaming of frost on someone's lawn
As he shaves, that would be all right.

I only mention this
To the caretaker of my absence,
Who dozes on a beige sofa.

While she knits us a bible
In which the blind remain blind,
Like shade trees. Filling with light,

Each leaf feels its way out
Each a mad bible of patience.

RHODODENDRONS

Winter has moved off
somewhere, writing its journals
in ice.

But I am still afraid to move,
afraid to speak,
as if I lived in a house
wallpapered with the cries of birds
I cannot identify.

Beneath the trees
a young couple sits talking
about the afterlife,
where no one, I think, is
whittling toys for the stillborn.
I laugh,

but I don't know.
Maybe the whole world is absent minded
or floating. Maybe the new lovers undress
without wondering how
the snow grows over the Andes,
or how a horse cannot remember those
frozen in the sleigh behind it,

but keeps running until the lines tangle,
while the dead sit coolly beneath their pet stars.

As I write this,
some blown rhododendrons are nodding
in the first breezes. I want
to resemble them, and remember nothing,
the way a photograph of an excavation
cannot remember the sun.

The wind rises or stops
and it means nothing.

I want to be circular;
a pond or a column of smoke
revolving, slowly, its ashes.

I want to turn back and go up
to myself at age 20,
and press five dollars into his hand
so he can sleep.
While he stands trembling on a street in Fresno,
suddenly one among many in the crowd
that strolls down Fulton Street,
among the stores that are closing,
and is never heard of again.

Telegraph Sam

NELS HANSON

Night: Telegraph Sam riding his black horse Derry Death sixty years after
the car, savoring the clip-clop and spark of the steel shoes on the asphalt
and the jagged epitaphs of flame they carve on the night's black marble.
Farmers with striped bib overalls loosen the shoulder straps as their wives
struggle to climb the dark stomachs at the sound of Death coming up the
road, hesitating, and then galloping on, leaving each farm house a red IOU
of fire.

"Billy, he's head for Albert's. You know Albert's mother's been sick, gastronatis or the like. They say old folks pick the coldest nights to go."

"Manda. Manda he's past Johnson's heading straight for Moore's whose boy ran off with that Eyetalian girl, stole the pickup, found it a week later turned sideways in a ditch. A boy's finger just laying there on the seat. A finger laying there by itself. Maybe it's the boy's body they've found."

Every farmer for a mile is out by his mail box watching Telegraph Sam barrel toward him, great horse wearing shoes of flame, a black horse he never feeds oats, just the rabbits he shoots, and as Sam approaches each house, each man starts mumbling the name of some relative, some friend on the brink of death, disaster, divorce, or murder, some hard-luck joe with his dead name suffocating in the burning letter Sam waves to all the folks as he gallops on.

At the end of the road there are two houses left—the Frys' and the Martens'. Georgy Fry is shaking, leaning against a fence post, baby girl in his arms, wife at his side. He keeps checking both of them to make sure that they are still breathing, that they are still alive and Sam isn't coming to tell him that his daughter and wife are dead. George's wife mumbles, "Momma Momma Momma Oh Momma." George pats his wife and whispers, "It'ld be your daddy first, your daddy any day before your momma. It's your daddy who died."

Telegraph Sam rides his black horse up to the center of the road, the place where the road ends and two dirt alley ways branch off, one to the Frys', the other to the Martens'. Sam stops, takes off his leather pilot's cap with his one good hand, and rolls his eyes up into his head looking, listening for the hum of an airplane wandering in some purple tunnel of the brain, one severed, bloody hand at the controls that lets up on the stick only at intervals to telegraph the name of some victim just bombed below.

George can see the letter in Telegraph's hand and Sam keeps bringing it forward and then pulling it back, like the announcer at a raffle who knows who has won but is trying to make it exciting. Maybe Sam is not sure whom the letter is for—his arm keeps jumping like a mad compass, first pointing toward the Frys and then toward the Martens and then the Frys again, and now hesitating in between, confused, trying to get its bearings.

"Giddy-up," Sam whispers, and trots Derry Death toward George Fry whose shaking hand has knocked his front fence down. Sam leans down from the tall horse and smiles at the Frys. He whispers, "Pretty baby, pretty baby," as George screams, "is not dead, is not dead, pretty baby is not dead," running his hand over the tiny mouth of his daughter, feeling for wind. Telegraph Sam is really looking at George's wife and each time he whispers "Pretty baby" he is secretly radioing the lost plane in his head to see if the torn hand can get the co-ordinates of the Fry woman. Now Sam lifts his ear to the wind and he can hear his lost fingers tapping out a message — "She's fogged in, can't get low enough for a year. It'll take a baby to kill her." Telegraph Sam bends low to George's wife's ear and just before he kicks his horse and starts to charge away toward the Martens', he speaks to her softly. "Seen your momma lately? Grover ain't that far, ought to take a trip to see her. Night all," Sam says politely, saluting George and then his wife. "Giddy-up Death!" he screams and his chrome spurs flash in the moonlight. George helps his wife to the house, every few steps stopping to put his head to her stomach, listening for a ticking he thinks he hears inside.

All along the road the neighbors are running toward the Martens' with flashlights and lanterns. They scream, "Joe Dan! Joe Dan! Oh it's Joe Dan!' as if they were in the football stadium in town and Joe Dan were dashing for a touchdown but tonight the field is dark and Joe Dan's cleat marks are grown over with the dead grass of three losing seasons.

Telegraph Sam whizzes forward in a trail of fire like a tracer bullet, Sam and Derry Death the black head clapped in darkness just in front of the fire, the fire only the blown hairs of the bullet that is itching, throbbing, sniffing one way and then the other for the chest and the breakable heart and the target of skin that is shaking and parting its thin soft hairs like the lace wings of a doomed insect caught in the radar of the bats.

Daniel can tell that Joe Dan his half-brother is dead. One of Daniel's hearts is dead, the slender, half-grown one on the right side that would have become famous if it had have lived. Daniel picks up a picture of Joe Dan winning the hundred yard dash and he presses his ear over the white chest but the music has stopped. There are bruises on Daniel's chest, the places where Daniel has beat the rhythm of Joe Dan's heart, trying to teach his own native heart to sing.

Daniel can tell that his brother is dead. The way the stars are not stars tonight but only the prints of shattered feet staggering, trying to cross the sky. And that airplane, that speck of light droning and crisscrossing from star to star, trying to find its way south for winter, that airplane is the hand of Daniel's brother sliding its way beneath the black ice. Joe Dan follows the track from star-print to star-print back the way he came, holding his breath, swimming, searching for the hole through which he fell. Daniel can feel his shoulder turn cold and he sees it blaze silver in the dark. It is where his brother touched him once, he knows it is his brother's hand reaching up through the ice, grabbing for the shoulder that pulled him from the caved-in well in a gone summer. Now Daniel grabs his own shoulder in order to be saved. Now, like then, he is down in that water with his brother, drowning.

In town, Mary Helen stumbles from parked car to parked car, knocking on the windows and burping sour kisses as she murmurs to the dark faces — "Doctor, can't you close this hole." Mary Helen reaches for her breast that has started to burn. She can see that it is rising to attention and shining with a silver glow, a silver medal, the cupped hand of Daniel's brother that once said "Sorry" after it had stolen her first warm glove of darkness. Closing her coat and putting her arms across her chest that is inflating like a rubber life preserver that will never be big enough, Mary Helen can't help but salute, not knowing to what, as she falls across a warm seat, at least sinking, at least crying one sweet tear as if she were going down with the ship.

Through the cracked boards of the ceiling, a silver light is moving between the legs of Daniel's mother as she walks back and forth across the rafters of Daniel's room, the dark floor of the attic.

Up the road great balls of fire are dancing toward the Martens' place and the way the voices keep yelling, "Joe Dan! Joe Dan! God All Mighty, it's Joe Dan!" the glowing flashlights and lanterns and torches could be baseballs thrown too fast and now caught fire, new stars flaming from Joe Dan's fingers as he takes his windup and flings strikes through the bat, through the catcher's glove, through the heart of the umpire, through the backstop, through the open legs of the girl behind the screen who is Joe Dan's target and the key to his concentration. The scoreboards in the girl's eyes are blank and burned out. Her yellow wrinkled legs propped open with a stick can't draw hungry bees in winter. Now the stars scream and bail out of their light, falling like the skeletons of zeppelin pilots or the black corpses of baseballs, just hitting ground after all these years.

In the attic, Daniel's mother Rhoda rummages through wedding dresses, baby clothes, and crutches. She brings down a wooden, velvet-lined case. There is a white flute inside. It is carved out of bone. It is the leg bone of her father he brought back with him from the war in France. He sat around in his rocking chair for two years waiting for plastic legs to be invented, carving a flute from his own leg. The way her father carved it, the flute will play only certain notes, certain songs, agree to play only certain nights, eat only certain kinds of wind. When you play the flute the round holes pull the fingers down as if each hole had a fishing pole and they could hook the fingers and reel them in and let them out, making the hand into a player piano. If you listen close, the flute almost talks — Rhonda's father said he could understand its language, a little bit like the language those French people talk only you don't have to be French to understand it. The flute talked to Rhoda's father. It told him that his wife wasn't plowing, that she was lying out in the field with Virgil the hired hand. It told him that Virgil would get killed in a pool room fight so he wouldn't have to kill him. The flute told Rhoda's father that he could seal the shaft of his wife's love, the gaping tunnel opening to enclose the blue flower of alfalfa — with one night's love work like a mason with red brick, Rhoda's father, his one plastic leg kicking holes in the wall, closed the dark valuable mine of his wife's wanting forever. By his rocker when it rains, a pool of water forms on the worn wooden floor where his wife sat in overalls listening to him play out her life on his carved leg, straining to hear some song of one of her sins still coming, but she never heard it played. One night Rhoda's father tried to play "Camp Town Races" and ended up watching his fingers dance across the flute, playing a tune he had never heard before:

Ol Red Marten died ready for death
So ready and waiting for the ol black breath
His plastic leg died fore his other one did

Rhoda's father gave the flute to Rhoda and went to bed.

The plane in the dark sky of Telegraph Sam's skull begins to dive and Sam's lost hand taps out a message with its finger. "Pilot to bombadier, pilot to bombadier, open bomb bay doors," and Sam answers back, screaming at the top of his voice, "Derry Death, good old Derry, set this town on fire!" Both rider and dark ridden horse leave the asphalt and the sparks of the hoofs and journey alone through the night like the nose cone of a rocket without the lost stages of its fire. Sam jumps the Martens' front fence and his horse Derry Death is so silent and calm that maybe there are great black wings cinched beneath the saddle that Sam has just undone. The neighbors running up the dirt alleyway suddenly fall back at the sound of long black feathers beating the air. In the wingpits of the black horse they see the waiting tragedies of their lives clinging like canisters of jellied gasoline in the soft dark down of a bomb bay.

Rhoda sits in her father's rocking chair and holds the flute in her hands. It is the leg bone of her father, it is what her mother wrapped her legs around when she scraped Rhoda from Red Marten's flesh, it is the translater of illwinds that speaks in a French accent none of the French can understand. Rhoda has played the flute once and then it didn't answer. Maybe she held it wrong or blew too softly. Maybe there is a secret word her father forgot to tell her. Once, alone in the house, in a locked attic above a house of locked rooms, after Joe Dan was born, "Who is his father?" and the flute scorched her lips and fell to the floor, not like dead bone against sawed dead nailed tame wood, making the noise they have to make whether or not anyone is listening, but clattering against the floor, sound dissected into its many concussions, not sound but the memory of sound, as if bone and wood had rehearsed or done it before in another kingdom. Still, silent, innocent against the floor, admitting no motive nor meaning, and yet so quiet Rhoda could almost hear the bone laughing, the floor and bone safe, sure they could not be convicted of conspiracy because she was the one who dropped it, Rhoda clenched the arms of the chair and leaned forward and saw her blood dripping from her seared lips falling far down through air, getting smaller like a body thrown off a building, the drops finally flattening against the floor far down below. The sound still clattered in her ears for a long time and for awhile walking across the barnyard, her hands swinging across her chest or throwing corn for chickens, her arm would stop in mid air and she would stare at it closely, the way it had been the first time, the remembered time, when she heard the sound of bone. (Rhoda knew she had heard it once before, she could remember, but she couldn't remember well enough to speak, to tell someone it had happened before, someone who would say it happened in a dream and think she was trying to act like a saint or a genius. Far away once a bone had clattered, hardly remembered but true, remembered only by her and still true, like the sound of scissor blades crossing in the distance, cutting the tube and the rushing of air and then the sound of your head plopping into the hands of the kind nurse holding you up.)

Now, holding the flute in her clenched fists, so hard and tight they would be charred before they could let go, now, filling the parts of her lungs air hasn't lived in for years, now, whether or not Joe Dan, her son, is dead, whether his bones drawling like the flute are trying to speak French lonely in the buried heaps of Dien Bien Phu, scraping bone against bone, intercourse of the grave, or whether, like Joe Dan's last letter said, he is still running from body to burning body, bending low to see if the last word a man says is really "Mother".

Telegraph Sam gallops up the concrete walk, the goggles of his leather pilot's cap drawn low, the plane in his head circling lower and lower to the one body that is glowing, his bloody hand that stayed behing squeezing the black stick of the controls.

"Play flute play, leg bone of my father," Rhoda whispers as she raises the flute to her trembling lips, unafraid of getting burned.

"Set this town on fire!" Sam screams, charging toward Rhoda, waving the letter like a bill to be paid, the balance of tears due on a boy's killed body, as he and Derry Death crash through the battle line of the house, the shovels, the fruit boxes, the milk stools, the cans full of gasoline, the barricade that Jake has set out.

Rhoda clenches her cheeks and the tunnel behind her mouth that leads to the nose. Her face twitches with her eyes closed as she forces the air out of her stomach up through her throat, all the pressure it will take to blow truth through the still silent flute of her father.

Sam reins his horse and hovers, throwing his arms out wide, his letter throbbing like a bomb he is ready to drop. Like a bright star rising, the chrome spur spins on its boot as he lifts his leg to kick the face of someone grappling for the horse's bit. "Five, four, three, two. . ." Sam shouts as

Derry Death's hoofs draw a flack of red spark, the steel shoes scraping against the concrete.

The flute trembles, Rhoda's bones that will someday be flutes shake as she feels her breath, the last bubble of it, the last hidden canteen of air bob up the tunnel of her throat. "AaaaLLLiiiiive!" shrieks the two-noted wail like the scream of someone falling through the dark forever.

And the black horse Derry Death, breaking the iron bit tempered in the fire of a hundred burning barns, in the flaming flesh of a trapped child, cooled in the flooded mouth of a drowned pregnant girl, rears and kicks great dusts of flame, rockets of spark that climb the ladders of their light and then fall back to the purple lake of gasoline Derry Death is standing in. Sam yells, "Derry, Derry Death, set this town on fire!" as he and his horse explode in a seizure of flame and Derry Death bolts back down the road, Sam tied to the stirrups. In the airplane falling through Telegraph Sam's brain, someone cries, "Bombadier to pilot, bombadier to pilot, we've been hit!" but the lost hand in the cockpit can't pull the plane up and Sam's face drifts down into the warm mane of the horse's neck, and flaming head to flaming head, Sam and Derry Death run through deep grass and dream of before the war, naked girl behind Sam, bare legs wrapped around Derry Death, just Derry then. Sam reaches out his flaming fingers to shake with his lost hand finally come back and Sam and Derry fall to the ground and do tricks in slow motion as they dance in the grass-fire oven amid the encore-clap of the dead.

On the front steps of the Martens', the gas burns itself out. All the neighbors stand around Rhoda who is still holding the flute in her mouth. Sitting forward in her father's rocking chair, left hand open and shaking, she waits for the letter that is just now coming to earth. "Daddy, look what I found!" cries Jessie Edwards before his mother yanks him by the arm and takes him back behind the house. Everyone's head is tilted back, watching the letter float down, slowly, like a parachute swinging a dead flyer. It is like the time at the county rodeo when Joe Dan got thrown and fell like the sun from the sky and everyone ran up to his stunned, cold body to see if they would live or not. The letter lands address down at Rhoda's feet. No one says a word. They know this could be a sign. Rhoda doesn't look at the letter but runs her fingers over the typed page, as if it were the face of her new born child she is afraid to look at at first. Slowly she brings it to her face. Her eyes squint, her lips move. She is either reading or beginning to lose her mind, already talking to herself. "Daddy come look!" shouts Jessie Edwards before his mother catches him again, tackling him from behind. No one notices. They watch Rhoda turn toward the torchlit faces, lifting the letter toward them with her outstretched arm, her lips trembling as she falls back, collapsing in her chair that rocks back and forth, her right hand still clutching the blackened flute that wheezes with the air Rhoda blows through her nostrills.

Edward Edwards slowly walks toward her chair. He is the smartest person north of town. He kneels at Rhoda's feet and picks up the fallen letter. He brings it close to his face, only an inch from his eyes — the words keep changing in the flickering torch light. He tilts the letter until it is flat and thin and he can peer with one squinted eye the length of the paper, moving it back and forth in the light to see if it is genuine, if there have been forgeries or erasures. He stands and turns to face the circle that has closed around him. He hands the letter to Bob Johnson who reads it and then gets out his glasses and reads it again and then looks up at Edwards as he passes it to his wife. "What is it, he's dead isn't he?" asks Naomi. No one answers. They pass the letter hand to hand over the heads of the children until each adult has brought the letter flush against his face, touched it by accident to his lips as if kissing the porthole of his lover's coffin. "What is it Daddy, huh Daddy?" Jessie Edwards pulls on his father's coat, looking at the letter that has come full circle, that his father holds again. Edward Edwards looks down at his son and the circle of boys who want to touch the letter, who would fight over it and tear it if he gave it to them. Maybe he shouldn't say anything and then he looks out across the alfalfa and the flames dying down, and the children with long sticks poking at the fire. "What does it say Daddy?" Jessie Edwards lowers his head and turns the blackened spur over in his hands. "Huh Daddy, what does it say?" Edward Edwards looks up toward Rhoda. Rosie Tuttle has sneaked between her mother's legs and slipped next to Rhoda's chair. She looks around and then touches Rhoda's flute. She screams, holding her little hand, as she runs back toward her mother.

"The United States Government regrets to inform you that on Saturday, January the 12th, 1964, in the service of his country." Edward Edwards hesitates, for a moment looking up at the waiting faces of the children they have taught not to lie. "In the service of his country, Joe Dan Marten died. But his name's been crossed out and Telegraph Sam's written in. It's addressed to his mother in the Old Folk's Home."

Everyone shakes a little, realizing they didn't read it wrong, relieved they weren't having a vision. As if reading it out loud has made it official, and true — Edward Edwards said it out loud and nothing happened — they look at one another and again and then they charge at Rhoda lifting her from the rocking chair onto their shoulders, everyone struggling to carry part of the weight. They hold her legs like goalposts as they carry her away, as the first person shouts, "Alive! Joe Dan is Alive!"

Daniel's forehead rests against the cold burning glass of the window. Down below he can see Jake his father standing by the burned down fence, staring at the torches moving across the vineyard and the flickering faces of people shouting, carrying his wife away. Their dark red mouths open like bullet holes in the flame. Jake cocks his head, as if listening to each voice, as if one of them is the one he's after. Jake falls to his knees and puts his cheek to the blackened cement, listening to the pounding feet of someone still running these twenty years. The way his mouth hangs open in anticipation, as if at any moment he will have the answer, Daniel remembers being sick as a child, lying between Rhoda and Jake, and waking in the night with fever to find Jake kneeling, mouth open like this, ear flat against Rhoda's naked body below her stomach. Daniel stares at the seat of Jake's pants that are shining with a bright silver glow. It is the place Joe Dan kicked him once for wearing his grandfather's old uniform. The blood dripping from the open gash on Jake's cheek is black in the dark. George Moore's tray shed bursts into flame. "Joe Dan is Alive!" rings like steel, like a commandment chiseled into the stone tablet of the night. If Jake could only believe it he would get down and pray. "Here Buster, here boy," Jake whispers as he kicks away the smouldering fence and stares out into the dark at the footprints Red Marten showed him. Even in the dark, with his eyes closed, Jake can follow them. Daniel has seen him late at night bending low to touch them with his cheek, the whitewashed footprints preserved in concrete. "Get a good smell Buster," he says kneeling, holding Buster in his arms. "Get the scent, get a good whiff, that a boy." Jake holds the dog's nose flat against the track, he holds Buster who didn't bark, Buster a dog can see in the dark, Buster The Dog who must have seen him. "Buster," whispers Jake, forcing his nose flat against the cold white footprint.

No wind blows. Dead leaves hang from the trees. In this silence set like a table by the flute's shrill divination, Daniel looks down at the table his right hand rests upon. There are the strewn papers, the yellowed plans of Jake's inventions — the army tank with wings, the huge wheeled statue of Hitler hollow inside. They could be antiques, found years later, just the way Jake left them. Daniel looks at the still hairs on the back of his hand. His hand is so still he wonders if it is worried whether it is alive or not. Daniel lifts one of his fingers. He wonders what Joe Dan's hand is doing right now.

"Get him Buster, after him boy!" cries Jake firing his shotgun in the air and then the pellets falling like rain against the dead grape leaves.

The white footprints, the stars have frozen black with ice. The airplane that was Joe Dan's searching hand drones fainter and fainter, its white palm slowly eaten away by the light-hungry dark. Daniel listens. In his chest he can hear the stutter of his orphaned heart kneeling by the body of its leader.

California Heartland:
The Exact Center

LAWSON FUSAO INADA

It doesn't matter to me
that "the exact geographical geographical center of California"
is located in the back of the Gomez family yard.
Or so they say.

I mean I don't know what in the world
they try to figure out that kind of stuff for,
or how, or even who *they* are,
except they seem to be continually obsessed
with the silly smack dab of things,
as if something were missing,
like a latter-day Miss McKenzie
proclaiming in her 5th grade grayness
that "we are now the most populous State in the Union."

So what's all the shouting for?

Besides, the Gomez family
doesn't live there anymore —
for what that's worth —
and the last I heard
Charles was in the Tico Tico
or possibly Pancho's Seven Seas.

And the funny thing is,
I got all this "through the grapevine" —
which is to be expected, in Fresno —
and maybe it was even "in the paper,"

but when I went by there
one hot day one summer —
which is something on which you can count —

this is what I found:

> no bronze plaque
> no bicentennial marker
> no famous arrowhead saying "Lookee Here"
> no nothing to even tell you that you *missed* it.

It makes you wonder.

Maybe there were some machinations at work,
some infamous fraud, some creative graft
of which only the "powers that be" are capable,
whereby the Gomez family, to wit, being unmistakably Mexican,
was heretofore denied the hoity-toity
glory and concession
as those "in the know"
hushed and hurriedly
moved the "mistaken" marker to the Mall,

where you can buy "Exact Center" decals
"for your listening pleasure"
   to show you were there.

I mean, what's a couple of crosstown blocks.
"Think metric."
Besides, it would be embarrassing for tourists
to park on "C" Street in the dust
and have those naked little kids
irrigate their whitewalls and their hubcaps.

So I stood there, beside the Gomez house,
in an awfully empty lot,
and saw:

> no Charles
> no Dolores
> no Pee Wee Vargas
> no Big Willie Murdock
> no Old Joe Lai
> no Little Lawson in
> no Pinocchio t-shirt
> no sign saying
> "No Families — Single Men Only"
> no "D" Street, even.

So later on, through the thick of my teeth,
through the grip of my throat,
this is what I sang:

> Even "D" Street
> or what it used to be
> mean little to me now,
> for what can you do
> with kite string,
> if it can ever be found
> in all that rubble,
> or Kenny's broken bat?
>
> These are fit for sacks,
> and weigh you down.
>
> Not far from here
> was home. In a year,
> the moonlight on these columns
> will not be seen
> but for the moons of headlights
> bobbing in a trough of cars.
>
> And I, here
> on no official reason
> but a whim,
> standing and swaying in a wind,
>
> can find no reason, no way,
> in the wind that blew
> a boy away,
> and blows him back again.

And, of course, as often follows
such singing, such tumultous singing,
which is our way of making music,
which is our way of making,
which is our way (It makes *you*. Wonder.),
which is the colorful blues
of mariachi
bon odori
making its way
through the tendrils of West Fresno,

bringing you the life
of fully awake on summer evenings,
the music permeating
the neighborhood
as a neighbor should;

well, it figures that I got to laughing,
slapping my self and laughing,
because here I was, you know,
I know, standing there in all my glory,
and I was:

> no inspector
> no surveyor
> no geographer
> no cartographer
> no geologist
> no archaeologist
> no anthropologist
> no apologist

but just the regular me, you know,
in regular clothes —
which is all the these
and then some —

and here I am, you know,
El Professor Inada
singing "yo no soy marinero" —
which I also am —

and driving a regular Chevy
instead of one of those common constipated jobs
with the State seal screaming "Eureka!"
through the streets of West Fresno;

just me, you know,
remembering the last time I saw Charles:

> We were We were digging in his backyard
> and found it,
> what we knew was there,
> what we were always looking for.

We lived, you see,
on the only hill in Fresno.
The *only* hill, mind you,
in *all* of Fresno.

Which means
there is something underneath.
Something special.

Which means
the regular kind of thing
irregular folks don't know about,
or avoid, at all costs.

Which is very expensive.

Because you can stand on that hill
and can't stand it:

there's nothing
but people around—
kids coming out of huts,
old folks husking
in back of shops—

and the heat is hot,
and if you don't like the kitchen
the hill is small enough
you can't see any
boulevards from off of it.

As a matter of fact,
the hill is easy to overlook
so you don't even have to name it,

but just leave it,
hightailing out of there
because those folks
are anyways and always

so you try to find
some bluffs or a **river**,

which, in Fresno,
there isn't any,

so you have to settle
down by the tracks,
which is your excuse for being
here and highballing
in the whitewall highrises
of the "other" side of town—

a sad state, of affairs.

And all the while,
this lovely hill is here.

So what Charles and I "found"
wasn't much—just the usual.

We knew it from before,
had felt it in the flesh and earth
as something natural,

You might say it was like
a hubcap, some bearings,
a way of measuring,
the way an ombligo
radiates with life.

You could look at it,
for what you could find.
You could feel it,
por seguro.

And since we knew the free way
and how an ugly road was coming,
and how invaders would arrive
with charts instead of hearts,

and since we knew
they would come and be gone,
in dust, in just,

we dusted our selves off
and went inside and out
and wherever we've been
with our families,

spreading the center among us.

The Gomez family, the Inadas,
are exactly where thay are,

where California starts from
and goes out, and out, and out.

From here, the going is easy.

Look at our faces, and smile.

Contributors to Part Four

ART CUELHO — Raised on a Riverdale farm, Cuelho is among the most prolific writers ever spawned by the valley. Among his books: *The Last Inch of Shade* (1974), *Some Magic in the Blues* (1975), *The Black Garden Follies* (1976), *The Valley Called Me Son* (1977), *Death's Legacy* (1977), and *Selected Road Poems, 1968-1976* (1978). He is the editor of the magazine, *Blackjack*, and recently expanded his activities as editor-publisher of *San Joaquin Grapevine*, a journal dedicated to writing from and about the valley.

JOAN DIDION — born in Sacramento in 1934. She graduated from U.C. Berkeley, with a degree in politics, in 1956. After several years as a magazine editor in New York, she published her first novel, *Run River*, in 1963. The excellence of her early magazine pieces led to the collection, *Slouching Towards Bethlehem* (1968). That book and her novels, *Play It As It Lays* (1970), and *The Book of Common Prayer* (1977), have established her as one of America's most respected and influential contemporary writers.

RICHARD DOKEY — Born in California, he lives in and teaches in Stockton. Educated at U.C. Berkeley, he has worked in a shipyard, for a railroad, in an ink manufacturing plant and as an assembly line worker for Squirt and Dr. Pepper. His short stories have been cited as distinct by Martha Foley and he has had work included in *Best American Short Stories*, *Southwest Review, Descant, Fiction Texas, Epoch,* and *South Dakota Review*, among other journals, have published his fiction.

LEONARD GARDNER — born in Stockton in 1933. Growing up there, he came to know the fields outside the city, the waterways, and the boxing sub-world that shaped his enormously successful first novel, *Fat City* (1969). A winner of the James D. Phelan Award and a Guggenheim Fellowship, Gardner studied literature and writing at San Francisco State College. He now lives in San Francisco, dividing his time between fiction and film writing.

NELS HANSON — a third generation Valley native. Born in Fowler in 1951, he grew up near Selma, where his parents had a house on one corner of his grandfather's farm. He studied writing at U.C. Santa Cruz, graduating in

1973, and in the graduate program at the University of Montana. In 1973 he won the James D. Phelan Award for a novel in progress, *The Long Slow Death of Joe Dan Marten,* from which "Telegraph Sam" is taken. And in 1975 his short stories earned an honorable mention in the Joseph Henry Jackson Award competition. His fiction has appeared in *Big Moon, Transpacific, Sundaze* and *Writing from the Inside.*

BILL HOTCHKISS – Raised on a small farm in California's Mother Lode country, Hotchkiss was born in Connecticut in 1936. He holds degrees from the universities of California and Oregon, plus San Francisco State University. He has worked as a fruit tramp, a fire-fighter, a wood-splitter, and an English teacher. Now on the faculty of Sierra College in Rocklin where the valley meets the foothills. His books of verse are *Steephollow Poems* (1966), *To Christ, Dionysus, Odin* (1969), *The Graces of Fire and Other Poems* (1974), and *Fever in the Earth* (1977).

LAWSON INADA – Born in West Fresno in 1938. His grandfather started the first fish store in Fresno. During World War II, Inada and his family lived in "relocation" camps in Arkansas, Colorado, and Fresno. "I went into the rest of the world, bringing Fresno with me." He is one of the poets influenced and aided by Phillip Levine. Published in many journals and anthologies, his widely-praised first volume *Before the War: Poems As They Happened* was published by William Morrow Co. in 1971.

GEORGE KEITHLEY – A native of Illinois, he has lived in Chico since 1962. Worked as a hotel dest clerk, groundskeeper at a race track and other varied tasks before becoming professor of English at Chico State University. He is the author of two prize-winning books of poetry: *The Donner Party* (1972), which was a Book-of-the-Month Club selection and from which an opera is being written, and *Song in a Strange Land* (1974). His full-length play about Aaron Burr, *The Best Blood of the Country* (1975) has won two playwriting awards. He has contributed poems to many journals.

DAVID KHERDIAN – Born in Racine, Wisconsin, in 1931, Kherdian has been closely associated with Fresno; he was co-editor of *Down at the Santa Fe Depot: 20 Fresno Poets* in 1970. He has edited eight contemporary American poetry anthologies, and compiled *A Bibliography of William Saroyan: 1934-1964* (1965). Since he began writing at the age of 35, six books of his poetry have been published: *Homage to Adana* (1970); *On the Death of My Father and Other Poems* (1970); *Looking Over Hills* (1973); *The Nonny Poems* (1974); *Any Day of Your Life* (1975); *I Remember Root River* (1978).

ALAN CHONG LAU — Born in Oroville, California, "where Ishi gave himself up." Later on his father ran a Chinese restaurant in Paradise, in the upper Sacramento Valley, where they were "the only Third World folks in town." After several campuses, and several years in Kyoto, Japan, studying brushpainting, Lau graduated from U.C. Santa Cruz with a degree in art. He now lives in Santa Cruz. With Lawson Inada and Garrett Hongo he has collaborated on a book of Valley-based poetry called *Down Highway 99: The Buddha Bandits.*

LARRY LEVIS — Born in Selma in 1946, Levis is a farm boy who now holds a Ph.D. from the University of Iowa and teaches at the University of Missouri. His first book, *The Wrecking Crew* (1972) won the United States Award given by the International Poetry Forum. In 1973, he was awarded a writing fellowship from the National Endowment for the Arts. His second collection of poetry, *The Afterlife,* was winner of the 1976 Lamont Poetry Selection.

MICHAEL LOPES — Born in Watsonville, California in 1943; attended public schools there and college in Santa Barbara, Berkeley, and Stony Brook, Long Island. Taught at Chico State College, where his interest in and writing about the Great Central Valley matured. Currently teaching at phillips Academy, Andover, Massachusetts. A volume of his poems, *Mr. & Mrs. Mephistopheles & Son,* was published in 1975.

WILMA ELIZABETH MCDANIEL — A native of Oklahoma, McDaniel came to the San Joaquin Valley with her family during the so-called Dust Bowl Migration of the 1930's. Called "the biscuit and gravy poet" by Eddie Lopez, she lives today in Tulare and she continues to draw her subjects from the people and places she knows well. Her books include *The Carousel Would Haunt Me* (1973), *The Red Coffee Can* (1974), *Letter to Cleotis* (1974), *The Wash Tub* (1976), and *The Coughdrop Saint* (1977).

KHATCHIK MINASIAN — Born in Fresno in 1913, he worked at a variety of jobs: fruit picker, baker, sign painter, box maker, steel rigger, etc. He began writing poetry at fifteen, and has been a regular contributor to various Armenian publications ever since; *The Hairenik Weekly, Ararat,* and *The Armenian Review* among others have published his verse, as has *The Nation.* His books include *A World of Questions and Things* (1950) and *The Simple Songs of Khatchik Minasian* (1950, 1969). He now lives in Palo Alto.

DEWAYNE RAIL — Born in Round Prairie, Oklahoma in 1944, he was seven when his family moved to Fresno. After twice returning to Oklahoma, they finally settled in Fresno in the late 1950's "with that feeling of perpetual discontent that has plagued all the members of my family since." Attended Fresno State where he studied with Peter Everwine and Phillip Levine. His poetry, which strongly reflects the land, has appeared in numerous periodicals.

WILLIAM RINTOUL — Born in Taft and reared in the West Side oilfields, he lives now in Bakersfield. He earns his living as a free-lance writer specializing in coverage of the oil and gas industry in California and Alaska. He is the author of *Spudding In: Recollections of Pioneer Days in the California Oilfields* (1976) and *Oildorado* (1978). His short stories have appeared in *Prairie Schooner, Cimarron Review, Mississippi Review, Minnesota Review, California Crossroads, The Mexican-American,* and *University of Kansas City Review.*

DENNIS SALEH — Born in Chicago, raised in Fresno, educated in California and Arizona, Saleh is the author of three books of poetry: *100 Chameleons* (1977), *Palmway* (1976), and *A Guide to Familiar American Incest* (1972). He has edited a collection of contemporary American poetry, *Just What the Country Needs, Another Poetry Anthology* (1971). He also designed and edited a book of record album graphics, *Rock Art* (1977). Saleh is another of the valley poets who studied with Phillip Levine at Fresno State College.

LUIS OMAR SALINAS — Born 17 miles from the gulf of Mexico in Robstown, Texas, he moved to California when he was nine. Attended Fresno State University where he studied poetry under Phillip Levine. Much of his writing has been involved with the Chicano revolution. First attracted literary notice when he wrote *Crazy Gypsy*. In 1973 he co-edited *From the Barrio*. He now lives, teaches and writes in Lindsay.

THOMAS SANCHEZ — third generation Californian, raised in Santa Clara and Sacramento Valleys, equal rights and anti-war activist in '60's and '70's, Master's Degree from San Francisco State University at age 22, Teaching there until violent 1969 Student-Teacher Strike. *Rabbit Boss*, widely anthologized and translated, is considered one of the most important historical novels of the American West. *Zoot-Suit Murders*, a political novel set in the Los Angeles Barrio during World War II, was recently published in America, England, France and Spain.

DENNIS SCHMITZ — A native of Iowa, where he was born in 1937, Schmitz has for the past twelve years lived and taught in Sacramento. He is on the faculty of the state university there. His writing has been much influenced by the region. In 1969 he won the Big Table Series of Younger Poets Award for *We Weep for Our Strangeness*, which was published that year. Two years later, *Double Exposures* was released, followed by *Monstrous Pictures of Whales* (1973) and *Goodwill, Inc.* (1976).

CHESTER SELTZER (AMADO JESUS MURO) — Born in Cleveland in 1915, he was the son of Louis B. Seltzer, editor of the *Cleveland Press* and grandson of the famed western writer Charles Alden Seltzer. He worked as a reporter and editor on more than 15 newspapers across the country, including a five-year stint with the *Bakersfield Californian*. He published fiction sketches using the nom de plume Amado Jesus Muro (a variation of his wife's maiden name). He was especially noted for his work on migrant laborers, which he researched by riding the rails and toiling the fields. Since his death in 1971, his literary reputation has grown enormously and he has been the subject of many scholarly studies. Paul Foreman calls him "an American B. Traven."

GARY SOTO — A native of Fresno, Soto burst onto the poetry scene in 1975 when he won the Discovery/*Nation* Award. Two years later he won the United States Award given by the International Poetry Forum for his first published book, *The Elements of San Joaquin*. His verse has also been printed in such journals as *The American Poetry Review, The New York Times Book Review,* and *Poetry*. Soto's poems are distinguised by both his Chicano heritage and by the influence of the harsh land he knows so well.

DON THOMPSON — A native of Bakersfield, where he was born in 1942, Thompson now works there for the county library and acts as librarian for the county jail and road camp. He holds an M.F.A. from the University of British Columbia. His fiction and poetry have appeared in such journals as *Kayak, Carolina Quarterly,* and *Fiction International*. Two collections of his poems have been published, *Toys of Death* (1971) and *Granite Station* (1977), the latter reflecting his continuing concern with the Valley's landscape.

GARY THOMPSON — Born in the midwest, he has lived over half his life in California. He graduated from California State University, Sacramento, then took an advanced degree from the University of Montana. For several years he has been teaching in the English Department at California State University, Chico, and publishing in literary journals such as *American Poetry Review, Phantasm,* and *Chicago Review*.

LUIS VALDEZ was born in Delano, California, in 1940, to migrant farmworker parents. In 1964 he graduated from San Jose State College, and the next year he was back in Delano, founding his now famous *Teatro Campesino* as a dramatic voice of the farmworkers movement. In 1969 the group moved to its permanent establishment in San Juan Bautista. As writer and director, Valdez has created an extraordinary body of work, blending bilingual dialogue, commedia-del-arte techniques, Mayan/Aztec imagery, and a keen awareness of social realities, to explore Chicano experience. In the process *El Teatro Campesino* has emerged as an international leader in alternative theatre. In 1976 they toured Europe performing his *La Carpa de Los Rasquachis* as an official American Bicentennial Event. He has also co-edited *Aztlan: An anthology of Mexican-American Literature* (1972). And in 1978 his play *Zoot Suit* premiered at the Mark Taper Forum in Los Angeles.

About the Editors

GERALD HASLAM. A native of Oildale, where he was born in 1937, and blooded a few years later. Haslam first attracted literary attention with the publication of OKIES: SELECTED STORIES, in 1973. He followed this with MASKS: A NOVEL (1976), also set in the valley. His most recent work is HAWK FLIGHTS: STORIES FROM THE WEST (1978). All his fiction reflects his background as a laborer on ranches, farms and in the oilfields. His stories have appeared in over thirty magazines, his non-fiction in over fifty. In addition to CALIFORNIA HEARTLAND, he has edited two previous collections, WESTERN WRITING (1974), and FORGOTTEN PAGES OF AMERICAN LITERATURE (1969). He currently lives in Petaluma, California, and teaches at Sonama State College.

JAMES D. HOUSTON. His father comes from Oklahoma, his mother from Alabama. They met in west Texas, and he was born in San Francisco. He has spent most of his life on the California coast, exploring this region via such works as GIG (1969), A NATIVE SON OF THE GOLDEN WEST (1971), THE ADVENTURES OF CHARLIE BATES (1973), and CONTINENTAL DRIFT, a novel he completed in 1977 with the aid of an NEA grant. With his wife Jeanne he also co-authored FAREWELL TO MANZANAR— the story of one Japanese-American family during and after the World War II internment — which became a NBC World Premiere Movie in 1976. Winner of the Joseph Henry Jackson Award and a Wallace Stegner Writing Fellowship, he teaches fiction writing at the University of California, Santa Cruz.

About the Illustrator

CLAYTON TURNER. Born in 1935 on a farm between Bristow and Kellyville, Oklahoma, in the same house where his mother had been born, Clay Turner migrated to the San Joaquin Valley as a child. On July 29, 1949, near Selma, he joined friends at a swimming hole. He climbed atop a wellhouse to dive, but slipped, landing upside down in the water, breaking his neck. He has been paralysed from the neck down ever since. "One day when I was 16 my parents put a magazine in front of me with a piece of paper on it. My mother stuck a pencil in my mouth and said, 'Clay, try to write your name.'" That was the beginning. Today Turner is not only an internationally exhibited artist, but a published short story writer as well. He owns his own gallery in Fresno. "I don't know what the worst thing in the world is," he says, "but I know one thing — it's not being without your arms and legs."